ntents

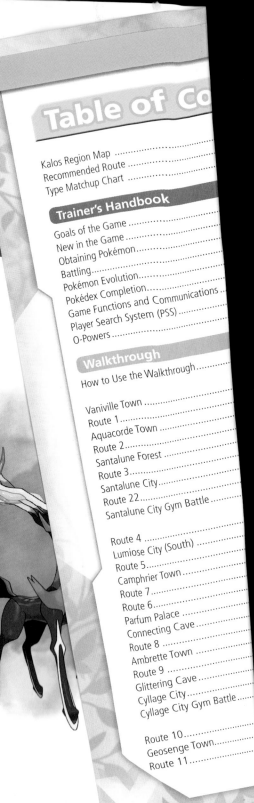

Table of Co[ntents]

Features Guide

Quick Location Index (Alphabetical)

Kalos Region Map

Sea Spirit's Den

Coumarine City Gym
Pokémon Center
Coumarine Hotel
Seaside Station
Hillcrest Station

Scary Hous

Azure Bay

Coumarine City

Shalour City Gym
Pokémon Center
Tower of Mastery

Route 12

Route 13

Shalour City

Kalos Power Plant

Reflection Cave

Parfum Palace

Route 11

Cyllage City Gym
Pokémon Center
Cycle Shop
Hotel Cyllage
Boutique

Battle Chateau

Route 6

Route 5

Route 10

Cyllage City

Geosenge Town

Route 7

Pokémon Center
Hotel Marine Snow

Camphrier Town

Pokémon
Day Care
Battle Chateau
Berry Fields

Pokémon Center
Shabboneau Castle
Name Rater
Hotel Camphrier

Route 8

Connecting Cave

Route 8

Route 9

Ambrette Town

Glittering Cave

Pokémon Center
Fossil Lab
Hotel Ambrette
Ambrette Aquarium

Key

- You can go to these locations using the field move Fly
- You can only go to these locations using the field move Surf
- You can ride Pokémon in these locations
- Use an unnamed path to access these locations

4

This is the map of the Kalos region, where your adventure awaits. All of the cities, towns, routes, caves, and other important places are shown. Routes are labeled in white, towns and cities in red, caves or naturally occurring locations in gray, and buildings in blue.

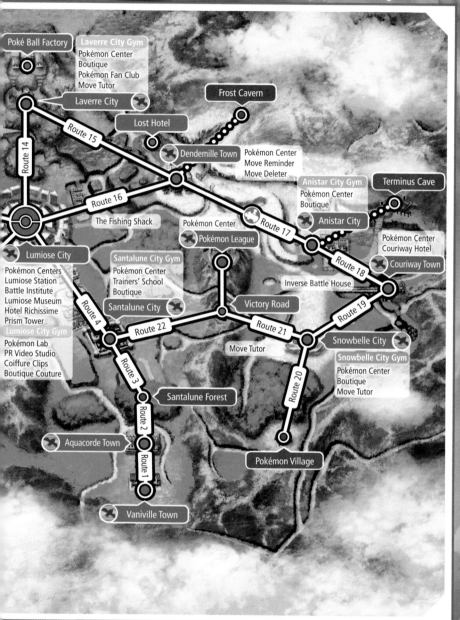

Poké Ball Factory

Laverre City Gym
Pokémon Center
Boutique
Pokémon Fan Club
Move Tutor

Laverre City

Frost Cavern

Lost Hotel

Route 15

Route 14

Dendemille Town

Pokémon Center
Move Reminder
Move Deleter

Anistar City Gym
Pokémon Center
Boutique

Terminus Cave

Route 16

The Fishing Shack

Route 17

Anistar City

Pokémon Center

Pokémon League

Route 18

Pokémon Center
Couriway Hotel

Couriway Town

Lumiose City

Pokémon Centers
Lumiose Station
Battle Institute
Lumiose Museum
Hotel Richissime
Prism Tower

Lumiose City Gym

Pokémon Lab
PR Video Studio
Coiffure Clips
Boutique Couture

Santalune City Gym
Pokémon Center
Trainers' School
Boutique

Santalune City

Victory Road

Inverse Battle House

Route 19

Route 4

Route 22

Route 21

Snowbelle City

Move Tutor

Snowbelle City Gym
Pokémon Center
Boutique
Move Tutor

Route 3

Route 20

Santalune Forest

Route 2

Aquacorde Town

Pokémon Village

Route 1

Vaniville Town

Y

5

Recommended Route

Below is the recommended route for your grand adventure through the Kalos region. Check this guide when you want to know how much progress you have made so far, or when you aren't sure where to go next.

Vaniville Town	p. 80

- Get dressed and go downstairs
- Meet your neighbors
- Leave Vaniville Town through the north gate

Route 1 (Vaniville Pathway)	p. 83

- Go to Aquacorde Town

Aquacorde Town	p. 84

- Meet up with your new friends
- Choose a Pokémon!
- Receive a Pokédex and the Prof's Letter
- Battle with Shauna

Vaniville Town	p. 82

- Deliver the Prof's Letter to your mom

Aquacorde Town	p. 87

- Explore Aquacorde Town

Route 2 (Avance Trail)	p. 88

- Battle a wild Pokémon
- Learn how to catch a wild Pokémon

Santalune Forest	p. 91

- Defeat Pokémon Trainers on your way to Route 3

Route 3 (Ouvert Way)	p. 94

- Receive the Adventure Rules from Serena/Calem

Santalune City	p. 97

- Check out the shops and Pokémon Center
- Battle Roller Skater Rinka for some Roller Skates
- Enter the Pokémon Gym or explore Route 22

Route 22 (Détourner Way)	p. 102

- Strengthen your Pokémon through battle

Santalune City	p. 104

Gym Battle 1: Gym Leader Viola

Route 4 (Parterre Way)	p. 106

- Meet Sina and Dexio

Lumiose City (South)   p. 108
- Battle Professor Sycamore
- Receive a new Pokémon and Mega Stone
- Meet Lysandre
- Meet Diantha and chat with Serena/Calem
- Meet Mr. Bonding

Route 5 (Versant Road)   p. 120
- Meet Korrina and Lucario
- Battle with Tierno
- Learn about Pokémon hordes

Camphrier Town   p. 126
- Meet the Name Rater
- Visit Shabboneau Castle

Route 7 (Rivière Walk)   p. 130
- Find the castle caretaker
- Visit the Berry fields

Route 6 (Palais Lane)   p. 139
- Travel to Parfum Palace

Parfum Palace   p. 141
- Help the palace's owner find his lost Furfrou
- Watch the fireworks and receive the Poké Flute

Route 7 (Rivière Walk)   p. 133
- Catch or defeat Snorlax
- Check out the Pokémon Day Care
- Visit the Battle Chateau
- Multi Battle with your friends

Connecting Cave (Zubat Roost)   p. 146
- Cut through the cave

Route 8 (Muraille Coast)   p. 148
- Get your Pokédex powered up
- Try a Sky Battle
- Meet Serena/Calem

Ambrette Town   p. 153
- Obtain TM94 Rock Smash
- Visit the Fossil Lab
- Visit the Ambrette Aquarium and get an Old Rod

Route 9 (Spikes Passage)   p. 158
- Ride the Rhyhorn across the rocks

Glittering Cave   p. 160
- Battle the Team Flare Grunts
- Join Serena/Calem in a Multi Battle against Team Flare
- Find the Fossil Lab assistant and receive a Fossil

Ambrette Town   p. 157
- Revisit the Fossil Lab to restore your Fossil

Route 8 (Muraille Coast)   p. 152
- Obtain the Dowsing Machine

Cyllage City   p. 166
- Ride off with a Bicycle
- Receive HM04 Strength
- **Gym Battle 2: Gym Leader Grant**

Route 10 (Menhir Trail)   p. 173
- Encounter more Team Flare members

Geosenge Town   p. 176
- Battle with Korrina

Route 11 (Miroir Way)   p. 179
- Receive a Holo Clip from Professor Sycamore

Reflection Cave   p. 181
- Meet up with Tierno and receive TM70 Flash
- Exit to Shalour City or delve deeper into the cave

Shalour City   p. 185
- Have a chat with Trevor and Tierno
- Meet the Mega Evolution guru
- Battle with Serena/Calem for one of Mega Evolution's secrets
- **Gym Battle 3: Gym Leader Korrina**
- Battle Korrina at the top of the Tower of Mastery
- Receive HM03 Surf

Route 12 (Fourrage Road)   p. 194
- Surf across the water
- Ride a Skiddo and reach items

Azure Bay   p. 197
- Obtain the Ampharosite

Coumarine City p. 200

- Receive a Holo Clip from Serena/Calem
- Reel in a Good Rod
- Take the monorail to the bluff
- Battle Serena/Calem outside the Pokémon Gym

Gym Battle 4: Gym Leader Ramos

- Get a Holo Clip from Lysandre
- Receive the Mountain Kalos Pokédex

Route 13 (Lumiose Badlands) p. 211

- Locate the Power Plant Pass
- Battle the Team Flare Grunt, then enter the Power Plant

Kalos Power Plant p. 214

- Battle your way to the Kalos Power Plant's center
- Defeat the Team Flare Admin and Aliana
- Meet the defenders of Kalos

Lumiose City (Center) p. 218

- Watch Prism Tower's lighting be restored
- Explore North Boulevard and the city

Gym Battle 5: Gym Leader Clemont

- Meet Professor Sycamore at Lysandre Café
- Receive a Holo Clip from Trevor

Route 14 (Laverre Nature Trail) p. 232

- Meet your friends and have a battle with Serena/Calem
- Check out the scary house

Laverre City p. 236

- Teach your Pokémon some battle-combo moves

Gym Battle 6: Gym Leader Valerie

Poké Ball Factory p. 244

- Enter the Poké Ball Factory and confront Team Flare
- Battle the Team Flare Admin in the northeast office
- Join forces with Serena/Calem to defeat Celosia and Bryony

Route 15 (Brun Way) p. 250

- See what Lysandre has to say
- Check out the Lost Hotel and Route 16

Lost Hotel p. 254

- Explore the Lost Hotel

Route 16 (Mélancolie Path) p. 258
- Obtain the Super Rod

Dendemille Town p. 262
- Have a chat with Professor Sycamore and Dexio
- Go north and investigate the Frost Cavern

Frost Cavern p. 266
- Cross the Frost Cavern's icy floors
- Battle against Team Flare

Dendemille Town p. 265
- Continue east to Route 17

Route 17 (Mamoswine Road) p. 273
- Hitch a ride on Mamoswine

Anistar City p. 276
- Have a chat with Sina and receive some Repeat Balls
- Learn the stories of the Legendary Pokémon
- Have a battle against Serena/Calem
  - **Gym Battle 7: Gym Leader Olympia**
- Receive a Holo Clip from the Team Flare Boss
- Fly back to Lumiose City

Lumiose City (North) p. 286
- Defeat the Team Flare Grunts inside Lysandre Café
- Find the secret door and enter Lysandre Labs

Lysandre Labs p. 289
- Test your skills against the head of Team Flare
- Defeat Team Flare Aliana
- Battle Team Flare Celosia and Bryony
- Battle Team Flare Mable
- Learn the story of Kalos's troubled past
- Battle Team Flare Xerosic

Geosenge Town (Second Visit) p. 298
- Defeat the Team Flare guard

Team Flare Secret HQ p. 299
- Battle the Team Flare Boss inside the secret headquarters
- Defeat the last of Team Flare
- Catch the Legendary Pokémon
- Defeat the Team Flare Boss

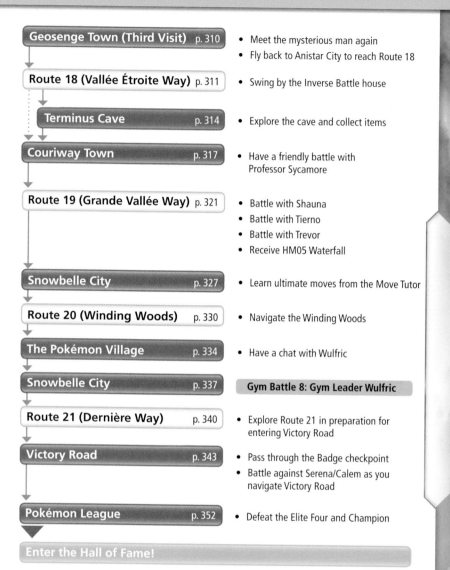

Geosenge Town (Third Visit) p. 310
- Meet the mysterious man again
- Fly back to Anistar City to reach Route 18

Route 18 (Vallée Étroite Way) p. 311
- Swing by the Inverse Battle house

Terminus Cave p. 314
- Explore the cave and collect items

Couriway Town p. 317
- Have a friendly battle with Professor Sycamore

Route 19 (Grande Vallée Way) p. 321
- Battle with Shauna
- Battle with Tierno
- Battle with Trevor
- Receive HM05 Waterfall

Snowbelle City p. 327
- Learn ultimate moves from the Move Tutor

Route 20 (Winding Woods) p. 330
- Navigate the Winding Woods

The Pokémon Village p. 334
- Have a chat with Wulfric

Snowbelle City p. 337

Gym Battle 8: Gym Leader Wulfric

Route 21 (Dernière Way) p. 340
- Explore Route 21 in preparation for entering Victory Road

Victory Road p. 343
- Pass through the Badge checkpoint
- Battle against Serena/Calem as you navigate Victory Road

Pokémon League p. 352
- Defeat the Elite Four and Champion

Enter the Hall of Fame!

Your adventure continues after you enter the Hall of Fame. Pack your Bag for another journey around the Kalos region!

Type Matchup Chart

Types are assigned both to moves and to the Pokémon themselves. These types can greatly affect the amount of damage dealt or received in battle, so if you learn how they line up against one another, you'll give yourself an edge in battle.

Attacking Pokémon's Move Type \ Defending Pokémon's Type	Normal	Fire	Water	Grass	Electric	Ice	Fighting	Poison	Ground	Flying	Psychic	Bug	Rock	Ghost	Dragon	Dark	Steel	Fairy
Normal													▲	×			▲	
Fire		▲	▲	●		●						●	▲		▲		●	
Water		●	▲	▲					●				●		▲			
Grass		▲	●	▲				▲	●	▲		▲	●		▲		▲	
Electric			●	▲	▲				×	●					▲			
Ice		▲	▲	●		▲			●	●					●		▲	
Fighting	●					●		▲		▲	▲	▲	●	×		●	●	▲
Poison				●				▲	▲				▲	▲			×	●
Ground		●		▲	●			●		×		▲	●				●	
Flying				●	▲		●					●	▲				▲	
Psychic							●	●			▲					×	▲	
Bug		▲		●			▲	▲		▲	●			▲		●	▲	▲
Rock		●				●	▲		▲	●		●					▲	
Ghost	×										●			●		▲		
Dragon															●		▲	×
Dark							▲				●			●		▲		▲
Steel		▲	▲		▲	●							●				▲	●
Fairy		▲					●	▲							●	●	▲	

Key

●	Very effective "It's super effective!"	× 2
No icon	Normal damage	× 1
▲	Not too effective "It's not very effective..."	× ½
×	No effect "It doesn't affect..."	× 0

- Fire-type Pokémon cannot be afflicted with the Burned condition.
- Grass-type Pokémon are immune to Leech Seed and powder and spore moves.
- Electric-type Pokémon cannot be afflicted with the Paralyzed condition.
- Ice-type Pokémon are immune to the Frozen condition and take no damage from hail.

- Poison-type Pokémon are immune to the Poison and Badly Poisoned conditions, even when switching in with Toxic Spikes in play. Poison-type Pokémon nullify Toxic Spikes (unless these Pokémon are also Flying type or have the Levitate Ability).
- Ground-type Pokémon are immune to Thunder Wave and take no damage from a sandstorm.
- Flying-type Pokémon cannot be damaged by Spikes when switching in, nor become afflicted with the Poison or Badly Poisoned conditions due to switching in with Toxic Spikes in play.
- Rock-type Pokémon take no damage from a sandstorm. Their Sp. Def also goes up in a sandstorm.
- Ghost-type Pokémon are not affected by moves that prevent Pokémon from fleeing from battle.
- Steel-type Pokémon take no damage from a sandstorm. They are also immune to the Poison and Badly Poisoned conditions. Even if switched in with Toxic Spikes in play, they will not be afflicted with the Poison or Badly Poisoned conditions.

Goals of the Game

Welcome! As an aspiring Pokémon Trainer, you have three primary goals in *Pokémon X* and *Pokémon Y*.

 Discover the secrets of Team Flare, a mysterious new organization in the Kalos region.

 Become the Champion of the Kalos region by collecting all eight Gym Badges and then defeating the Elite Four and the current Champion, who wait at the illustrious Pokémon League.

3 Complete the Kalos region's Pokédex by catching all 450 Pokémon native to the region.

To reach these lofty goals, you'll need to master the fine arts of raising Pokémon and battling with them. You've come to the right place, because this chapter is dedicated to helping you become the best Trainer the Kalos region has ever seen!

New in the Game

Pokémon X and *Pokémon Y* boast many new features that you'll want to know about. This section brings you up to speed on these all-new, exciting features.

Pokédex types

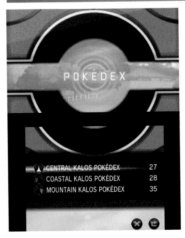

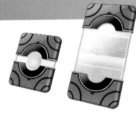

Anyone who's played a Pokémon game knows what a Pokédex is for. This vital device records critical data on every Pokémon encountered during the adventure. In *Pokémon X* and *Pokémon Y*, the Kalos region is loaded with Pokémon, so you'll end up with three different classifications of the Pokédex by the time you get to the Pokémon League!

Central Kalos Pokédex: This Pokédex records data on the many Pokémon who are encountered around the heart of Kalos.

Coastal Kalos Pokédex: Once you reach Kalos's breathtaking coastline, your Pokédex will be upgraded to include Coastal Kalos Pokédex entries.

Mountain Kalos Pokédex: The moment you begin to explore Kalos's towering mountains, your Pokédex will be enhanced to include data on the Pokémon that dwell in these scenic locations.

Customize your look

Let's get started with some quick questions...
Are you a boy? Or are you a girl?

The very first time you play *Pokémon X* or *Pokémon Y*, you get to customize your character's appearance. First, decide if you want to play as a male or female character, and then select a skin tone. Later, you'll be able to change your hairstyle and other options, including your hair color, eye color, and clothing. To perfect your look, visit the many clothing boutiques around the region.

NOTE *The gender that you select at the game's onset determines the gender of a valued friend who appears at many points during your adventure. If you choose the male character, you will journey with Serena, while those who choose the female character share their experiences with Calem.*

Roller Skates

Kalos is a sprawling region full of bustling cities, quaint little towns, and many other intriguing locations in between. Exploring this huge region on foot is a time-consuming process, but never fear—you'll receive some snazzy Roller Skates early in your adventure to help you get around.

After you score your Roller Skates, use the Circle Pad to skate around at a swift pace. Roller Skates can be used practically anywhere outdoors, but they often aren't available while exploring indoor areas. They also don't roll very well through some terrains, like sand and tall grass, so remember that you can always kick off your wheels with the +Control Pad, and dash around using ⓑ.

With Roller Skates, you can grind along special rails that appear in certain areas. Grinding on these rails sometimes lets you cross obstacles and reach more items. Some rails feature small kinks, and you'll fall while grinding along them if you don't have enough speed. Whenever you see a rail, slap on your Roller Skates and find out where it leads!

It's also possible to learn a variety of Roller Skate tricks, but you must seek out special characters who teach these flashy moves. You won't be able to use some Roller Skate tricks until you're told about them, so get out there and talk to everyone you can find!

Riding Pokémon

Another new feature in *Pokémon X* and *Pokémon Y* is the ability to ride on the back of certain Pokémon, like Rhyhorn and Mamoswine. By riding a Pokémon, you can comfortably cross even the harshest terrain. This fun new feature helps you explore every nook and cranny of the Kalos region.

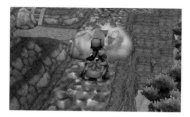

Sometimes you'll encounter rocks while riding a Pokémon, but these obstacles are no match for your larger Pokémon mounts. Simply press Ⓐ to smash any rocks that get in your way.

NOTES *You cannot ride a Pokémon while using items, such as the Dowsing Machine. Put away anything you're holding before climbing aboard!*

Though you may be off the ground, you aren't beyond the reach of wild Pokémon! When they get caught underfoot, they sometimes lash out and you may find yourself drawn into battles.

New applications on the Touch Screen

Pokémon X and *Pokémon Y* take full advantage of the Nintendo 3DS system's Touch Screen interface with brand new applications that will enhance your Pokémon experience like never before. Switch between screens using Ⓛ and Ⓡ to find the Player Search System, Super Training, and Pokémon-Amie. These three applications are explained in greater detail elsewhere, but here is a quick taste of what each can do for you.

Player Search System: Connect with the world, as you trade, battle, chat, and share O-Powers (p. 72).

Super Training: Train the Pokémon on your team in two different modes to improve their base stats (p. 21).

Pokémon-Amie: Play with and care for the Pokémon on your team to make them more affectionate (p. 19).

Shops and boutiques

If you thought that choosing your character at the game's onset was cool, you haven't seen anything yet! *Pokémon X* and *Pokémon Y* take customization to greater heights by letting you customize your look at special shops, including numerous clothing boutiques and the hair salon in Lumiose City.

When visiting the hair salon, let the stylist know what you'd like. You can change your hair color or hairstyle in a variety of ways. You can find the salon in Lumiose City's South Boulevard.

Boutiques are special shops that sell all sorts of clothing and accessories. Each boutique has its own style, and some purchases may have a pretty price to match. The selection of items available at a boutique changes daily, so visit them often! The boutique's inventory also varies based on your character's gender.

NOTE *Not a fan of shopping? You may want to reconsider that stance. The more you shop and the more you do in Lumiose City in particular, the more fashionable and knowledgeable you will appear to others. Certain shops and facilities won't be available to you until you are deemed stylish enough.*

Pokémon-Amie

Pokémon-Amie is a unique Touch Screen mode that becomes available early in the adventure. This mode helps your Pokémon feel more affectionate toward you through a variety of fun activities, including petting your Pokémon and feeding it delicious snacks called Poké Puffs. Affectionate Pokémon will perform better than ever before in battle, as you can learn about in the guide to Pokémon-Amie following the walkthrough (p. 366).

 When feeding Poké Puffs to your Pokémon, use the stylus to hold the Poké Puff up to the Pokémon's face until it finishes eating. Don't let the Poké Puff drop!

Your Pokémon also responds to your voice and expressions in Pokémon-Amie. Try entertaining your Pokémon by calling its name or making faces. Try all sorts of things, for you never know how your Pokémon might react!

Pokémon-Amie also lets you play fun minigames once you have three or more healthy Pokémon on your team, including Berry Picker, Head It, and Tile Puzzle. These simple minigames are easy to grasp, yet challenging to master. Play together with your Pokémon to earn more Poké Puffs.

The Decorate option lets you change your wallpaper or show off fancy Décor items, such as cushions. You can also set out Poké Puffs in the hopes of attracting nearby Pokémon to visit. Visiting Pokémon may give you new Décor items or more Poké Puffs, so they're always welcome. Have fun decorating with Décor items and customizing your Pokémon-Amie experience!

NOTE For an in-depth guide to all you can do in Pokémon-Amie, turn to page 366. There you will learn more about the games you can play, the rewards you can earn, and the benefits of having affectionate Pokémon.

Super Training

The world of Pokémon raising has been turned upside down by genius inventor Clemont's latest, greatest invention— Super Training! This mode becomes available early in the adventure. You can use it to improve your Pokémon's base stats and battle-worthiness anywhere, anytime. Learn more about it on page 372.

Super Training's main mode is a virtual sports game in which your Pokémon faces off against Balloon Bots. To toughen up your Pokémon, dodge the balls that are launched by the Balloon Bots while simultaneously shooting balls into the opponent's goal. It sounds simple, but there's a surprising amount of skill involved!

Perform well in Super Training to earn special training bags for use in Core Training. In Core Training, your Pokémon hits a training bag to become stronger. This process is automatic, but you can accelerate it by tapping the training bag over and over until your Pokémon knocks it for a loop. The result of Core Training will vary based on the training bag that was used. Try them all!

NOTE *For an in-depth guide to what you can accomplish in Super Training, turn to page 372. There you can read more about different shots, the effects of the different training bags you can win, and what it takes to make a Fully Trained Pokémon.*

Obtaining Pokémon

Now that you've learned about some of the new features in *Pokémon X* and *Pokémon Y*, it's time to review the basics. Most of this will seem very familiar to series fans, but it's worth reviewing. Finding Pokémon friends is the first thing you'll need to know about.

Catching Wild Pokémon

Wild Pokémon love nature, and their many different habitats include tall grass, flower fields, caves, deserts, wetlands, lakes, and rivers. They may also appear along with certain phenomena in the field, such as rustling bushes or shaking trash cans. When you find a place where it looks like a Pokémon might appear, rush over to check it out.

Main areas for finding Pokémon

Tall Grass

Very Tall Grass

Yellow Flowers

Purple Flowers

Red Flowers

Caves

Deserts

Swamps

Water Surface

Fishing

Special places where wild Pokémon appear

*Use field move Rock Smash

> **NOTE** These special encounters can generally be avoided, if you choose not to investigate shaking trash cans or cracked rocks, or stay far from shadows that appear on the ground or bushes that shake. But they are also the only ways to find some Pokémon, so work up the courage to check them out!

Throw Poké Balls to catch Pokémon

When you discover a wild Pokémon, throw a Poké Ball to catch it. But a Pokémon won't just meekly hop into the Poké Ball you've thrown. Pokémon that are still full of energy are likely to escape from the Poké Ball. Use the following techniques to catch Pokémon successfully.

Tips for catching Pokémon

1 Reduce HP

A Pokémon's HP is a measure of how tired it is. Use moves to attack a Pokémon and lower its HP. When the Pokémon's HP is lowered, even a little bit, it's easier to catch. When the HP bar is red, it means the Pokémon is weak. That's the best time to throw a Poké Ball!

2 Inflict status conditions

Some Pokémon moves and Abilities inflict status conditions on their targets (p. 36). A Pokémon with a status condition, such as Poison or Paralysis, is easier to catch. Lower the target's HP and use status conditions to maximize your chances of success.

3 Use the right Poké Ball

Many different kinds of Poké Balls exist. Each kind of Poké Ball performs differently. They are each specialized for a certain use. Always choose a Poké Ball that's effective for the location or kind of Pokémon you want to catch. It's a basic Pokémon-catching principle.

NOTE *A critical capture is a phenomenon where a Pokémon is caught after the Poké Ball rocks only once. Catching many different kinds of Pokémon will improve your chances for a critical capture, so fill your Pokédex and show those wild Pokémon what you're made of.*

Poké Ball data

Many different types of Poké Balls can be found in the Kalos region. Each Poké Ball's special effects depend on factors such as Pokémon type or the location of the battle. Learn the ins and outs of each Poké Ball so you can use the right one for the Pokémon you're aiming to catch.

Basic Poké Balls

Poké Ball

The most basic device you can use to catch Pokémon.

How to make it available at Poké Marts:
Sold from the beginning of your adventure

Great Ball

Better at catching Pokémon than the Poké Ball.

How to make it available at Poké Marts:
Obtain one Gym Badge

Ultra Ball

Better at catching Pokémon than the Great Ball.

How to make it available at Poké Marts:
Obtain three Gym Badges

Master Ball

It is the ultimate Ball that is sure to catch any wild Pokémon.

How to get one:
Given as a reward for saving the Poké Ball Factory
Given as a jackpot prize at the Loto-ID Center

Premier Ball

Same as a regular Poké Ball. Given as a bonus at Poké Marts.

How to get one:
Buy 10 Poké Balls at one time

Poké Balls with special features

Quick Ball

More effective when thrown at the very beginning of a battle.

Shops that carry this Ball:
Poké Marts in Coumarine City and Snowbelle City, Poké Ball Boutique in Lumiose City

Timer Ball

The more turns that have elapsed in battle, the more effective it is.

Shops that carry this Ball:
Poké Marts in Coumarine City and Snowbelle City, Poké Ball Boutique in Lumiose City

Heal Ball

Restores a caught Pokémon's HP and status.

Shops that carry this Ball:
Poké Marts in Lumiose City (North Pokémon Center) and Snowbelle City, Poké Ball Boutique in Lumiose City

Dusk Ball

Good for catching Pokémon at night and in caves.

Shops that carry this Ball:
Poké Marts in Cyllage City and Snowbelle City, Poké Ball Boutique in Lumiose City

Net Ball

Good for catching Bug- and Water-type Pokémon.

Shops that carry this Ball:
Poké Marts in Cyllage City, Lumiose City (North Pokémon Center), and Snowbelle City, Poké Ball Boutique in Lumiose City

Dive Ball

Good for catching Pokémon that live in the water.

Shops that carry this Ball:
Poké Ball Boutique in Lumiose City

Nest Ball

The lower the Pokémon's level, the more effective it is.

Shops that carry this Ball:
Poké Marts in Cyllage City, Lumiose City (North Pokémon Center), and Snowbelle City, Poké Ball Boutique in Lumiose City

Luxury Ball

Your friendship with the caught Pokémon will grow faster (p. 37).

Shops that carry this Ball:
Poké Ball Boutique in Lumiose City

Repeat Ball

Good for catching Pokémon of a species you've caught before.

Shops that carry this Ball:
Poké Marts in Coumarine City and Snowbelle City, Poké Ball Boutique in Lumiose City

Other ways to obtain Pokémon

The main way to get Pokémon is catching them with a Poké Ball, but there are many other ways to obtain Pokémon as well. Knowing all the ways to obtain Pokémon is crucial for completing the Pokédex.

Other methods for obtaining Pokémon:

Evolve them through battle

Fennekin gained 160 Exp. Points!

Pokémon build up Experience Points when they take part in battles. After getting a certain number of Experience Points, Pokémon will level up. Some Pokémon evolve at a certain level.

Evolve them by meeting certain conditions

Congratulations! Your Helioptile evolved into Heliolisk!

Pokémon evolve in many different ways, such as by befriending their Trainer or using stones that have special powers.

Link Trade

Trade Pokémon with friends, family, and people all over the world (p. 70). This way you can both get Pokémon you want. Some Pokémon can only be evolved by trading them, in fact.

Get them through story events

Sometimes people you talk to during the story will entrust you with Pokémon. These can be Pokémon that are hard to encounter in the wild, so make sure to take them up on any offers.

Trade with people in towns

Some people in towns will ask you to trade them a certain Pokémon. Many of these Pokémon are hard to find, so go along with their suggestion.

Get Pokémon Eggs from the Pokémon Day Care

Leave two Pokémon at the Pokémon Day Care, and sometimes an Egg will be discovered at the Day Care (p. 134). What luck!

Restore Fossils

You may find ancient Pokémon Fossils during your adventure. Restoring a Fossil yields a living Pokémon!

Battling

Pokémon grow stronger as they battle

Pikachu grew to Lv. 4!

Winning a battle gives Pokémon Experience Points. When they gain enough points, they'll level up, and their stats—Attack, HP, and so forth—will increase. Have them battle to help them grow stronger.

 You gain Experience Points not only from defeating other Pokémon in battle but also when you successfully catch a Pokémon.

Pokémon use moves

Fennekin used Tail Whip!

Pokémon can learn all kinds of moves, which are useful both in battle and while traveling on your adventure. There are more than 600 different moves, each with its own effects. The maximum number of moves a Pokémon can know at one time is four. This means you'll want to put some hard thought into which moves you want your Pokémon to know to bring out its unique characteristics.

How to teach new moves to Pokémon

Level them up

Pikachu learned Play Nice!

A Pokémon can learn certain moves at different levels. Once it reaches the required level, it can learn the move.

Use a TM or HM

TMs & HMs
HM05 Waterfall

The user charges at the target and may make it flinch. This can also be used to climb a waterfall.

TYPE		POWER	80
CATEGORY		ACCURACY	100
		PP	15

TMs and HMs are items that teach moves to Pokémon. You can use the same one over and over on different Pokémon.

Learn moves from Move Tutors

Yes
No

A special move...
Should I teach it a battle-combo move?

Seek out Move Tutors during your travels. They know moves that they're willing to teach your Pokémon.

Battle types

During your adventures in *Pokémon X* or *Pokémon Y*, you'll experience the following eight battle formats: Single Battle, Double Battle, Multi Battle, Triple Battle, Rotation Battle, Sky Battle, Horde Encounter, and Inverse Battle. If you want to win, you'll need to learn the rules of every format.

Single Battle

Each side battles with one Pokémon at a time

Each Pokémon Trainer sends out one Pokémon with which to battle. The straightforward nature of Single Battle, in which you focus on attacking and exploiting your opponent's weaknesses, is what makes this such a fun battle format. But if you want to become a Pokémon battle master, you'll need to think carefully about how to raise your Pokémon, what items to give them to hold, and much more. You can get an explanation of a move if you hold ⓛ when choosing the move.

★ Double Battle

Each side battles with two Pokémon at a time

Each Pokémon Trainer sends out two Pokémon with which to battle. In Double Battles, attacks that can hit both of the opposing Pokémon become very useful. Double Battles require you to know more about moves and their effects than you need for Single Battles. It's important to come up with good ways to combine a Pokémon's moves, held item, and Ability in order to achieve victory in Double Battles.

★ Multi Battle

Up to four Trainers battle it out

Two to four Trainers can take part in Multi Battles. Like Double Battles, there are two Pokémon on each side, but if you are battling alongside an ally, you will only be able to control the actions of your own Pokémon. Try to use Pokémon, moves, and Abilities that will complement those of your partner if you are battling two to a side.

★ Triple Battle

Each side battles with three Pokémon at a time

Each Pokémon Trainer sends out three Pokémon with which to battle. The Pokémon in the middle can target any of the opposing Trainer's three Pokémon. The Pokémon on the left and right have a limited range. Each can target only the Pokémon directly in front of itself and the Pokémon in the middle, but not the Pokémon on the far side of its position. Triple Battles can be extremely demanding, as they require you to shift your Pokémon around in order to exploit your opponent's weaknesses.

★ Rotation Battle

In this evolved form of the Single Battle format, each side battles with three Pokémon at a time

The Rotation Battle is an evolved form of the Single Battle format. Each Pokémon Trainer sends out three Pokémon with which to battle. Only one Pokémon can attack per turn, but you can choose to use a move from any of your Pokémon. What makes Rotation Battles unique is that Pokémon can move and attack on the same turn. For example, if you choose a move from a Pokémon in the back, it will rotate to the front and use its move on the same turn.

★ Sky Battle

Each side battles with one Flying or levitating Pokémon

In this all-new battle format, each Trainer sends out one Flying or levitating Pokémon with which to battle. Only Flying-type Pokémon or Pokémon with the Levitate Ability can participate in Sky Battles, but that does not guarantee that all Flying types or levitating Pokémon are able to rise to this challenge. The battle plays out just like a Single Battle, except that only Flying or levitating Pokémon may be used. Many of the Flying-type Pokémon share common weaknesses, so it's important to exploit those of your opponent while seeking to defend your own.

Horde Encounter

Take on a horde of Pokémon

Like Sky Battles, Horde Encounters are new to *Pokémon X* and *Pokémon Y*. In a Horde Encounter, you send out one Pokémon with which to battle against a large group of opposing Pokémon. It seems unfair, but the Pokémon you encounter in Horde Encounters are often far less experienced than your Pokémon. Still, moves that target multiple Pokémon are extremely useful in this type of battle. Try to take out the whole horde in one move! If you want to catch one of them, you'll need to defeat them individually, because you can't throw a Poké Ball while more than one opponent still stands against you. Pokémon appearing in Horde Encounters sometimes have rare Abilities that you won't find otherwise, so consider this tactic.

★ Inverse Battle

Experience a reverse type matchup

This all-new battle format flips the Type Matchup Chart (p. 12) on its head by reversing the strengths and weaknesses of Pokémon types and move types. For example, Fire-type moves are usually super effective against Grass-type Pokémon, but in an Inverse Battle, they will not be very effective at all. It seems like a simple twist, but one false move could lead to defeat. Inverse Battles play out just like Single Battles, with each Trainer sending out one Pokémon with which to battle.

> **NOTE** *These new battle formats aren't the only exciting changes that will affect your battles in* Pokémon X *and* Pokémon Y. *Enjoy discovering new features, like moves that affect the background of the battle field. If your Pokémon's moves destroy rocks or trees or other scenery during battle, you might just find a special item in the aftermath!*

Pokémon Types

Pokémon can be classified into 18 types, such as Normal, Fire, Water, Grass, and the newly discovered Fairy type! The matchups between these types are a key factor in determining a battle's outcome. Master the intricate knowledge of all the different types!

Examples of the 18 Pokémon types

Normal

Furfrou and others

Fire

Fennekin and others

Water

Froakie and others

Grass

Chespin and others

Electric

Helioptile and others

Ice

Cubchoo and others

Fighting

Pancham and others

Poison

Skrelp and others

Ground

Diggersby and others

Flying

Noibat and others

Psychic

Espurr and others

Bug

Scatterbug and others

Rock

Tyrunt and others

Ghost

Pumpkaboo and others

Dragon

Axew and others

Dark

Inkay and others

Steel

Honedge and others

Fairy

Flabébé and others

Pokémon moves have types

Both Pokémon and their moves have types. This Froakie is typical of most Pokémon. Although it belongs to the Water type, it can learn moves from other types as well. When it uses moves of its own type, however, they get a 50% boost in power!

Example: Froakie

The move's type is used when attacking

When Froakie attacks Pancham with Bounce, look at Bounce's type—the Flying type.

The Pokémon's type is used when defending

When Pancham attacks Froakie, look at Froakie's type—the Water type.

Pokémon type:	Type of the move Bounce
Water	Flying

Matchups and building a strong team

Types have good or bad matchups

Types interact like a big game of rock-paper-scissors. For instance, Water is strong against Fire, but weak against Grass. If the attacking Pokémon's move type is strong against the defending Pokémon's type, the move does increased damage.

Froakie
Water

Fennekin
Fire

Chespin
Grass

Good type matchups mean increased damage!

Froakie
Water

Fennekin
Fire

Froakie attacks with a Water-type move:

Deals increased damage because it's a good type matchup.

Bad type matchups mean decreased damage!

Froakie
Water

Chespin
Grass

Froakie attacks with a Water-type move:

Deals reduced damage because it's a bad type matchup.

 Exploiting your opponent's weakness and using moves that have a type advantage is one of the fundamental strategies in Pokémon battles. For example, by targeting a Lv. 35 Braixen's weakness, a Frogadier that's only Lv. 30 can deal massive damage to the Braixen!

Use type advantages to increase attack damage

It's super effective!

Under the right conditions, your moves will do at least 50% more damage than usual. If you can keep dishing out that kind of damage, victory is sure to be within your reach.

Battle messages describe the damage range

Message	Matchup	Damage
It's super effective!	Good	2–4 times damage
It's not very effective...	Not good	Half damage or less
(No message)	Normal	Regular damage
It doesn't affect...	Bad	No damage
A critical hit!		1.5 times damage

Use status conditions to gain an advantage

Pokémon can be affected by status conditions such as Sleep and Poison. These conditions can immobilize a Pokémon or eat away at its HP. Wear down your opponent by hitting Pokémon with moves that inflict status conditions.

Status conditions cause physical changes

Status condition examples

Poison
The target's HP decreases each turn. This condition does not wear off on its own.

Paralysis
There's a 25% chance that the target can't attack. The target's Speed is also lowered. This condition does not wear off on its own.

Sleep
Excluding the use of specific moves, the target becomes unable to attack. This condition can wear off during battle.

Frozen
Excluding the use of specific moves, the target becomes unable to attack. This condition can wear off during battle.

Burned
The target's HP decreases each turn. The target's Attack is also lowered. This condition does not wear off on its own.

Confused
The target will sometimes attack itself. This condition can wear off during battle.

Infatuation
The target becomes infatuated by a Pokémon of the opposite gender and is unable to attack 50% of the time. Once the Pokémon that inflicted the Infatuation status is defeated, the condition wears off.

 If one of your Pokémon is affected by a status condition, heal it as soon as you can. By leaving a status condition alone, your Pokémon might lose HP each turn or be unable to attack, putting you in a tricky position. Keep items that heal status conditions, such as Antidotes and Awakenings, on hand so that you can be ready to heal your Pokémon as soon as they are inflicted with a status condition.

Give Pokémon items to hold

Each Pokémon can hold a single item. Consider giving your Pokémon an item that has an effect in battle to gain an advantage, or an item that increases what you receive after battle. It's always a good idea to give your Pokémon an item to hold.

Examples of useful held items

Quick Claw

Allows the holder to attack first sometimes.

Amulet Coin

Doubles the prize money if the holding Pokémon is brought into battle at least once.

Lucky Egg

Gain 50% more Experience Points after a battle.

Pokémon and Trainers become friends

Very connected to each other! That's what it looks like to me!

Friendship is the bond of trust that can grow between a Pokémon and its Trainer. Keep a Pokémon happy and it will grow to like you, but a mistreated Pokémon will dislike you. Two things Pokémon definitely don't like are fainting in battle and swallowing down herbal medicines. Certain characters you meet will check how friendly you and your Pokémon are.

How to improve your friendship with your Pokémon

Use Pokémon-Amie:

Every activity in Pokémon-Amie increases friendship.

Travel together:

Put a Pokémon in your party and go on an adventure together.

Level it up:

Battle with a Pokémon and have it level up.

Use stat-boosting items on it:

Use items such as Protein or Zinc to boost base stats.

Use items on it during battles:

Use items such as X Attack and X Defend during battles.

Teach it a new move:

Use a TM or HM to teach it a new move.

Battle Gym Leaders with it:

Use it in major battles, such as those with Gym Leaders.

Have it hold a Soothe Bell:

Have it hold a Soothe Bell that you can receive from an old woman in Shalour City.

Get it a massage:

Take it to get a massage in Cyllage City.

Use your O-Powers:

Use the Befriending Powers you obtain from Mr. Bonding to improve your friendship.

Benefits of friendship

Pokémon evolve

What?
Pichu is evolving!

Many species of Pokémon evolve when leveled up while they're on friendly terms with you. There are other conditions that affect these Evolutions, though, like the time of day.

They can learn more moves

Yes
No

Would you like your Pokémon to learn that move?

If you are friendly with them, you can teach some of your Pokémon special moves, including battle-combo moves, the strongest Dragon-type move, and the ultimate moves for evolutions of your first Pokémon partners.

Pokémon have different Abilities

Each Pokémon species has various Abilities. For instance, Vivillon can have the Shield Dust or Compound Eyes Abilities. Some Abilities take effect during battle, while other Abilities come in handy as you explore the region.

Sandile's
Intimidate!

When a Pokémon's Ability is triggered in battle, messages appear for both your Pokémon and your opponent's Pokémon, so it's clear when an Ability activates.

Examples of Abilities and their effects

Ability	**Pickup**

May pick up an item while it's in your party. The Pokémon's level determines what items you're likely to find.

Pokémon with this Ability:
Bunnelby, Diggersby, and others

Ability	**Intimidate**

Lowers opponent's Attack by 1 when the Pokémon enters battle. This can reduce the amount of damage done by physical moves.

Pokémon with this Ability:
Sandile, Krokorok, and others

Battling online and Link Battles

Pokémon X and *Pokémon Y* provide plenty of options when it comes to battling against other players. The most common way to battle is through the PSS (Player Search System)—just tap the icon of any player who appears in the PSS and then choose Battle to send that player an invite. You can ask Friends, Acquaintances, or even random Passersby for battles this way.

You can also use the Battle Spot feature to find players to battle with. Simply open the PSS menu by tapping the center button at the top of the PSS screen. On the PSS menu screen, choose Battle Spot to begin your search for players who are looking to participate in online battles at the same time as you. Sometimes this is a better option than just randomly asking players to battle, because you know that everyone who's using Battle Spot is interested in testing their skills against other players.

IR and local wireless battles

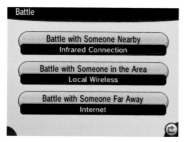

No Internet connection? No problem! When other players are close by, you can challenge them to an IR (infrared) or local wireless battle. Open the PSS menu and select Battle to set up a local battle.

Pokémon Global Link Battles

When you're looking to expand your online battle experience, take a look at the PGL (p. 404). You'll find competitive players participating in Online Competitions, hoping to capture fame in the worldwide rankings. Check it out at www.pokemon-gl.com!

Introducing the *Pokémon Bank* and *Poké Transporter* applications for the Nintendo 3DS!

Each time the Pokémon series has leaped to a new generation, players needed a way to move beloved Pokémon from past games to the newest. Now, that is about to change as Pokémon takes to the cloud! When your Pokémon are stored in the cloud, they'll be saved on the Internet. Even if you lose your Game Card or your save data is corrupted, your Pokémon will be safe and ready to be brought to your new game at any time.

Pokémon Bank

Pokémon Bank is a downloadable application for the Nintendo 3DS system that lets you store up to 3,000 Pokémon online in the cloud. With advanced search functions, you can quickly find the Pokémon you want and transfer multiple Pokémon at a time. You can also transfer between different copies of *Pokémon X* or *Pokémon Y*. There will be an annual fee associated with this application.

Poké Transporter

Poké Transporter is available for free with *Pokémon Bank*. It lets you transfer from other Game Cards *(Pokémon Black, White, Black 2,* and *White 2)* and send your Pokémon to *Pokémon Bank*, ready to be transferred to *Pokémon X* or *Pokémon Y*. No more worries about having problems with or losing old hardware now that Pokémon can be stored safely in the cloud.

Pokémon Evolution

Mega Evolution and Mega Stones

Mega Evolution is an all-new feature in *Pokémon X* and *Pokémon Y*. This powerful yet temporary transformation is unlike any other form of evolution known to Trainers. Only certain Pokémon can take advantage of Mega Evolution, but before that can happen, those Pokémon must be given the proper Mega Stone to hold. Even then, you'll find that there are more secrets to making Mega Evolution possible.

Once you've obtained all you need for Mega Evolution and have given a suitable Pokémon the proper Mega Stone to hold, Mega Evolution becomes available for that Pokémon during battle. Simply tap the Mega Evolution button that appears at the bottom of the Touch Screen before selecting a move for your Pokémon to use. The Pokémon's Mega Stone will then react to your Mega Ring, evolving the Pokémon into a truly formidable form. The Pokémon then carries out its move on the same turn.

Mega Evolution can have astounding effects. Mega Evolved Pokémon will take on powerful new appearances, but the effects of Mega Evolution are not all on the surface. Mega Evolving can change Pokémon's stats, Abilities, and even their types. Some Mega Evolutions are exclusive to *Pokémon X* and some are exclusive to *Pokémon Y*. Some Pokémon even have more than one Mega Evolution! Unleash Mega Evolution to transform your Pokémon during battle and make them more powerful!

> **NOTE** *Mega Evolution can only be used during battle, and the effect wears off when the battle ends. You can only Mega Evolve one Pokémon per battle, even if you have more than one Pokémon in your team capable of Mega Evolution. You can switch your Mega Evolved Pokémon in and out of battle, though, without undoing their transformation. But if a Mega Evolved Pokémon faints during the battle, it will return to its usual form.*

Leveling up Pokémon

Most people raise their Pokémon by battling with them. At the same time, Trainers want to use their highest level Pokémon in battle. Interested in some tips for raising lower-level Pokémon as quickly as possible? Here are some techniques to help you build a strong team of Pokémon without needing to have them all participate in battle directly.

Effective Pokémon-raising techniques

Switch out the Pokémon after a battle begins

As long as a Pokémon appears in the battle even once, it will receive Experience Points. You can use this to your advantage by putting a lower-level Pokémon in the lead position of your party, and then switching it out for a more powerful Pokémon as soon as the battle begins.

Revive a fainted Pokémon before a battle ends

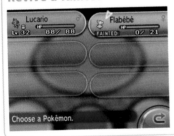

If a lower-level Pokémon faints during battle, switch in another Pokémon for it, and then use Revive on it. As long as you revive the fainted Pokémon before the battle ends, it will receive Experience Points.

Trade Pokémon with another Trainer

Pokémon that you obtain via Link Trades receive 50% more Experience Points than Pokémon obtained through regular means. Ask someone to trade you a Pokémon that you'd like to raise so you can get this Experience Point bonus.

Use Exp. Point Power

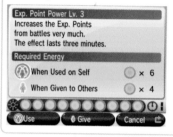

Exp. Point Power Lv. 3
Increases the Exp. Points
from battles very much.
The effect lasts three minutes.

Required Energy

When Used on Self   × 6

When Given to Others   × 4

Use   Give   Cancel

Use the O-Power called Exp. Point Power that you can obtain from Mr. Bonding, and your Pokémon will level up faster than ever. The more you use your O-Powers, the stronger they will get—and if you raise this O-Power to Lv. 3, your Pokémon can receive two times the Experience Points they would otherwise! See page 74 for more on O-Powers.

Hold off on evolving your Pokémon

Huh? Flabébé
stopped evolving!

Pressing ® when your Pokémon appears to be evolving will surprise it and cause it to stop evolving. This is called Evolution cancellation. A Pokémon that has been prevented from evolving in this way will get a bit more Experience Points after a battle than it would have in its evolved form.

Play often with your Pokémon

Pokémon that are feeling affectionate, thanks to playing together in Pokémon-Amie, will also receive an extra bonus when Experience Points are being dealt out. Keep all the Pokémon on your team feeling well-loved and you'll be rewarded by seeing them level up faster! See page 366 for more on Pokémon-Amie.

Raising Pokémon also gets easier with an Exp. Share or Lucky Egg

Some special items enable you to raise both your lead Pokémon and your supporting Pokémon at the same time. Two such useful items are the Lucky Egg and Exp. Share. Give the Lucky Egg to your main Pokémon, and use the Exp. Share to watch your supporting Pokémon grow!

How to use the Exp. Share and Lucky Egg

Exp. Share

Share Experience Points

The Exp. Share in *Pokémon X* and *Pokémon Y* functions differently than in recent games in the series—all of the Pokémon in your party, not just one, gain Experience Points without actually participating in battle. When you get the Exp. Share, it appears in your Bag in the Key Items Pocket. It is set to the On position when you receive it, but you can turn it Off later if you wish. You do not give it to any Pokémon; it remains in your Bag and affects every Pokémon in your party as long as it is turned On.

How to get one:
It's given to you by Alexa right before you enter Route 4 after obtaining the first Gym Badge.

Lucky Egg

Get more Experience Points than usual

The Lucky Egg is an item that gives 50% more Experience Points than usual. It is most effective if you have your main Pokémon hold it.

How to get one:
At Coumarine City, show a girl in the Coumarine Hotel a Pokémon with whom you have a high friendship bond.

Natures and Characteristics

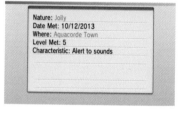

Nature: Jolly
Date Met: 10/12/2013
Where: Aquacorde Town
Level Met: 5
Characteristic: Alert to sounds

Each individual Pokémon has its own Nature and Characteristic. A Pokémon's Nature affects how its stats increase when it gains a level. A Pokémon's Characteristic indicates which stat will grow the most. Catch a lot of Pokémon and you may find one with the perfect Nature and Characteristic for how you hope to raise it.

How Pokémon Natures affect stat growth

Nature	Attack	Defense	Speed	Sp. Atk	Sp. Def
Hardy					
Lonely	◎	▲			
Brave	◎		▲		
Adamant	◎			▲	
Naughty	◎				▲
Bold	▲	◎			
Docile					
Relaxed		◎	▲		
Impish		◎		▲	
Lax		◎			▲
Timid	▲		◎		
Hasty		▲	◎		
Serious					
Jolly			◎	▲	
Naive			◎		▲
Modest	▲			◎	
Mild		▲		◎	
Quiet			▲	◎	
Bashful					
Rash				◎	▲
Calm	▲				◎
Gentle		▲			◎
Sassy			▲		◎
Careful				▲	◎
Quirky					

◎ Gains more upon leveling up　▲ Gains less upon leveling up

How Pokémon Characteristics affect stat growth

HP grows most	Attack grows most	Defense grows most	Speed grows most	Sp. Attack grows most	Sp. Defense grows most
Loves to eat.	Proud of its power.	Sturdy body.	Likes to run.	Highly curious.	Strong willed.
Takes plenty of siestas.	Likes to thrash about.	Capable of taking hits.	Alert to sounds.	Mischievous.	Somewhat vain.
Nods off a lot.	A little quick tempered.	Highly persistent.	Impetuous and silly.	Thoroughly cunning.	Strongly defiant.
Scatters things often.	Likes to fight.	Good endurance.	Somewhat of a clown.	Often lost in thought.	Hates to lose.
Likes to relax.	Quick tempered.	Good perseverance.	Quick to flee.	Very finicky.	Somewhat stubborn.

Pokémon Eggs and Egg Groups

Leave two Pokémon at the Pokémon Day Care on Route 7, and sometimes an Egg will be discovered. Many Pokémon species in the Kalos Pokédex can be obtained by hatching them from Eggs. Use these steps to discover Eggs and get the Pokémon you're after.

Steps leading to Egg discovery

1 Deposit Pokémon

Try leaving two Pokémon of opposite gender.

2 Take the Egg

If the male and female Pokémon left at the Day Care get along well, an Egg will be discovered.

2 Hatch the Egg

Put the Egg in your party and carry it around on your adventure. Eventually, a Pokémon will hatch from the Egg.

The man at the Pokémon Day Care will give you clues about whether an Egg will be found

The two seem to get along.

When you leave two Pokémon at the Pokémon Day Care, the man outside tells you how well they get along. His words also reveal how likely it is that an Egg will be discovered.

The Day-Care Man's messages

The two seem to get along very well!	Eggs are likely to be found.
The two seem to get along.	Eggs may be found.
The two don't really seem to like each other very much.	Eggs are unlikely to be found.
The two prefer to play with other Pokémon more than with each other.	Eggs will not be found.

Egg Groups

To find Eggs, you can leave two Pokémon of the same species but opposite genders at the Pokémon Day Care. This is the simplest method. You can also pair off Pokémon by Egg Group. You can find an Egg from two different species of Pokémon if they have opposite genders and the same Egg Group. The Pokémon which hatches from the Egg will be of the same species as the female Pokémon you left at the Pokémon Day Care, or an earlier evolution form in its line.

> **TIPS**
>
> *With a Ditto, you can find almost any kind of Egg! Ditto are commonly found in Pokémon Village, so be sure to catch one. It will allow you to find Eggs even for Pokémon of unknown gender, where normally no Eggs can be found.*
>
> ---
>
> *Eggs don't just inherit their species from the Pokémon that are left at the Pokémon Day Care. A Pokémon that hatches from an Egg can also inherit moves that it would normally only learn at a higher level, if both of the Pokémon left at the Day Care know it. It can also inherit moves that would normally be impossible to learn, or only available from a TM, from the male Pokémon left at the Pokémon Day Care. Even Abilities and Hidden Abilities are inheritable from the female Pokémon left at the Pokémon Day Care.*

Some Pokémon belong to more than one Egg Group. Consult the following tables when you want to find an Egg after dropping off a pair of Pokémon at the Pokémon Day Care. This information will be indispensable when you want to pass along Egg Moves!

Key to the Tables

- Numbers represent the Pokémon's place in the National Pokédex
- Pokémon listed as ♂ are only male, while those listed as ♀ are only female
- Pokémon listed as ♂/♀ have both male and female
- Pokémon listed as "Unknown" do not have a known gender

Grass Group

Grass Egg Group only

	Amoonguss	♂/♀
	Bellossom	♂/♀
	Bellsprout	♂/♀
	Carnivine	♂/♀
	Exeggcute	♂/♀
	Exeggutor	♂/♀
	Foongus	♂/♀
	Gloom	♂/♀
	Lilligant	♀
	Maractus	♂/♀
	Oddish	♂/♀
	Petilil	♀
	Sunflora	♂/♀
	Sunkern	♂/♀
	Tangela	♂/♀
	Tangrowth	♂/♀
	Victreebel	♂/♀
	Vileplume	♂/♀
	Weepinbell	♂/♀

Grass and Bug Egg Groups

	Paras	♂/♀
	Parasect	♂/♀

Grass and Human-Like Egg Groups

	Cacnea	♂/♀
	Cacturne	♂/♀

Grass and Monster Egg Groups

	Abomasnow	♂/♀
	Bayleef	♂/♀
	Bulbasaur	♂/♀
	Chikorita	♂/♀
	Grotle	♂/♀
	Ivysaur	♂/♀
	Meganium	♂/♀
	Snover	♂/♀
	Torterra	♂/♀
	Tropius	♂/♀
	Turtwig	♂/♀
	Venusaur	♂/♀

Grass and Fairy Egg Groups

	Breloom	♂/♀
	Cherrim	♂/♀
	Cherubi	♂/♀
	Cottonee	♂/♀
	Hoppip	♂/♀
	Jumpluff	♂/♀
	Roselia	♂/♀
	Roserade	♂/♀
	Shroomish	♂/♀
	Skiploom	♂/♀
	Whimsicott	♂/♀

Grass and Mineral Egg Groups

	Ferroseed	♂/♀
	Ferrothorn	♂/♀

Grass and Field Egg Groups

	Nuzleaf	♂/♀
	Seedot	♂/♀
	Serperior	♂/♀
	Servine	♂/♀
	Shiftry	♂/♀
	Snivy	♂/♀

Grass and Water 1 Egg Groups

	Lombre	♂/♀
	Lotad	♂/♀
	Ludicolo	♂/♀

Grass and Amorphous Egg Groups

	Phantump	♂/♀
	Trevenant	♂/♀

There is no crossover between the Grass Egg Group and the following Egg Groups:

- Flying
- Dragon
- Water 2
- Water 3
- Ditto
- No Eggs Discovered

Bug Group

Bug Egg Group only

Accelgor	♂/♀		Nincada	♂/♀
Ariados	♂/♀		Ninjask	♂/♀
Beautifly	♂/♀		Pineco	♂/♀
Beedrill	♂/♀		Pinsir	♂/♀
Burmy	♂/♀		Scatterbug	♂/♀
Butterfree	♂/♀		Scizor	♂/♀
Cascoon	♂/♀		Scolipede	♂/♀
Caterpie	♂/♀		Scyther	♂/♀
Combee	♂/♀		Sewaddle	♂/♀
Durant	♂/♀		Shelmet	♂/♀
Dustox	♂/♀		Shuckle	♂/♀
Escavalier	♂/♀		Silcoon	♂/♀
Flygon	♂/♀		Spewpa	♂/♀
Forretress	♂/♀		Spinarak	♂/♀
Galvantula	♂/♀		Swadloon	♂/♀
Gligar	♂/♀		Trapinch	♂/♀
Gliscor	♂/♀		Venipede	♂/♀
Heracross	♂/♀		Venomoth	♂/♀
Joltik	♂/♀		Venonat	♂/♀
Kakuna	♂/♀		Vespiquen	♀
Karrablast	♂/♀		Vibrava	♂/♀
Kricketot	♂/♀		Vivillon	♂/♀
Kricketune	♂/♀		Volcarona	♂/♀
Larvesta	♂/♀		Weedle	♂/♀
Leavanny	♂/♀		Whirlipede	♂/♀
Ledian	♂/♀		Wormadam	♀
Ledyba	♂/♀		Wurmple	♂/♀
Metapod	♂/♀		Yanma	♂/♀
Mothim	♂		Yanmega	♂/♀

Bug and Grass Egg Groups

Paras	♂/♀
Parasect	♂/♀

Bug and Human-Like Egg Groups

Illumise	♀
Volbeat	♂

Bug and Mineral Egg Groups

Crustle	♂/♀
Dwebble	♂/♀

Bug and Water 1 Egg Groups

Masquerain	♂/♀
Surskit	♂/♀

Bug and Water 3 Egg Groups

Drapion	♂/♀
Skorupi	♂/♀

There is no crossover between the Bug Egg Group and the following Egg Groups:

- Flying
- Fairy
- Dragon
- Amorphous
- Water 2
- Ditto
- Monster
- No Eggs Discovered

Have Pokémon inherit level-up moves

The two Pokémon you leave at the Pokémon Day Care can pass on a move they have learned to a Pokémon hatched from an Egg. Usually, newly hatched Pokémon only know the moves that the Pokémon would know at Lv. 1. However, if both of the two Pokémon you left at the Pokémon Day Care have learned a move that the hatched Pokémon can learn by leveling up, the hatched Pokémon will know that move. This is a great way to give Pokémon powerful moves from the start.

Remember: If both Pokémon at the Day Care know the same level-up move, the hatched Pokémon may know that level-up move.

Flying Group

● **Flying Egg Group only**

Aerodactyl	♂/♀	Rufflet	♂
Braviary	♂	Sigilyph	♂/♀
Chatot	♂/♀	Skarmory	♂/♀
Crobat	♂/♀	Spearow	♂/♀
Dodrio	♂/♀	Staraptor	♂/♀
Doduo	♂/♀	Staravia	♂/♀
Fearow	♂/♀	Starly	♂/♀
Fletchinder	♂/♀	Swellow	♂/♀
Fletchling	♂/♀	Taillow	♂/♀
Golbat	♂/♀	Talonflame	♂/♀
Honchkrow	♂/♀	Tranquill	♂/♀
Hoothoot	♂/♀	Unfezant	♂/♀
Mandibuzz	♀	Vullaby	♀
Murkrow	♂/♀	Xatu	♂/♀
Natu	♂/♀	Zubat	♂/♀
Noctowl	♂/♀		
Noibat	♂/♀		
Noivern	♂/♀		
Pidgeot	♂/♀		
Pidgeotto	♂/♀		
Pidgey	♂/♀		
Pidove	♂/♀		

● **Flying and Fairy Egg Groups**

Togekiss	♂/♀
Togetic	♂/♀

● **Flying and Dragon Egg Groups**

Altaria	♂/♀
Swablu	♂/♀

● **Flying and Field Egg Groups**

Farfetch'd	♂/♀
Swoobat	♂/♀
Woobat	♂/♀

● **Flying and Water 1 Egg Groups**

Ducklett	♂/♀
Pelipper	♂/♀
Swanna	♂/♀
Wingull	♂/♀

● **Flying and Water 3 Egg Groups**

Archen	♂/♀
Archeops	♂/♀

There is no crossover between the Flying Egg Group and the following Egg Groups:

● Grass
● Bug
● Human-Like
● Monster
● Mineral
● Amorphous
● Water 2
● Ditto
● No Eggs Discovered

Have Pokémon inherit TM moves

The male Pokémon you leave at the Pokémon Day Care can pass on a move that it has learned to the Pokémon that hatches from a found Egg if the hatched Pokémon is able to learn that move regularly from a TM.

Remember: A move that the male Pokémon knows and that the hatched Pokémon could learn from a TM can be passed on.

Teach your Pokémon Egg Moves

Pokémon from Eggs may hatch already knowing moves that they usually can't learn, called Egg Moves. For example, Riolu can't learn the move Bullet Punch by leveling up. But if a male Pokémon left at the Pokémon Day Care knows Bullet Punch, the Riolu that hatches from the Egg found there might know the move Bullet Punch. Many Egg Moves are unexpected, letting you take opponents by surprise.

Remember: A move that the male Pokémon knows and that the hatched Pokémon can learn as an Egg Move can be passed on.

Human-Like Group

Human-Like Egg Group only

Abra	♂ / ♀	Machop	♂ / ♀
Alakazam	♂ / ♀	Magmar	♂ / ♀
Beheeyem	♂ / ♀	Magmortar	♂ / ♀
Bisharp	♂ / ♀	Makuhita	♂ / ♀
Conkeldurr	♂ / ♀	Medicham	♂ / ♀
Croagunk	♂ / ♀	Meditite	♂ / ♀
Drowzee	♂ / ♀	Mr. Mime	♂ / ♀
Electabuzz	♂ / ♀	Pawniard	♂ / ♀
Electivire	♂ / ♀	Sableye	♂ / ♀
Elgyem	♂ / ♀	Sawk	♂
Gothita	♂ / ♀	Throh	♂
Gothitelle	♂ / ♀	Timburr	♂ / ♀
Gothorita	♂ / ♀	Toxicroak	♂ / ♀
Gurdurr	♂ / ♀		
Hariyama	♂ / ♀		
Hawlucha	♂ / ♀		
Hitmonchan	♂		
Hitmonlee	♂		
Hitmontop	♂		
Hypno	♂ / ♀		
Jynx	♀		
Kadabra	♂ / ♀		
Machamp	♂ / ♀		
Machoke	♂ / ♀		

Human-Like and Grass Egg Groups

Cacnea	♂ / ♀
Cacturne	♂ / ♀

Human-Like and Bug Egg Groups

Illumise	♀
Volbeat	♂

Human-Like and Field Egg Groups

Buneary	♂ / ♀
Chimchar	♂ / ♀
Infernape	♂ / ♀
Lopunny	♂ / ♀
Lucario	♂ / ♀
Mienfoo	♂ / ♀
Mienshao	♂ / ♀
Monferno	♂ / ♀
Spinda	♂ / ♀

There is no crossover between the Human-Like Egg Group and the following Egg Groups:

- Flying
- Monster
- Fairy
- Dragon
- Mineral
- Amorphous
- Water 1
- Water 2
- Water 3
- Ditto
- No Eggs Discovered

Pokémon Eggs found with the help of incense

In general, the Pokémon hatched from Eggs you find at a Pokémon Day Care will be the first in their Evolutionary line. However, there are exceptions. For example, dropping off a female Wobbuffet and a male Pokémon from the Amorphous Group will not result in finding a Wynaut Egg, although Wynaut is the pre-Evolution of Wobbuffet. It will be a Wobbuffet Egg. To get a Wynaut Egg, you'll need to give one of the Pokémon a Lax Incense before you drop it off, which you can get at the stand in Coumarine City.

Eggs that require incense

Egg Discovered	Female Pokémon	Male Pokémon Egg Group	Necessary Item
Azurill	Marill or Azumarill	Fairy Group or Water Group 1	Sea Incense
Wynaut	Wobbuffet	Amorphous Group	Lax Incense
Budew	Roselia or Roserade	Fairy Group or Grass Group	Rose Incense
Chingling	Chimecho	Amorphous Group	Pure Incense
Bonsly	Sudowoodo	Mineral Group	Rock Incense
Mime Jr.	Mr. Mime	Human-Like Group	Odd Incense
Happiny	Chansey or Blissey	Fairy Group	Luck Incense
Munchlax	Snorlax	Monster Group	Full Incense
Mantyke	Mantine	Water Group 1	Wave Incense

Monster Group

● Monster Egg Group only

🐾	Aggron	♂ / ♀
🐾	Amaura	♂ / ♀
🐾	Aron	♂ / ♀
🐾	Aurorus	♂ / ♀
🐾	Avalugg	♂ / ♀
🐾	Bastiodon	♂ / ♀
🐾	Bergmite	♂ / ♀
🐾	Cranidos	♂ / ♀
🐾	Cubone	♂ / ♀
🐾	Kangaskhan	♀
🐾	Lairon	♂ / ♀
🐾	Larvitar	♂ / ♀
🐾	Lickilicky	♂ / ♀
🐾	Lickitung	♂ / ♀
🐾	Marowak	♂ / ♀
🐾	Pupitar	♂ / ♀
🐾	Rampardos	♂ / ♀
🐾	Shieldon	♂ / ♀
🐾	Snorlax	♂ / ♀
🐾	Tyranitar	♂ / ♀

● Monster and Grass Egg Groups

🐾	Abomasnow	♂ / ♀
🐾	Bayleef	♂ / ♀
🐾	Bulbasaur	♂ / ♀
🐾	Chikorita	♂ / ♀
🐾	Grotle	♂ / ♀
🐾	Ivysaur	♂ / ♀
🐾	Meganium	♂ / ♀
🐾	Snover	♂ / ♀
🐾	Torterra	♂ / ♀
🐾	Tropius	♂ / ♀
🐾	Turtwig	♂ / ♀
🐾	Venusaur	♂ / ♀

● Monster and Dragon Egg Groups

🐾	Axew	♂ / ♀
🐾	Charizard	♂ / ♀
🐾	Charmander	♂ / ♀
🐾	Charmeleon	♂ / ♀
🐾	Druddigon	♂ / ♀
🐾	Fraxure	♂ / ♀
🐾	Gabite	♂ / ♀
🐾	Garchomp	♂ / ♀
🐾	Gible	♂ / ♀
🐾	Grovyle	♂ / ♀
🐾	Haxorus	♂ / ♀
🐾	Heliolisk	♂ / ♀
🐾	Helioptile	♂ / ♀
🐾	Sceptile	♂ / ♀
🐾	Treecko	♂ / ♀
🐾	Tyrantrum	♂ / ♀
🐾	Tyrunt	♂ / ♀

● Monster and Field Egg Groups

🐾	Ampharos	♂ / ♀
🐾	Exploud	♂ / ♀
🐾	Flaaffy	♂ / ♀
🐾	Loudred	♂ / ♀
🐾	Mareep	♂ / ♀
🐾	Nidoking	♂
🐾	Nidoran ♀	♀
🐾	Nidoran ♂	♂
🐾	Nidorino	♂
🐾	Rhydon	♂ / ♀
🐾	Rhyhorn	♂ / ♀
🐾	Rhyperior	♂ / ♀
🐾	Whismur	♂ / ♀

● Monster and Water 1 Egg Groups

🐾	Blastoise	♂ / ♀
🐾	Croconaw	♂ / ♀
🐾	Feraligatr	♂ / ♀
🐾	Lapras	♂ / ♀
🐾	Marshtomp	♂ / ♀
🐾	Mudkip	♂ / ♀
🐾	Slowbro	♂ / ♀
🐾	Slowking	♂ / ♀
🐾	Slowpoke	♂ / ♀
🐾	Squirtle	♂ / ♀
🐾	Swampert	♂ / ♀
🐾	Totodile	♂ / ♀
🐾	Wartortle	♂ / ♀

There is no crossover between the Monster Egg Group and the following Egg Groups:

- ● Bug
- ● Flying
- ● Human-Like
- ● Fairy
- ● Mineral
- ● Amorphous
- ● Water 2
- ● Water 3
- ● Ditto
- ● No Eggs Discovered

Either one of the two Abilities can be inherited

You don't know which Ability a Pokémon hatched from an Egg will have until it hatches. For example, Axew can have either the Rivalry or Mold Breaker Ability. Sometimes when you leave a female Haxorus with the Mold Breaker Ability at the Pokémon Day Care, the Egg that hatches will be an Axew with the Rivalry Ability. This is the basic rule about the Abilities of Pokémon hatched from Eggs.

Remember: The Ability of a Pokémon hatched from an Egg is more likely to be the Ability of the female Pokémon left at the Pokémon Day Care.

Fairy Group

Fairy Egg Group only

▨	Aromatisse	♂/♀
▨	Audino	♂/♀
▨	Blissey	♀
▨	Chansey	♀
▨	Clefable	♂/♀
▨	Clefairy	♂/♀
▨	Flabébé	♀
▨	Floette	♀
▨	Florges	♀
▨	Jigglypuff	♂/♀
▨	Minun	♂/♀
▨	Plusle	♂/♀
▨	Slurpuff	♂/♀
▨	Spritzee	♂/♀
▨	Swirlix	♂/♀
▨	Wigglytuff	♂/♀

Fairy and Grass Egg Groups

▨	Breloom	♂/♀
▨	Cherrim	♂/♀
▨	Cherubi	♂/♀
▨	Cottonee	♂/♀
▨	Hoppip	♂/♀
▨	Jumpluff	♂/♀
▨	Roselia	♂/♀
▨	Roserade	♂/♀
▨	Shroomish	♂/♀
▨	Skiploom	♂/♀
▨	Whimsicott	♂/♀

Fairy and Flying Egg Groups

▨	Togekiss	♂/♀
▨	Togetic	♂/♀

Fairy and Mineral Egg Groups

▨	Carbink	Unknown
▨	Froslass	♀
▨	Glalie	♂/♀
▨	Snorunt	♂/♀

Fairy and Field Egg Groups

▨	Delcatty	♂/♀
▨	Granbull	♂/♀
▨	Mawile	♂/♀
▨	Pachirisu	♂/♀
▨	Pikachu	♂/♀
▨	Raichu	♂/♀
▨	Skitty	♂/♀
▨	Snubbull	♂/♀

Fairy and Amorphous Egg Groups

▨	Castform	♂/♀

Fairy and Water 1 Egg Groups

▨	Azumarill	♂/♀
▨	Manaphy	Unknown
▨	Marill	♂/♀
▨	Phione	Unknown

There is no crossover between the Fairy Egg Group and the following Egg Groups:

- Bug
- Human-Like
- Monster
- Dragon
- Water 2
- Water 3
- Ditto
- No Eggs Discovered

Hidden Abilities can be inherited

Certain Pokémon have rare Abilities called "Hidden Abilities." If you are lucky enough to get one, you can pass on these Hidden Abilities. If you leave a female Pokémon with a Hidden Ability at the Pokémon Day Care, you may find an Egg that hatches into a Pokémon with the same Ability. For Example, Watchog can have the Hidden Ability Analytic. If you discover an Egg when you leave a female Watchog with the Analytic Ability at the Pokémon Day Care, you may find an Egg of a Patrat with Run Away, Keen Eye, or the same Hidden Ability, Analytic.

Remember: You can sometimes hatch a Pokémon with a Hidden Ability if and only if the female Pokémon left at the Pokémon Day Care had that Hidden Ability.

Dragon Group

● Dragon Egg Group only

	Bagon	♂/♀
	Deino	♂/♀
	Goodra	♂/♀
	Goomy	♂/♀
	Hydreigon	♂/♀
	Salamence	♂/♀
	Shelgon	♂/♀
	Sliggoo	♂/♀
	Zweilous	♂/♀

● Dragon and Flying Egg Groups

	Altaria	♂/♀
	Swablu	♂/♀

● Dragon and Monster Egg Groups

	Axew	♂/♀
	Charizard	♂/♀
	Charmander	♂/♀
	Charmeleon	♂/♀
	Druddigon	♂/♀
	Fraxure	♂/♀
	Gabite	♂/♀
	Garchomp	♂/♀
	Gible	♂/♀
	Grovyle	♂/♀
	Haxorus	♂/♀
	Sceptile	♂/♀
	Treecko	♂/♀

● Dragon and Field Egg Groups

	Arbok	♂/♀
	Ekans	♂/♀
	Scrafty	♂/♀
	Scraggy	♂/♀
	Seviper	♂/♀

● Dragon and Water 1 Egg Groups

	Dragonair	♂/♀
	Dragonite	♂/♀
	Dratini	♂/♀
	Feebas	♂/♀
	Horsea	♂/♀
	Kingdra	♂/♀
	Milotic	♂/♀
	Seadra	♂/♀

● Dragon and Water 2 Egg Groups

	Gyarados	♂/♀
	Magikarp	♂/♀

There is no crossover between the Dragon Egg Group and the following Egg Groups:

- ● Grass
- ● Bug
- ● Human-Like
- ● Fairy
- ● Mineral
- ● Amorphous
- ● Water 3
- ● Ditto
- ● No Eggs Discovered

Special pairings can result in two differing Eggs

It is usually a given that only one kind of Pokémon can be hatched from a particular Pokémon pairing, but that doesn't mean that there aren't certain special conditions which defy this common sense. If you drop off a Nidoran ♀ with a male Pokémon from either the Monster Group or the Field Group, the Egg that you find could be either a Nidoran ♀ or a Nidoran ♂. This also works if you leave the male Pokémon at the Day Care with a Ditto.

Remember: Certain Pokémon have the chance of hatching different Pokémon from the Eggs that you find.

Mineral Group

Mineral Egg Group only

Aegislash	♂/♀		Lunatone	Unknown		Crustle	♂/♀
Baltoy	Unknown		Magnemite	Unknown		Dwebble	♂/♀
Beldum	Unknown		Magneton	Unknown			
Boldore	♂/♀		Magnezone	Unknown			
Bronzong	Unknown		Metagross	Unknown			
Bronzor	Unknown		Metang	Unknown			
Claydol	Unknown		Nosepass	♂/♀			
Cryogonal	Unknown		Onix	♂/♀			
Doublade	♂/♀		Porygon	Unknown			
Electrode	Unknown		Porygon2	Unknown			
Garbodor	♂/♀		Porygon-Z	Unknown			
Geodude	♂/♀		Probopass	♂/♀			
Gigalith	♂/♀		Roggenrola	♂/♀			
Golem	♂/♀		Shedinja	Unknown			
Golett	Unknown		Solrock	Unknown			
Golurk	Unknown		Steelix	♂/♀			
Graveler	♂/♀		Sudowoodo	♂/♀			
Honedge	♂/♀		Trubbish	♂/♀			
Klang	Unknown		Vanillish	♂/♀			
Klefki	♂/♀		Vanillite	♂/♀			
Klink	Unknown		Vanilluxe	♂/♀			
Klinklang	Unknown		Voltorb	Unknown			

Mineral and Bug Egg Groups

Crustle	♂/♀
Dwebble	♂/♀

Mineral and Fairy Egg Groups

Froslass	♀
Glalie	♂/♀
Snorunt	♂/♀

Mineral and Amorphous Egg Groups

Cofagrigus	♂/♀
Yamask	♂/♀

There is no crossover between the Mineral Egg Group and the following Egg Groups:

- Flying
- Human-Like
- Monster
- Dragon
- Field
- Water 1
- Water 2
- Water 3
- Ditto
- No Eggs Discovered

Mineral and Grass Egg Groups

Ferroseed	♂/♀
Ferrothorn	♂/♀

Use a new item to help control Abilities

A new item in *Pokémon X* and *Pokémon Y* is the Ability Capsule. If you can obtain it, this wondrous item will allow a Pokémon with two possible Abilities to switch which Ability it has. It is not possible to switch to a Hidden Ability, but this item will still be a great help in battle and when trying to pass along certain Abilities to hatched Pokémon.

Remember: You can use an item called an Ability Capsule to change the Ability of your Pokémon.

Pokémon Evolution

Field Group

Field Egg Group only

Absol	♂/♀	Hippopotas	♂/♀	Samurott	♂/♀
Aipom	♂/♀	Hippowdon	♂/♀	Sandile	♂/♀
Ambipom	♂/♀	Houndoom	♂/♀	Sandshrew	♂/♀
Arcanine	♂/♀	Houndour	♂/♀	Sandslash	♂/♀
Beartic	♂/♀	Jolteon	♂/♀	Sawsbuck	♂/♀
Blaziken	♂/♀	Kecleon	♂/♀	Sentret	♂/♀
Blitzle	♂/♀	Krokorok	♂/♀	Shinx	♂/♀
Bouffalant	♂/♀	Krookodile	♂/♀	Simipour	♂/♀
Braixen	♂/♀	Leafeon	♂/♀	Simisage	♂/♀
Bunnelby	♂/♀	Liepard	♂/♀	Simisear	♂/♀
Camerupt	♂/♀	Lillipup	♂/♀	Skiddo	♂/♀
Chesnaught	♂/♀	Linoone	♂/♀	Skuntank	♂/♀
Chespin	♂/♀	Litleo	♂/♀	Slaking	♂/♀
Cinccino	♂/♀	Luxio	♂/♀	Slakoth	♂/♀
Combusken	♂/♀	Luxray	♂/♀	Smeargle	♂/♀
Cubchoo	♂/♀	Mamoswine	♂/♀	Sneasel	♂/♀
Cyndaquil	♂/♀	Manectric	♂/♀	Spoink	♂/♀
Darmanitan	♂/♀	Mankey	♂/♀	Stantler	♂/♀
Darumaka	♂/♀	Meowstic	♂/♀	Stoutland	♂/♀
Deerling	♂/♀	Meowth	♂/♀	Stunky	♂/♀
Delphox	♂/♀	Mightyena	♂/♀	Swinub	♂/♀
Dewott	♂/♀	Miltank	♀	Sylveon	♂/♀
Diggersby	♂/♀	Minccino	♂/♀	Tauros	♂
Diglett	♂/♀	Munna	♂/♀	Teddiursa	♂/♀
Donphan	♂/♀	Musharna	♂/♀	Tepig	♂/♀
Drilbur	♂/♀	Ninetales	♂/♀	Torchic	♂/♀
Dugtrio	♂/♀	Numel	♂/♀	Torkoal	♂/♀
Dunsparce	♂/♀	Oshawott	♂/♀	Typhlosion	♂/♀
Eevee	♂/♀	Panpour	♂/♀	Umbreon	♂/♀
Electrike	♂/♀	Pansage	♂/♀	Ursaring	♂/♀
Emboar	♂/♀	Pansear	♂/♀	Vaporeon	♂/♀
Emolga	♂/♀	Patrat	♂/♀	Vigoroth	♂/♀
Espeon	♂/♀	Persian	♂/♀	Vulpix	♂/♀
Espurr	♂/♀	Phanpy	♂/♀	Watchog	♂/♀
Excadrill	♂/♀	Pignite	♂/♀	Weavile	♂/♀
Fennekin	♂/♀	Piloswine	♂/♀	Zangoose	♂/♀
Flareon	♂/♀	Ponyta	♂/♀	Zebstrika	♂/♀
Furfrou	♂/♀	Poochyena	♂/♀	Zigzagoon	♂/♀
Furret	♂/♀	Primeape	♂/♀	Zoroark	♂/♀
Girafarig	♂/♀	Purrloin	♂/♀	Zorua	♂/♀
Glaceon	♂/♀	Purugly	♂/♀		
Glameow	♂/♀	Pyroar	♂/♀		
Gogoat	♂/♀	Quilava	♂/♀		
Growlithe	♂/♀	Quilladin	♂/♀		
Grumpig	♂/♀	Rapidash	♂/♀		
Heatmor	♂/♀	Raticate	♂/♀		
Herdier	♂/♀	Rattata	♂/♀		

Field Group

Field and Grass Egg Groups

Nuzleaf	♂ / ♀
Seedot	♂ / ♀
Serperior	♂ / ♀
Servine	♂ / ♀
Shiftry	♂ / ♀
Snivy	♂ / ♀

Field and Flying Egg Groups

Farfetch'd	♂ / ♀
Swoobat	♂ / ♀
Woobat	♂ / ♀

Field and Human-Like Egg Groups

Buneary	♂ / ♀
Chimchar	♂ / ♀
Infernape	♂ / ♀
Lopunny	♂ / ♀
Lucario	♂ / ♀
Mienfoo	♂ / ♀
Mienshao	♂ / ♀
Monferno	♂ / ♀
Pancham	♂ / ♀
Pangoro	♂ / ♀
Spinda	♂ / ♀

Field and Monster Egg Groups

Ampharos	♂ / ♀
Exploud	♂ / ♀
Flaaffy	♂ / ♀
Loudred	♂ / ♀
Mareep	♂ / ♀
Rhydon	♂ / ♀
Nidoran ♀	♂ / ♀
Nidoran ♂	♂ / ♀
Nidorino	♂
Rhydon	♂ / ♀
Rhyhorn	♂ / ♀
Rhyperior	♂ / ♀
Whismur	♂ / ♀

Field and Fairy Egg Groups

Dedenne	♂ / ♀
Delcatty	♂ / ♀
Granbull	♂ / ♀
Mawile	♂ / ♀
Pachirisu	♂ / ♀
Pikachu	♂ / ♀
Raichu	♂ / ♀
Skitty	♂ / ♀
Snubbull	♂ / ♀

Field and Dragon Egg Groups

Arbok	♂ / ♀
Ekans	♂ / ♀
Scrafty	♂ / ♀
Scraggy	♂ / ♀
Seviper	♂ / ♀

Field and Water 1 Egg Groups

Bibarel	♂ / ♀
Bidoof	♂ / ♀
Buizel	♂ / ♀
Delibird	♂ / ♀
Dewgong	♂ / ♀
Empoleon	♂ / ♀
Floatzel	♂ / ♀
Golduck	♂ / ♀
Piplup	♂ / ♀
Prinplup	♂ / ♀
Psyduck	♂ / ♀
Quagsire	♂ / ♀
Sealeo	♂ / ♀
Seel	♂ / ♀
Spheal	♂ / ♀
Walrein	♂ / ♀
Wooper	♂ / ♀

Field and Water 2 Egg Groups

Wailmer	♂ / ♀
Wailord	♂ / ♀

There is no crossover between the Field Egg Group and the following Egg Groups:

- Bug
- Mineral
- Amorphous
- Water 3
- Ditto
- No Eggs Discovered

Pokémon may inherit Natures

The Pokémon hatched from an Egg may inherit the Nature of the female Pokémon that was left at the Pokémon Day Care. You will be able to pass along a Pokémon's Nature with certainty if it is holding an item called an Everstone. Natures affect how a Pokémon's stats grow upon leveling up.

Remember: Pokémon hatched from Eggs can inherit Natures from the Pokémon left at the Pokémon Day Care.

Amorphous Group

Amorphous Egg Group only

Banette	♂/♀		Koffing	♂/♀
Chandelure	♂/♀		Lampent	♂/♀
Chimecho	♂/♀		Litwick	♂/♀
Drifblim	♂/♀		Magcargo	♂/♀
Drifloon	♂/♀		Misdreavus	♂/♀
Duosion	♂/♀		Mismagius	♂/♀
Dusclops	♂/♀		Muk	♂/♀
Dusknoir	♂/♀		Pumpkaboo	♂/♀
Duskull	♂/♀		Ralts	♂/♀
Eelektrik	♂/♀		Reuniclus	♂/♀
Eelektross	♂/♀		Rotom	Unknown
Frillish	♂/♀		Shuppet	♂/♀
Gallade	♂		Slugma	♂/♀
Gardevoir	♂/♀		Solosis	♂/♀
Gastly	♂/♀		Spiritomb	♂/♀
Gengar	♂/♀		Swalot	♂/♀
Gourgeist	♂/♀		Tynamo	♂/♀
Grimer	♂/♀		Weezing	♂/♀
Gulpin	♂/♀		Wobbuffet	♂/♀
Haunter	♂/♀			
Jellicent	♂/♀			
Kirlia	♂/♀			

Amorphous and Fairy Egg Groups

Castform	♂/♀

Amorphous and Mineral Egg Groups

Cofagrigus	♂/♀
Yamask	♂/♀

Amorphous and Water 1 Egg Groups

Gastrodon	♂/♀
Shellos	♂/♀
Stunfisk	♂/♀

There is no crossover between the Amorphous Egg Group and the following Egg Groups:

- Grass
- Bug
- Flying
- Human-Like
- Monster
- Dragon
- Field
- Water 2
- Water 3
- Ditto
- No Eggs Discovered

Use your special Abilities and O-Powers to help hatch Eggs

There is an O-Power called Hatching Power that will aid you by making Pokémon Eggs hatch faster than usual. For Egg enthusiasts, this O-Power will be a great boon. And like all other O-Powers, the more you use it, the stronger it will become. It is not an easy O-Power to obtain, though. You will have to obtain every other O-Power first and fulfill certain other conditions. If you are up to this challenge, Mr. Bonding will bestow this power upon you. Don't forget that you can also use the O-Powers of those around you. See page 72 for more information. Having a Pokémon in your party with certain Abilities will also help you hatch an Egg that you are carrying around. Abilities like Flame Body or Magma Armor will keep the Egg warm, and make it hatch faster.

Remember: You can obtain a special O-Power that will help you to hatch Eggs more quickly. You can also use Abilities to help an Egg hatch faster.

Water Group 1

Water Egg Group 1 only

Clamperl	♂/♀
Froakie	♂/♀
Frogadier	♂/♀
Gorebyss	♂/♀
Greninja	♂/♀
Huntail	♂/♀
Mantine	♂/♀
Palpitoad	♂/♀
Politoed	♂/♀
Poliwag	♂/♀
Poliwhirl	♂/♀
Poliwrath	♂/♀
Seismitoad	♂/♀
Tympole	♂/♀

Water 1 and Grass Egg Groups

Lombre	♂/♀
Lotad	♂/♀
Ludicolo	♂/♀

Water 1 and Bug Egg Groups

Masquerain	♂/♀
Surskit	♂/♀

Water 1 and Flying Egg Groups

Ducklett	♂/♀
Pelipper	♂/♀
Swanna	♂/♀
Wingull	♂/♀

Water 1 and Monster Egg Groups

Blastoise	♂/♀
Croconaw	♂/♀
Feraligatr	♂/♀
Lapras	♂/♀
Marshtomp	♂/♀
Mudkip	♂/♀
Slowbro	♂/♀
Slowking	♂/♀
Slowpoke	♂/♀
Squirtle	♂/♀
Swampert	♂/♀
Totodile	♂/♀
Wartortle	♂/♀

Water 1 and Fairy Egg Groups

Azumarill	♂/♀
Manaphy	Unknown
Marill	♂/♀
Phione	Unknown

Water 1 and Dragon Egg Groups

Dragalge	♂/♀
Dragonair	♂/♀
Dragonite	♂/♀
Dratini	♂/♀
Feebas	♂/♀
Horsea	♂/♀
Kingdra	♂/♀
Milotic	♂/♀
Seadra	♂/♀
Skrelp	♂/♀

Water 1 and Field Egg Groups

Bibarel	♂/♀
Bidoof	♂/♀
Buizel	♂/♀
Delibird	♂/♀
Dewgong	♂/♀
Empoleon	♂/♀
Floatzel	♂/♀
Golduck	♂/♀
Piplup	♂/♀
Prinplup	♂/♀
Psyduck	♂/♀
Quagsire	♂/♀
Sealeo	♂/♀
Seel	♂/♀
Spheal	♂/♀
Walrein	♂/♀
Wooper	♂/♀

Water 1 and Amorphous Egg Groups

Gastrodon	♂/♀
Shellos	♂/♀
Stunfisk	♂/♀

Water 1 and Water 2 Egg Groups

Alomomola	♂/♀
Inkay	♂/♀
Malamar	♂/♀
Octillery	♂/♀
Relicanth	♂/♀
Remoraid	♂/♀

Water 1 and Water 3 Egg Groups

Carracosta	♂/♀
Clauncher	♂/♀
Clawitzer	♂/♀
Corphish	♂/♀
Corsola	♂/♀
Crawdaunt	♂/♀
Kabuto	♂/♀
Kabutops	♂/♀
Omanyte	♂/♀
Omastar	♂/♀
Tirtouga	♂/♀

There is no crossover between the Water Egg Group 1 and the following Egg Groups:

- Human-Like
- Mineral
- Ditto
- No Eggs Discovered

Water Group 2

Water Egg Group 2 only

	Barboach	♂ / ♀
	Basculin	♂ / ♀
	Carvanha	♂ / ♀
	Chinchou	♂ / ♀
	Finneon	♂ / ♀
	Goldeen	♂ / ♀
	Lanturn	♂ / ♀
	Lumineon	♂ / ♀
	Luvdisc	♂ / ♀
	Qwilfish	♂ / ♀
	Seaking	♂ / ♀
	Sharpedo	♂ / ♀
	Whiscash	♂ / ♀

Water 2 and Dragon Egg Groups

	Gyarados	♂ / ♀
	Magikarp	♂ / ♀

Water 2 and Field Egg Groups

	Wailmer	♂ / ♀
	Wailord	♂ / ♀

Water 2 and Water 1 Egg Groups

	Alomomola	♂ / ♀
	Octillery	♂ / ♀
	Relicanth	♂ / ♀
	Remoraid	♂ / ♀

There is no crossover between the Water Egg Group 2 and the following Egg Groups:

- Grass
- Bug
- Flying
- Human-Like
- Monster
- Fairy
- Mineral
- Amorphous
- Water 3
- Ditto
- No Eggs Discovered

Water Group 3

Water Egg Group 3 only

	Anorith	♂ / ♀
	Armaldo	♂ / ♀
	Barbaracle	♂ / ♀
	Binacle	♂ / ♀
	Cloyster	♂ / ♀
	Cradily	♂ / ♀
	Kingler	♂ / ♀
	Krabby	♂ / ♀
	Lileep	♂ / ♀
	Shellder	♂ / ♀
	Starmie	Unknown
	Staryu	Unknown
	Tentacool	♂ / ♀
	Tentacruel	♂ / ♀

Water 3 and Bug Egg Groups

	Drapion	♂ / ♀
	Skorupi	♂ / ♀

Water 3 and Flying Egg Groups

	Archen	♂ / ♀
	Archeops	♂ / ♀

Water 3 and Water 1 Egg Groups

	Carracosta	♂ / ♀
	Corphish	♂ / ♀
	Corsola	♂ / ♀
	Crawdaunt	♂ / ♀
	Kabuto	♂ / ♀
	Kabutops	♂ / ♀
	Omanyte	♂ / ♀
	Omastar	♂ / ♀
	Tirtouga	♂ / ♀

There is no crossover between the Water Egg Group 3 and the following Egg Groups:

- Grass
- Human-Like
- Monster
- Fairy
- Dragon
- Mineral
- Field
- Amorphous
- Water 2
- Ditto
- No Eggs Discovered

Ditto Group

● **Ditto Group**

Ditto	Unknown

The Ditto Group is a special Group. Ditto is not a part of any other Egg Group, yet if you drop it off at a Pokémon Day Care with almost any other Pokémon, you will find an Egg for that Pokémon. You cannot find a Ditto Egg.

No Eggs Discovered Group

● **No Eggs Discovered**

None of the Pokémon in the No Eggs Discovered Group belong to any other Egg Group

Arceus	Unknown	Mew	Unknown
Articuno	Unknown	Mewtwo	Unknown
Azelf	Unknown	Mime Jr.	♂/♀
Azurill	♂/♀	Moltres	Unknown
Bonsly	♂/♀	Munchlax	♂/♀
Budew	♂/♀	Nidoqueen	♀
Celebi	Unknown	Nidorina	♀
Chingling	♂/♀	Palkia	Unknown
Cleffa	♂/♀	Pichu	♂/♀
Cobalion	Unknown	Raikou	Unknown
Cresselia	♀	Rayquaza	Unknown
Darkrai	Unknown	Regice	Unknown
Deoxys	Unknown	Regigigas	Unknown
Dialga	Unknown	Regirock	Unknown
Elekid	♂/♀	Registeel	Unknown
Entei	Unknown	Reshiram	Unknown
Genesect	Unknown	Riolu	♂/♀
Giratina	Unknown	Shaymin	Unknown
Groudon	Unknown	Smoochum	♀
Happiny	♀	Suicune	Unknown
Heatran	♂/♀	Terrakion	Unknown
Ho-Oh	Unknown	Thundurus	♂
Igglybuff	♂/♀	Togepi	♂/♀
Jirachi	Unknown	Tornadus	♂
Keldeo	Unknown	Tyrogue	♂
Kyogre	Unknown	Unown	Unknown
Kyurem	Unknown	Uxie	Unknown
Landorus	♂	Victini	Unknown
Latias	♀	Virizion	Unknown
Latios	♂	Wynaut	♂/♀
Lugia	Unknown	Xerneas	Unknown
Magby	♂/♀	Yveltal	Unknown
Mantyke	♂/♀	Zapdos	Unknown
Meloetta	Unknown	Zekrom	Unknown
Mesprit	Unknown		

Pokédex Completion

Complete the Kalos region Pokédex by catching 450 kinds of Pokémon

In the world of *Pokémon X* and *Pokémon Y*, the number of wild Pokémon species in the Kalos region is truly vast. You must register 450 Pokémon species to complete the Kalos Pokédex, so prepare to take on a challenge!

Have Professor Sycamore rate your Pokédex completion

Professor Sycamore provides a lot of feedback as you complete the Kalos Pokédex. The professor tells you how complete your Kalos Pokédex is. He'll give you advice on completing your Pokédex along with words of support.

How to have Professor Sycamore rate your Pokédex

1. Visit any Pokémon Center and access the PC.

2. Choose "Professor's PC" to have Professor Sycamore rate your Kalos Pokédex.

TIP When you complete the Kalos Pokédex, Professor Sycamore will give you an Oval Charm. He's not the only one impressed with your progress, though. Visit the following friendly characters, who will reward you for working hard at your Pokédex:

- A Scientist in Shalour City gives you an Eviolite if you've seen 40 or more Pokémon in the Coastal Kalos Pokédex.

- A Monsieur in Dendemille Town gives you a Shell Bell if you've seen 70 or more Pokémon in the Mountain Kalos Pokédex.

- The Game Director in Coumarine Hotel will recognize you for completing each section of your Pokédex.

Game Functions and Communications

How to use the game menus

Throughout your journey, you can press ⊗ to see the main menu on the Touch Screen. Once you learn what the different options are and what information they contain, you'll have no problem finding your way.

Menu Screen

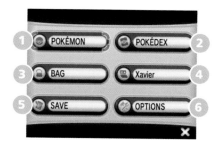

Using the game functions

1 Pokémon

Displays the Pokémon currently in your party. You can also access detailed info on each.

2 Pokédex

A device that records Pokémon data, including how many you've seen and caught and where to find Pokémon.

3 Bag

Stores the items you've collected. Open it to use the items inside.

4 Trainer Info

Shows how far you've come as a Trainer. You can check which Gym Badges have been obtained and other data.

5 Save

Tap here to save your game. Remember to save often!

6 Options

Adjust the gameplay options to your liking.

Pokémon data

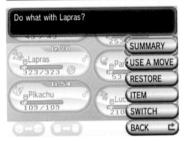

Tap "Pokémon" on the menu to see a list of your current party Pokémon. You can also view more info about your Pokémon or use field moves, such as Fly or Rock Smash. To use these field moves, select a Pokémon, tap "USE A MOVE," and then choose the move.

What you can do with the party Pokémon screen

SUMMARY
Shows where you caught the Pokémon, its moves, its stats, and more.

USE A MOVE
Lets your Pokémon use a field move, such as Fly or Rock Smash.

RESTORE
Lets you restore your Pokémon's HP or heal its status conditions with items kept in your Bag.

ITEM
Lets you give a Pokémon an item to hold or take away its held item.

SWITCH
Move a Pokémon around in your lineup. The top-left Pokémon is the first Pokémon and the top-right Pokémon is the second Pokémon to join in a battle.

Pokémon data under "SUMMARY"

From the party Pokémon screen, choose SUMMARY to view a Pokémon's info. There are two separate pages of info.

Stats and Learned Moves

The top screen shows the Pokémon's stats and Ability. The lower screen shows the moves it knows.

Trainer Memo and Ribbons

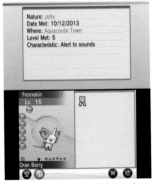

The top screen shows the Pokémon's Nature, Characteristic, and more. The lower screen shows any Ribbons it has earned.

Bag and Key Items

Your Bag is where you store the items you collect on your journey. The Bag has five Pockets. Items are automatically placed into the correct Pocket for their type. You can also sort the items in each Pocket by selecting the third icon from the right on the bottom of the Touch Screen.

Contents of your Bag

ITEMS Pocket
Store items for Pokémon to hold, Evolution stones, and more.

BERRIES Pocket
Store Berries you obtain on your journey.

MEDICINE Pocket
Store items that restore HP/PP or cure status conditions.

KEY ITEMS Pocket
Store important items acquired on your journey, like the Bicycle and the Dowsing Machine.

TMs & HMs Pocket
Store TMs & HMs.

 You can sort items in Pockets so that you can find them easily. You can sort by type, name, and quantity.

Register frequently used Key Items for quick access

Register frequently used Key Items, such as the Town Map or Dowsing Machine, by selecting the Key Item and then choosing "REGISTER." You can use a registered Key Item just by pressing Ⓨ. You can register up to four Key Items. If you have registered more than one item, please select the one you want by using the +Control Pad.

Saving and deleting saved data

The Save menu lets you save your data when you want to take a break from playing your *Pokémon X* or *Pokémon Y* game. When you save your data, you'll see the save screen shown below, where you can check details about your game.

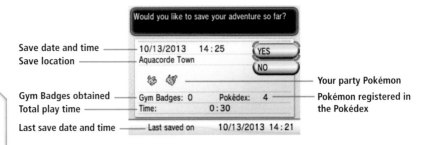

Would you like to save your adventure so far?

Save date and time — 10/13/2013   14:25   YES
Save location — Aquacorde Town   NO

Your party Pokémon

Gym Badges obtained — Gym Badges: 0   Pokédex: 4 — Pokémon registered in
Total play time — Time: 0:30   the Pokédex

Last save date and time — Last saved on   10/13/2013 14:21

Save your game anytime

Before battling a Gym Leader

It's a good idea to save the game before battling a Gym Leader. If you forget to save before the battle and then you end up losing, you'll have to go through the Gym again. Save the game before that ultimate battle, and then if you need another go-round, you'll be ready to start right at the battle with the Gym Leader.

Before battling the Elite Four

It's an equally good idea to save the game before battling the Elite Four in the Pokémon League. You can choose the order in which to challenge them. Save your data before entering any of the private chambers of the Elite Four.

Before trying to catch a valuable Pokémon

When you know you are about to face a rare Pokémon, it's a good idea to save the game before trying to catch it. That way, if you unluckily make the Pokémon faint, you can try again.

How to delete your saved data

If you want to delete your saved data and start over, press ✚ + ⑧ + ⓧ. After you delete it, you can't restore it, so be very sure it's what you want to do before deleting it.

Options menu

The Options menu lets you adjust game settings to suit your preferences, making it easier to play. For instance, if the game text scrolls too slowly, you can increase the speed. If there's a game feature you want to change, open the Options menu and adjust it to your preference.

What you can do at the Options menu

1 Text Speed
Choose from slow, normal, or fast text speeds.

2 Battle Effects
Choose whether you want to see animations when Pokémon use their moves and when they are affected by status conditions.

3 Battle Style
When you defeat one Pokémon on a team, you'll be asked whether you want to switch your own Pokémon. If you want to automatically stay with your current Pokémon, select "SET" to stop being asked this question.

4 Battle BG
Select the wallpaper you want to see on the lower screen during battles.

5 Button Mode
You can disable the ⓛ and ⓡ buttons, or set ⓛ to function as ⓐ. This also disables ⓡ.

6 Forced Save
Choose whether or not you must save before PSS battles and other communication features.

Player Search System (PSS)

The PSS (Player Search System) is a new feature in *Pokémon X* and *Pokémon Y*. This multipurpose menu appears on the lower screen as you play. Its primary function is to help you interact with other *Pokémon X* and *Pokémon Y* players, whether they're playing right nearby or in another part of the world.

Main PSS screen

 PSS Menu button
Tap this button to open the PSS menu and call up a list of the many actions you can perform through the PSS.

2 Internet connection
Tap this button to connect to the Internet and use various PSS functions that require an Internet connection.

3 Friends
Players whom you've registered as friends will appear here. You can choose to register other players as Friends after you have battled or traded with them a couple of times. You'll also see different icons indicating what they are currently doing.

4 Acquaintances
Any players with whom you've traded or battled will automatically become acquaintances of yours and appear here whenever they're playing. This helps you find these players and trade or battle with them again.

5 Passersby
Players who are playing in your area or who are online at the same time as you are listed here. Go ahead and say hello!

6 Menu buttons
For convenience, the buttons along the bottom row call up the same menus that can be visited by pressing ⊗ (Pokémon, Pokédex, Bag, and so on).

> **TIP** *The icons of players who are currently playing will appear brighter and farther to the left. Players who are not currently playing will appear farther to the right, and their icons will be shaded. When there are more icons than can fit on a single screen, you will be able to scroll through multiple screens of icons by dragging your stylus across the screen.*

Functions on the main PSS screen

The PSS is a powerful tool with many functions. Here's how to use it.

Communicate with other players

Tap any player who appears in the PSS, and you'll bring up a list of interactive actions that you can perform with them. Tap the player's name in the upper left to view their profile, and tap the button in the upper right to compliment other players on their profile by sending them a "Nice!". You can view his or her Trainer PR Video if the player has agreed to share it with you.

Battle with other players

Battling other players is a fine way to hone your skills and discover new tactics that you never knew were possible. The easiest way is to just tap a player and then choose Battle. You can adjust a variety of settings to create the desired battle experience.

Trade Pokémon with other players

One of the coolest things you can do with the PSS is trade Pokémon with other players. This is a great way to receive Pokémon you didn't know about, and it will help you fill out your Pokédex with the greatest of ease. You can choose Trade from any player's profile on the PSS main screen.

Game Chat with friends

When you become friends with someone, you will be able to use Game Chat to talk to one another in real time while you battle and trade, as long as the Parental Controls on your Nintendo 3DS system allow for it. Hear the delight in your friends' voices when they see the great Pokémon you gave them, or the frustration when you beat them handily in battle!

 On the PSS screen, tap and hold a player's icon to quickly add them to your favorites.

Functions on the main PSS screen

Link Battles and Battle Spot—More on battling

While you can challenge anyone directly by selecting them from the PSS main screen, you can also select Battle on the first page of the PSS menu to choose to battle someone via Internet, Local Wireless, or Infrared Connection. You'll be able to set the battle format and rules and even set a handicap if one seems necessary. This is a great way to battle friends or family, but what about when no one is around to battle with? That's where Battle Spot comes in. Battle Spot will use your Internet connection to instantly connect you to another player in the world who is looking for a battle at the same time as you. Now you can turn on your game, anytime day or night, and find other Trainers from around the globe to battle with just the tap of a button!

Link Trades, Wonder Trades, and the GTS

There are several ways you can trade in *Pokémon X* and *Pokémon Y*. You can simply select anyone from the PSS screen and select Trade from the options that appear, of course. Or you could open the PSS menu and tap Trade, which will give you the options of trading with someone via Internet, Local Wireless, or Infrared Connection. You can also utilize the GTS (Global Trade System) and Wonder Trade. The GTS, on the second page of the PSS menu, allows you to deposit a Pokémon for trading and input certain requirements for the Pokémon you would like to receive in return. On the other hand, you can search for Pokémon that other players have deposited and see if you can offer them any Pokémon that match their request.

You can limit Pokémon by species, level, gender, and more. You can even search for Pokémon you've never seen before nor registered in your Pokédex. Just scroll down past all of the alphabetical options!

Wonder Trade is a new kind of trading that is available in *Pokémon X* and *Pokémon Y*, and it can also be accessed from the PSS menu. Select Wonder Trade from the first page of the PSS menu and you can deposit any Pokémon you like. You don't get to specify what kind of Pokémon you will get in return, but unlike the GTS, you won't have to wait to find a match either. You will instantly be paired up with another player around the world who is also looking for a trade and your Pokémon will be swapped instantaneously. Don't you wonder what you might get?

Let everyone know you're happy

From the first page of the PSS menu, you can select Shout-Out. A Shout-Out is a brief, 16-character message you can send out to the world. Tell everyone about what's made you happy or your latest victory. It will appear to everyone on the PSS and you'll be able to see others' Shout-Outs as well. But don't get any ideas: inappropriate words or messages cannot be included in your Shout-Out if you want others to be able to see it.

Stay connected to the Pokémon community

Access the Holo Caster by tapping the PSS actions button and then choosing Holo Caster. By checking the Holo Caster regularly, you can stay clued in on all the latest news and events.

Game Sync

You can Game Sync directly from the PSS. Game Sync allows you to sync up your progress in the game with the PGL (Pokémon Global Link), a linked website that players around the world can use to show their progress in the game, upload photos they've taken with Phil the Photo Guy, cash in Poké Miles, and more! Select Game Sync to create your Game Sync ID to use online at www.pokemon-gl.com.

O-Powers

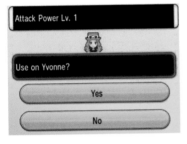

O-Powers are special powers that are activated through the PSS. You may use these powers on yourself or others anytime by opening the PSS menu and then selecting O-Power. You can also use O-Powers on others who are playing at the same time by selecting their icon and then tapping O-Power from among the options that appear. Each O-Power has its own special benefits, and you can share these benefits with other players. It's an outstanding way to make new friends—and the more that you use your O-Powers, the more powerful they will become!

View your favorites

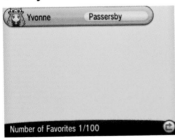

You can favorite other players, so that they are always easy to find. When you connect to the Internet, there may be hundreds and thousands of other ambitious Trainers online at the same time as you. Consider registering Trainers that you want to interact with again to your favorites list. You can always remove them later if you need to free up some space.

Edit your profile

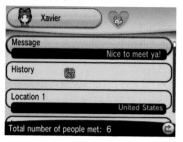

Your PSS profile is visible to other players, so it's a good idea to keep it up to date. Access your profile from the PSS menu by choosing Profile. You can change your icon and default greeting, and even answer some cool Mini Survey questions to help personalize your profile.

Change your settings

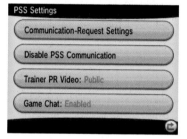

In the PSS Settings, you adjust your settings to decide just how much you want to share or not share with others. Younger players should review these settings with a parent or guardian!

Trainer PR Videos

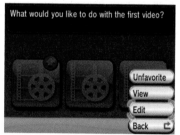

Trainer PR Videos are short films that you can create while visiting Lumiose City. Simply visit the PR Video Studio on the South Boulevard to film your personal Trainer PR Video. Afterward, you'll be able to edit and modify your video by accessing any PC in the Kalos region. Other players can view your Trainer PR Video through the PSS if you choose to share it with other players, so work on wowing people with cool videos that really show off your style! You can ask to view the Trainer PR Videos of other players by tapping their icon and then selecting "Trainer PR Video" from the options that appear.

More about O-Powers

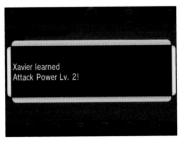

During your journey through the Kalos region, you'll meet a distinguished gentleman named Mr. Bonding who teaches you all about O-Powers. These unique powers grant valuable benefits, like reducing the cost of items at shops or increasing the Experience Points your Pokémon receive after battles. Keep an eye out for Mr. Bonding whenever you visit a new city or town, as he'll teach you a new O-Power each time you meet him.

O-Power Energy

O-Powers require energy to use. Pay attention to each O-Power's energy requirement when you select it. The energy requirement may be different depending on whether you're using the O-Power on yourself or giving its benefits to another player. Your supply of O-Power energy is shown at the bottom of the menu and will slowly regenerate over time. The more experienced you become in the world of *Pokémon X* and *Pokémon Y*, the faster your energy will regenerate.

> **TIP** *O-Powers have levels. Their effects will become greater and greater with each new level, and the only way to level them up is by using them. There are fifteen powers in total that Mr. Bonding can share with you, and all can be raised from Lv. 1 to Lv. 3. So put them to use as often as you can!*

How to Use the Walkthrough

This walkthrough is mostly illustrated with the male main character, but the information applies equally to the female main character.

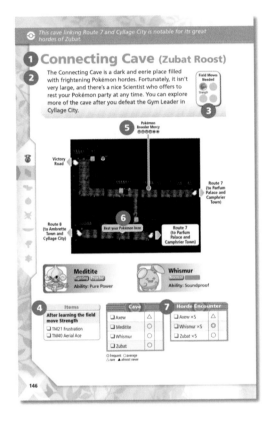

1 Location name

The name of the location.

2 Location guide

Here's your guide to the special features of various locations!

③ Field moves needed

Check these icons to see what moves you need to access every area on the map and collect all the items.

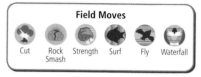

④ Items

This checklist shows you all of the items you can find by searching the area. At times, you must meet certain conditions to get an item, and those conditions are included. For cities and towns, you'll find the items sold by the clerks in the Poké Marts in Pokémon Centers.

⑤ Trainers waiting to challenge you

Find out where you can encounter Pokémon Trainers who will challenge you if they spot you.

The Poké Balls beneath each Trainer's name indicate how many Pokémon that Trainer has in his or her party. Trainers who challenge you to special battles (like Sky Battles) are also marked, as are those who can be challenged to rematches.

⑥ Restore your Pokémon's health

You'll sometimes find people in homes or places along routes that can restore your Pokémon's health. These locations are marked on each map. When Pokémon in your party are unwell, do your best to reach these spots and have your loyal Pokémon restored to full health.

⑦ Pokémon encounters

See the Pokémon that appear in the area. This information helps you complete your Pokédex.

Pokémon Encounter Rate	
◎	Frequent
○	Average
△	Rare
▲	Almost never

Version Differences	
X	Only appears in *Pokémon X*
Y	Only appears in *Pokémon Y*

8 **1** Swing by Cassius's house

Enter the very first cottage you see in Camphrier Town for a surprising dose of modern technology. A group of gifted computer buffs are keeping a powerful machine running here. Speak with Cassius, who runs the PC storage system, to learn that the contraption is actually the server on which your PC Boxes are stored! Cassius gladly tells you all about PC Boxes, and one of the girls gives you TM46 Thief just for stopping by.

9 **NOTE** *After meeting Cassius, you'll notice that the option on your PC screen has changed from "Someone's PC" to "Cassius's PC."*

You can access your PC Boxes by inspecting Cassius's server.

2 Meet the Name Rater

Speak to the man in the suit in the Pokémon Center, and he'll introduce himself as the official Name Rater. This mysterious man gets a thrill out of critiquing the nicknames that you've given to your Pokémon. The Name Rater also has the power to change your Pokémon's nicknames if you like. What a guy!

3 Chat with the locals

Once you're done talking to the Name Rater, move on to talk to other locals around Camphrier Town. You never know who you will meet. Talk to everyone, and you'll receive lots of neat gifts, including an Ultra Ball, a Berry Juice, and a Sweet Heart.

127

8 Completion guide

What do you need to move forward? Get step-by-step descriptions of key events in each city, route, or location. If you follow these steps in order, you'll be able to complete the entire game! Combine this with the Recommended Route chart and your progress should be a breeze.

9 Extra information

You want more hints? Get 'em right here! The info may include effective ways to use the items you receive or behind-the-scenes stories.

10 Gym battle preparation

A little preparation before challenging a Gym Leader will make it much easier to take home a win. The information in this section will help you prepare thoroughly. If at first you don't succeed, try again.

11 Gym battle guide

Get some hints on the tricks of each Gym and the best ways to attack the weak points of each Gym Leader's Pokémon.

12 Gym Leader's Pokémon

Find out about the Pokémon that each Gym Leader will use in battle, including their weaknesses. This gives you the info you need to choose appropriate Pokémon and moves so you can target your opponent's weaknesses relentlessly! (The artwork for some Pokémon is purposefully omitted.)

13 Gym Badges

Take a look at the Gym Badge you get for defeating a Gym Leader, plus the effects of the Gym Badge.

14 TMs received from the Gym Leaders

Get an outline of the TM you get for defeating Gym Leaders.

Vaniville Town

Vaniville Town is a small, quiet community nestled in the Kalos region's lush southern hills. You've only just moved here, and you couldn't ask for a nicer place to live. It is here that your great adventure begins!

Field Moves Needed

Route 1
(to Aquacorde Town)

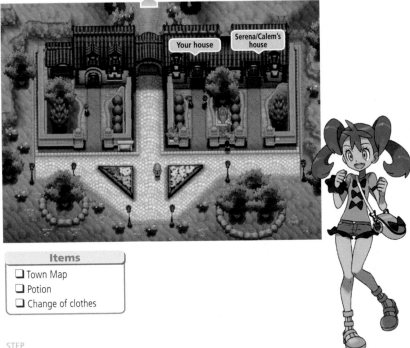

Your house

Serena/Calem's house

Items
❑ Town Map
❑ Potion
❑ Change of clothes

STEP
1 **Check out your room**

Rise and shine! You've just moved to a new town, but that's no excuse for sleeping in so late. Take a few moments to rub the sleep from your eyes, then check out your bedroom. A state-of-the-art Wii U system is all hooked up, and you can turn on the TV to see a movie, a game show, or something else. Take a look.

Head to your computer desk and press Ⓐ to view a few helpful hints for your adventure.

STEP 2 » Go downstairs

Go have a look at yourself in the mirror, and change out of your pajamas.

You can't just hang around your room all day! Head downstairs to speak to your mom. She's glad to see that you're up and about, but she asks that you change out of your pajamas before you leave the house. Not a bad idea!

STEP 3 » Get dressed

...And changed out of his pajamas!

Sprint back upstairs and return to your bedroom. Stand in front of the mirror and press Ⓐ to change clothes. Ah, much better!

STEP 4 » Explore your house

Why don't you step out and say hello to the neighbors?

Go back downstairs to speak to your mom again. Now that you've changed out of your pajamas, your mom suggests that you go outside and say hi to your neighbors. Feel free to check out the rest of your home before heading outdoors.

STEP 5 » Meet your neighbors

Welcome to Vaniville Town!

It doesn't take long for you to run into your neighbors—they're waiting right outside your front door. Serena/Calem* and Shauna are pleased to meet you, and they seem really friendly. They tell you that an esteemed professor named Sycamore has heard about you, and then they invite you to join them in the neighboring town of Aquacorde.

*The identity of your neighbor depends on which gender you chose in the beginning of the game. If you opted to play a boy, then Serena will accompany you on your journey. If you chose to play a girl, then Calem will be one of your friends.

STEP
⑥ Check out Vaniville Town

Your new friends have rushed off to Aquacorde Town, but there's no need for you to keep pace. Take a moment to say hi to the folks in Vaniville Town before you leave. Don't be shy—stroll right into your neighbors' homes and introduce yourself!

TIPS *Hold ⑧ while moving to walk faster toward your next destination.*

Turn on the TVs in your neighbors' homes to watch informative programming. Some shows provide hints that will help you in your adventure.

NOTE *The Rhyhorn your mom brought home from her racing days is fast asleep at the moment, but you can climb onto its back if you like.*

STEP
⑦ Leave Vaniville Town through the north gate

After you've spoken to everyone in Vaniville Town, it's time to travel to Aquacorde Town. Proceed through Vaniville Town's north gate to reach Route 1, which leads to Aquacorde Town.

AFTER VISITING AQUACORDE:
⚙ Get ready to hit the road

Give your mom the Prof's Letter and she will get you all ready to set out on your big adventure with a Town Map, a Potion, and a change of clothes. Then it's back to Aquacorde Town—and beyond—with the best wishes of your mom and her Rhyhorn!

NOTE *The Town Map shows all the great places awaiting you in the Kalos region. Each city and town will turn blue as you visit it, and eventually you can instantly return to places you've visited before by using the field move Fly.*

Route 1 (Vaniville Pathway)

Route 1 is one of the smallest routes you'll ever see. This straight pathway simply connects Vaniville Town and Aquacorde Town. Though short, it makes for a pleasant stroll.

Field Moves Needed

Aquacorde Town

Vaniville Town

STEP
1 Go to Aquacorde Town

Your journey to Aquacorde Town is short and sweet. Just travel north along Route 1, and you'll be there before you know it.

TIP *Have you checked out the Player Search System (PSS) yet? It appears by default on the bottom screen when you do not have the field menu open. You'll be able to see other players nearby or other players online at the same time as you. You'll have to wait until you get your first Pokémon to use all the features, but then you'll be able to trade and battle with others instantaneously. You can already edit your profile, though, if you'd like to distinguish yourself on the PSS! For more information on the PSS, see page 68.*

Aquacorde Town

Welcome to Aquacorde Town. There's even more to see and do in this town than in Vaniville. Here you'll find shops that sell vital wares to beginner Pokémon Trainers. If only you had a Pokémon of your own!

Field Moves Needed

Route 2
(to Santalune Forest)

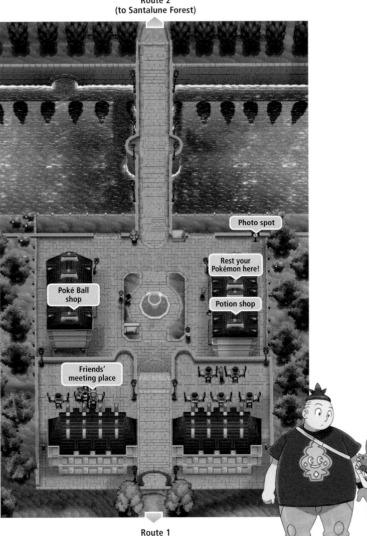

Photo spot

Rest your Pokémon here!

Poké Ball shop

Potion shop

Friends' meeting place

Route 1
(to Vaniville Town)

Items
❑ Pokédex
❑ Potion
❑ Prof's Letter

Poké Ball Shop	
Poké Ball	200

Potion Shop	
Potion	300

STEP 1 » Meet up with your new friends

Hey, Xavier! This way! Over here!

Your friends call out to you as you enter Aquacorde Town. Go west to find them sitting at an outdoor table, excitedly talking to one another.

STEP 2 » Choose a Pokémon!

The Fire-type Pokémon Fennekin

Shauna and Serena/Calem introduce you to two more friends: Tierno and Trevor. The group insists on giving you a nickname, but is kind enough to let you decide it for yourself. After that, they waste no time getting to the good stuff: letting you pick your very own Pokémon partner!

Chespin
Grass
Ability: Overgrow

Fennekin
Fire
Ability: Blaze

Froakie
Water
Ability: Torrent

NOTES *Each Pokémon partner has its own strengths and weaknesses, so choose the one you like best.*

Super Training and Pokémon-Amie are now available on the Touch Screen. See pages 366 and 372 for more information on these special new features that will allow you to power up your Pokémon partners.

STEP
3 » Receive your Pokédex

Give your new Pokémon a nickname if you like. Afterward, Trevor will hand you an important item called a Pokédex. This device gives you detailed information on all of the Pokémon you encounter. The mysterious Professor Sycamore has challenged you to fill your Pokédex by finding every Pokémon in the Kalos region!

STEP
4 » Receive the Prof's Letter

Before the meeting concludes, Tierno gives you one last item: a letter from Professor Sycamore to your mom. With that, Tierno and Trevor race off to explore Lumiose City, leaving you to deliver the letter. Better hurry back to your house!

STEP
5 » Battle with Shauna

On your way back to Vaniville Town, you're suddenly waylaid by none other than your newfound friend, Shauna. Right away, Shauna wants to try a Pokémon battle! Luckily for you, the Pokémon Shauna uses will be of the type that's weak against the type you've selected. Use a move that is the same type as your Pokémon to make short work of Shauna's Pokémon!

TIP *When a Pokémon uses an attack that is the same type as one of its types, the damage dealt will go up by half! So, if a Fire-type Pokémon uses a Fire-type move, it will do far more damage than if a Fire-type move is used by a Grass-type Pokémon with the same stats.*

NOTE *When you are viewing a summary of your Pokémon's moves from the battle menu, you will see that attacks are color-coded to match their type.*

Vs. Shauna's Pokémon

If you chose Chespin:	If you chose Fennekin:	If you chose Froakie:
Froakie ♂ Lv. 5 [Water]	**Chespin** ♂ Lv. 5 [Grass]	**Fennekin** ♂ Lv. 5 [Fire]
Weak to: [Grass] [Electric]	Weak to: [Fire] [Ice] [Poison] [Flying] [Bug]	Weak to: [Water] [Ground] [Rock]

STEP
⑥ Deliver the Prof's Letter

Did you make it through your first Pokémon battle victoriously? After Shauna heals your Pokémon, retrace your steps to your house in Vaniville Town. Don't forget: you've still got to get your mom's go-ahead before you hit the road on your own!

AFTER RETURNING TO VANIVILLE TOWN:
✳ Explore Aquacorde Town

Xavier obtained a Potion!

Armed with the Town Map, you're all set to begin exploring the region. Back in Aquacorde Town, speak to all of the townsfolk to receive lots of advice. One kind young man will even hand you a valuable Potion. Be sure to visit all of the local shops as well! When you're all ready, continue north to Route 2.

TIP *Buy 10 Poké Balls from the shop with the green Poké Ball sign hanging above it in Aquacorde Town, and you'll receive a free Premier Ball. This trick works anywhere you can buy Poké Balls. And don't hesitate to buy more Potions—they're sure to come in handy!*

You'll find many Pokémon hiding among the tall grass that grows in tufts along this trail.

Route 2 (Avance Trail)

This route is a bit longer than Route 1, and it features tall grass that wild Pokémon just love to hide in. You're certain to encounter a few wild Pokémon as you make your way through here, but never fear— your Pokémon partner is by your side!

Field Moves Needed

Santalune Forest

Youngster Austin
◉◉◉◉◉◉

Aquacorde Town

Items
☐ Poké Ball ×10

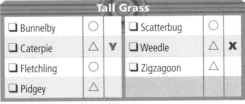

Tall Grass					
☐ Bunnelby	○		☐ Scatterbug	○	
☐ Caterpie	△	▼	☐ Weedle	△	✕
☐ Fletchling	○		☐ Zigzagoon	△	
☐ Pidgey	△				

◎ frequent ○ average △ rare ▲ almost never

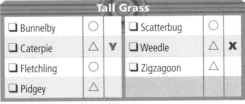

Bunnelby

Normal

Abilities: Pickup
Cheek Pouch

Fletchling

Normal Flying

Ability: Big Pecks

Scatterbug

Bug

Abilities: Shield Dust
Compound Eyes

STEP
1 Battle a wild Pokémon

You're certain to be surprised by a wild Pokémon as you trudge through Route 2's very first patch of tall grass. Your Pokémon partner is a bit more experienced, however, and is ready to take on this wild Pokémon. Don't hold back!

STEP
2 How to catch a wild Pokémon

Your friends Shauna and Serena/Calem are just a few paces ahead. Your timing couldn't be better, for your neighbor is about to show you how to catch wild Pokémon! Watch and learn how to use Poké Balls to catch a wild Pokémon after it has been weakened in battle.

STEP
3 Catch a wild Pokémon

Now that you've learned how to catch a wild Pokémon and received some Poké Balls, why not try catching one yourself? Enter the second patch of tall grass, and you're sure to be ambushed again by another wild Pokémon. This time, rather than defeating the wild Pokémon, try to weaken it so that its health is yellow or red, then fling a Poké Ball at it.

TIPS Always try to weaken wild Pokémon before attempting to catch them with a Poké Ball.

Use Potions to heal your Pokémon, or return to the northeastern shop in Aquacorde Town and let your Pokémon rest there for free. You can always return to your home in Vaniville Town and speak to your mother to heal your Pokémon at any time.

STEP
④ Battle Youngster Austin

As you near Route 2's north end, a young Pokémon Trainer challenges you. You can't catch his Pokémon, so simply focus on defeating it with powerful attacks. After the battle, head north into Santalune Forest.

 NOTE Only wild Pokémon can be caught with Poké Balls. Don't try to catch other Trainers' Pokémon—it's just bad manners!

 TIP While battling a Pokémon Trainer, pay attention to the number of Poké Balls that appear beneath his or her Pokémon's stats. Each Poké Ball represents one Pokémon you'll face during the battle.

The gentle light filtering through this sun-dappled forest makes it a popular spot for nature walks.

Santalune Forest

This lush forest is filled with tall grass, making it a wonderful area for Pokémon catching. Of course, this has also attracted a number of Pokémon Trainers who are eager to test their skills! Several valuable items can be found in the forest's nooks and crannies.

Field Moves Needed

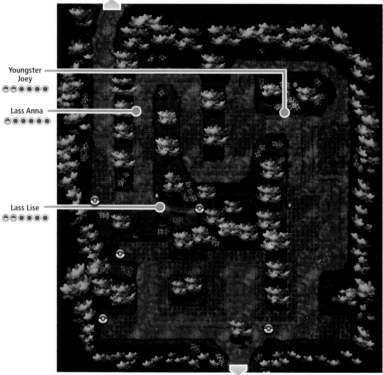

Route 3
(to Santalune City)

Youngster Joey

Lass Anna

Lass Lise

Route 2
(to Aquacorde Town)

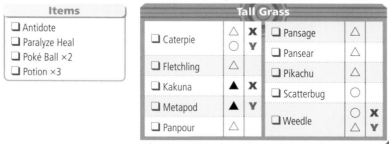

Items
❑ Antidote
❑ Paralyze Heal
❑ Poké Ball ×2
❑ Potion ×3

Tall Grass				Tall Grass		
❑ Caterpie	△	X		❑ Pansage	△	
	◎	Y		❑ Pansear	△	
❑ Fletchling	△			❑ Pikachu	△	
❑ Kakuna	▲	X		❑ Scatterbug	◯	
❑ Metapod	▲	Y		❑ Weedle	◯	X
❑ Panpour	△				△	Y

◎ frequent ◯ average △ rare ▲ almost never

91

Panpour
Water
Ability: Gluttony

Pansage
Grass
Ability: Gluttony

Pansear
Fire
Ability: Gluttony

Pikachu
Electric
Ability: Static

STEP
① Search the forest for items

Shauna catches up to you as you enter the forest and asks if she can tag along. She offers to heal your Pokémon at any time, so she's a welcome companion. Approach the Poké Ball on the nearby ground and inspect it to claim your first item from the forest: a Potion.

TIP   *Search the forest thoroughly to discover many more items. Check the map for their locations.*

STEP
② Catch lots of wild Pokémon

With Shauna by your side and a forest full of Pokémon, nothing should stop you from adding several new entries to your Pokédex. Search the tall grass and do your best to catch as many new Pokémon as possible. If you're really lucky, you might even catch a Pikachu!

NOTES   *There's no pressing need to catch Pokémon that you've already caught, though it's good to have some to trade with (see p. 70). If you see a small Poké Ball icon next to a wild Pokémon's name in battle, then that means you've already caught one like it. Save your Poké Balls for new species!*

You can carry up to six Pokémon with you in your party. If you already have six Pokémon in your party when you catch a new Pokémon, it will be sent to your PC Box and you won't be able to add it to your party until you visit a Pokémon Center.

STEP
3 Defeat Pokémon Trainers on your way to Route 3

Come on, Scatterbug--let's powder this punk!

A forest so full of wild Pokémon has lured many a Pokémon Trainer into its depths. Expect to have your skills tested as you explore deeper into the forest. Fight hard to beat each Trainer you encounter and have Shauna heal your team after every battle.

 TIP

Pokémon that you receive in trades will get extra Exp. Points from battles, enabling them to level up faster than Pokémon you catch in the wild. Catch extra Pokémon and trade them on the GTS or with a friend to get Pokémon you want in your team. These new teammates will quickly become strong allies!

Route 3 (Ouvert Way)

Route 3 lies just south of Santalune City and connects to Santalune Forest. Additional species of wild Pokémon can be caught here on your way to the big city ahead. Once you are able to use Cut in the field, you can slash through the prickly thorns up north and claim a special item.

Field Moves Needed

Cut   Surf

Santalune City

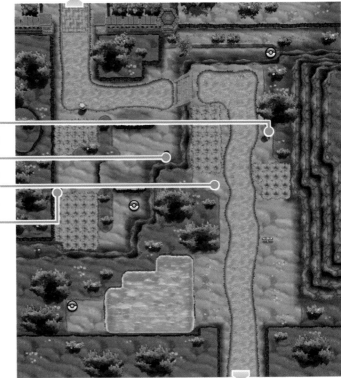

Preschooler Ella

Schoolgirl Bridget

Preschooler Oliver

Schoolboy Brighton

Santalune Forest

Items

First visit

☐ Adventure Rules

☐ Super Potion

After learning the Cut field move

☐ Revive

After learning the Surf field move

☐ Dawn Stone

Azurill

`Normal` `Fairy`

Abilities: Thick Fat
Huge Power

Burmy

`Bug`

Ability: Shed Skin

Tall Grass		
❑ Azurill	△	
❑ Bidoof	○	
❑ Bunnelby	○	
❑ Burmy	△	
❑ Dunsparce	▲	
❑ Fletchling	○	
❑ Pidgey	△	
❑ Pikachu	▲	

Fishing		
Old Rod		
❑ Magikarp	◎	
Good Rod		
❑ Corphish	○	
❑ Goldeen	◎	
Super Rod		
❑ Crawdaunt	▲	
❑ Gyarados	◎	
❑ Seaking	○	

Water Surface		
❑ Marill	○	
❑ Masquerain	◎	

◎ frequent ○ average
△ rare ▲ almost never

STEP
① Receive the Adventure Rules from Serena/Calem

Upon arriving at Route 3, all of your friends gather 'round for a quick meeting. Everyone makes plans to catch Pokémon, except for Serena/Calem, who has her/his eye set on challenging the Leader of the Pokémon Gym within the city ahead. Before the meeting ends, Serena/Calem hands you a helpful handbook that's filled with rules that every Pokémon Trainer should know.

STEP
② Take on Pokémon Trainers

The path to Santalune City is lined with Pokémon Trainers, all of them ready to test their skills against you. Fight hard as you journey toward the city gate, for every battle you win makes your Pokémon stronger!

 Shauna isn't around to heal your Pokémon anymore, so don't hesitate to use Potions and heal your Pokémon as needed.

 Don't worry if any of your Pokémon have fainted. You can heal them soon at the Pokémon Center in Santalune City!

Catch more wild Pokémon

You can catch several new species of wild Pokémon in the tall grass along Route 3. After tackling all of the Trainers, take stock of your Pokémon party and see if they're feeling well enough to risk going after some of the wild Pokémon that hide in Route 3's tall grass. Of course, you can always return to catch more wild Pokémon later.

NOTE *Roller Skater Rinka passes you as you head toward the city. Looks like she's having fun zipping around on her Roller Skates!*

Many beginning Trainers gather in this friendly city to start a Pokémon journey.

Santalune City

Ah, Santalune City. This bustling community is a hub of Pokémon Trainer activity. From the Pokémon Center to the Trainers' School, young Trainers will find plenty of support here. And they'll need it if they hope to challenge the Leader of the local Pokémon Gym!

Field Moves Needed

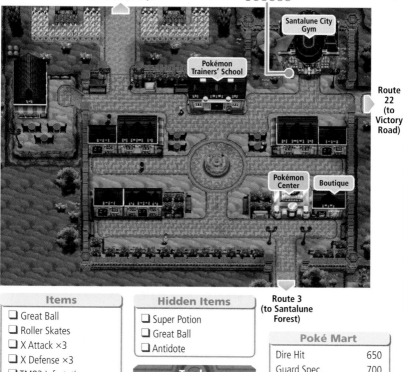

Route 4
(to Lumiose City)

Roller Skater Rinka
◉◉◉◉◉◉

Santalune City Gym

Pokémon Trainers' School

Route 22 (to Victory Road)

Pokémon Center

Boutique

Route 3
(to Santalune Forest)

Items
❑ Great Ball
❑ Roller Skates
❑ X Attack ×3
❑ X Defense ×3
❑ TM83 Infestation
❑ Exp. Share

Hidden Items
❑ Super Potion
❑ Great Ball
❑ Antidote

Trade
❑ Farfetch'd (Quacklin')

Poké Mart	
Dire Hit	650
Guard Spec.	700
X Accuracy	950
X Attack	500
X Defense	550
X Sp. Atk	350
X Sp. Def	350
X Speed	350

TIP *You'll need a Dowsing Machine to find Hidden Items. When you get one, visit again to find these great items.*

NOTE *The items available to purchase from the left clerk are not listed and increase after you defeat the Gym Leader. See page 410 for what items you can buy based on your current number of Badges.*

STEP
1 » Heal your Pokémon

The Pokémon Center is one of Santalune City's main attractions. It's the first shop you see when entering the city, so pop in and speak with the receptionist to quickly heal your Pokémon, free of charge.

> **NOTE** *Whenever you rest your Pokémon at a Pokémon Center, their HP and PP are fully restored, and all status conditions are removed. Nice!*

STEP
2 » Log on to the PC

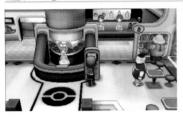

Examine the computer terminal next to the reception desk to log on and sort your Pokémon. Using this special PC, you can swap Pokémon in your party with others that are stored in your PC Boxes. You can also log on to Professor Sycamore's account for a quick evaluation of your Pokémon-catching progress.

STEP
3 » Check out the Poké Mart

A shop known as the Poké Mart is found behind the reception counter to the right. The clerk on the left offers vital items, including Potions and Poké Balls. The clerk on the right sells other items that can give you an edge in battle.

STEP
4 » Find the fitting room

Now check out the fitting room on the Pokémon Center's left side. Here you can change clothes to customize your appearance. Your mom packed a fresh shirt and pants for you to try out, but you'll need to do a little shopping if you want more style options. Lucky for you, there's a boutique that sells clothing right next door to the Pokémon Center!

STEP
5 Pop by the boutique

If you'd like, check the items at the back of the shop.

This fashionable shop stands right beside the Pokémon Center. Head inside to check their selection of hats. You don't need to make a purchase, but it's fun to browse!

TIP *The inventory at each boutique across Kalos can change from day to day. Visit them often and buy favorites when you see them, because they may be gone the next day!*

STEP
6 Grab a Great Ball

Xavier obtained a Great Ball!

Talking to people you meet on the street or in houses can be very rewarding! A Schoolboy in a house on the city's east side will graciously part with a Great Ball, which can be used to catch a wild Pokémon with greater ease.

STEP
7 Trade Pokémon with Cliff

Yes
No

So how about it? Why don't you trade a Bunnelby for my Farfetch'd?

Enter a house on the city's west side to speak with a Hiker named Cliff, who wishes to trade Pokémon with you. Go ahead and make the trade, because the Pokémon you receive from Cliff is quite rare.

TIP *The Beauty in the house west of the Pokémon Center will tell you how close you are to your Pokémon. Some Pokémon need to be very friendly with you to evolve or to perform well in battle!*

NOTES *Pokémon you receive from trades with other characters or other players earn bonus Experience Points from battles, allowing them to level up faster than normal.*

If you trade Pokémon with another player, that player becomes an Acquaintance of yours and will appear on your PSS home screen whenever he or she is nearby or online.

STEP
⑧ Stop by the Trainers' School

Enter the building at the city's north end to visit the Trainers' School. Here you'll receive many more useful tips on how to succeed in Pokémon battles. Check out the white board and you might learn something very useful. The teacher will even hand you three X Attacks and three X Defenses just for stopping by!

STEP
⑨ Battle Roller Skater Rinka for some Roller Skates

Now that you've explored the whole town, all that's left is to challenge the Gym Leader of the local Pokémon Gym. But before you may enter the Gym, you must triumph over a particular Pokémon Trainer. Roller Skater Rinka stands right in front of the Gym's door—defeat her in a Pokémon battle, and she'll not only skate out of your way, but she'll also give you a free pair of Roller Skates!

 Use the Circle Pad to snap on your Roller Skates and travel along roads. Use the +Control Pad to kick off your Roller Skates and walk or dash around again.

STEP
⑩ Enter the Pokémon Gym or Explore Route 22

You now face an important choice: should you enter the Pokémon Gym and challenge the Gym Leader (see p. 104), or explore Route 22 to the east? How about exploring Route 22 first, as there are more wild Pokémon to catch there, and more Trainers to face? Remember, every battle makes your Pokémon stronger!

AFTER DEFEATING GYM LEADER VIOLA:

 Receive the Exp. Share from Alexa

As you approach Route 4 after defeating the Santalune City Gym Leader, Viola, you're drawn into conversation with Viola's older sister, Alexa. There are no hard feelings. In fact, Alexa congratulates you on your victory and gives you a very valuable item!

TIP
Now that you have the Exp. Share, all of the Pokémon in your party can receive 50% of the Experience Points gained from battle, even if they don't participate. Just leave the Exp. Share on and it will do all the work!

Route 22 (Détourner Way)

When it comes to training up your Pokémon for your first Gym battle, you couldn't ask for a better place than Route 22. Located right next to Santalune City, this path is lined with talented Trainers who are eager to test your battle prowess. More species of wild Pokémon can be obtained from the tall grass here as well. Consider exploring this route before taking on the Gym Leader in Santalune City.

Field Moves Needed

Cut Surf
Waterfall Strength

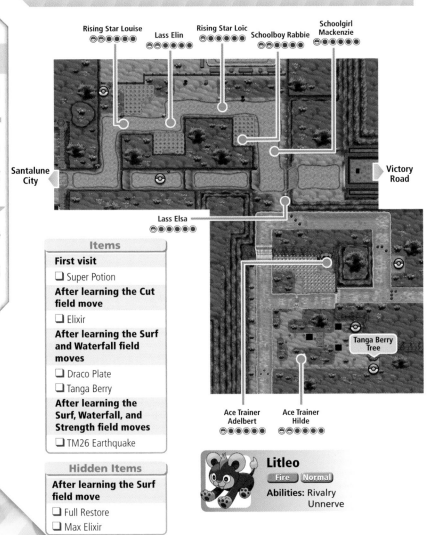

Rising Star Louise
Lass Elin
Rising Star Loïc
Schoolboy Rabbie
Schoolgirl Mackenzie
Santalune City
Victory Road
Lass Elsa
Tanga Berry Tree
Ace Trainer Adelbert
Ace Trainer Hilde

Items

First visit
❑ Super Potion

After learning the Cut field move
❑ Elixir

After learning the Surf and Waterfall field moves
❑ Draco Plate
❑ Tanga Berry

After learning the Surf, Waterfall, and Strength field moves
❑ TM26 Earthquake

Hidden Items

After learning the Surf field move
❑ Full Restore
❑ Max Elixir

Litleo
Fire Normal
Abilities: Rivalry
Unnerve

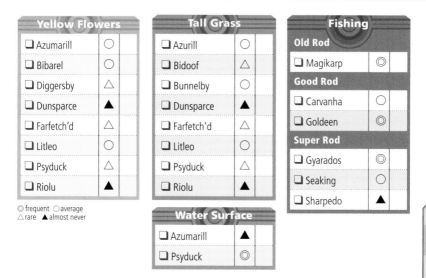

Yellow Flowers		
❑ Azumarill	◎	
❑ Bibarel	○	
❑ Diggersby	△	
❑ Dunsparce	▲	
❑ Farfetch'd	△	
❑ Litleo	○	
❑ Psyduck	△	
❑ Riolu	▲	

◎ frequent ○ average
△ rare ▲ almost never

Tall Grass		
❑ Azurill	○	
❑ Bidoof	△	
❑ Bunnelby	○	
❑ Dunsparce	▲	
❑ Farfetch'd	△	
❑ Litleo	○	
❑ Psyduck	△	
❑ Riolu	▲	

Water Surface		
❑ Azumarill	▲	
❑ Psyduck	◎	

Fishing		
Old Rod		
❑ Magikarp	◎	
Good Rod		
❑ Carvanha	○	
❑ Goldeen	◎	
Super Rod		
❑ Gyarados	◎	
❑ Seaking	○	
❑ Sharpedo	▲	

STEP
1 Strengthen your Pokémon through battle

This route is a great place to train your Pokémon. Challenge the Trainers along the winding path and trudge through Route 22's tall grass to engage in even more battles. When you're happy with the strength of your party, return to Santalune City to rest up before entering the Pokémon Gym.

Swap out your Pokémon during battles to give them Experience Points. They don't even need to take action—Pokémon gain Experience Points just by entering the fray! Or just from being in your party if you use the Exp. Share you got from Viola's cool journalist sister, Alexa.

Return to the Pokémon Center to rest your Pokémon as often as you like.

Electric-, Flying-, and Rock-type Pokémon will be of the most value to you when challenging the Gym Leader of Santalune City.

Santalune City Gym Battle

Gym Battle Tips

✓ Bring lots of Potions

✓ Use Electric-, Flying-, and Rock-type Pokémon

✓ Use a Pikachu if you have one

Gym Leader Viola

Lass Charlotte
◉◉◉◉◉◉

Youngster Zachary
◉◉◉◉◉◉

Youngster David
◉◉◉◉◉◉

Santalune City Gym Leader

Viola
Bug-type Pokémon User

Use Electric-, Flying-, and Rock-type moves to deal massive damage

Work your way around the Gym's giant web, following the water droplets as they lead you among and around Trainers waiting to challenge you. Defeat each Trainer in turn to approach the Gym Leader, Viola. If you like, you may return to the web's center and exit the Gym at any time to rest your Pokémon at the Pokémon Center.

Like all of the Gym's Trainers, Viola uses Bug-type Pokémon, which are vulnerable to Flying- and Rock-type moves. Beware of Viola's final Pokémon, Vivillon, which will use Infestation to deal steady damage and prevent you from swapping out your Pokémon. Use Potions to keep your Pokémon in the battle!

Viola's Pokémon

Surskit
♀ Lv. 10 `Bug` `Water`
Weak to: `Electric` `Flying` `Rock`

Vivillon
♀ Lv. 12 `Bug` `Flying`
Weak to: `4x! Rock` `Fire` `Electric` `Ice` `Flying`

Bug Badge
Pokémon up to Lv. 30, including those received in trades, will obey you.

TM83 Infestation
The target is infested and attacked for four to five turns. The target can't flee during this time.

TIP *Although pure Bug-type Pokémon are not weak to Electric types, both of Viola's dual-type Pokémon are. Did you manage to catch a Pikachu in Santalune Forest? If you did, having it use Electric-type moves will end this battle in a flash! Any Pikachu you catch probably knows Thunder Shock. Plus, with Pikachu's Static Ability, Pokémon that come into direct contact with it may be paralyzed, making them less likely to attack!*

Route 4 (Parterre Way)

This lovely path connects Santalune and Lumiose Cities. Its geometric gardens are fun to explore, and keen adventurers will find valuable items hidden among the flora. Trainers and wild Pokémon abound, so be ready to battle at any moment!

Field Moves
Needed

Lumiose City

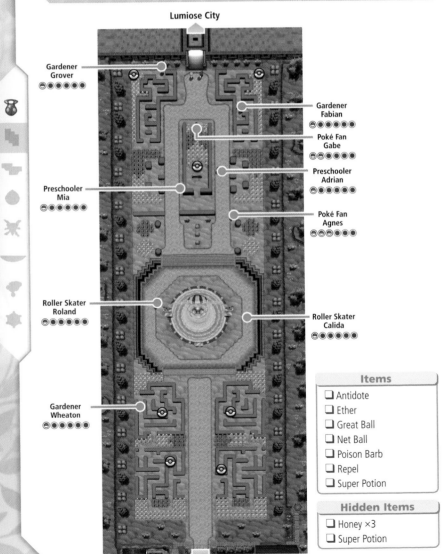

Gardener
Grover

Gardener
Fabian

Poké Fan
Gabe

Preschooler
Adrian

Preschooler
Mia

Poké Fan
Agnes

Roller Skater
Roland

Roller Skater
Calida

Gardener
Wheaton

Santalune City

Items
❑ Antidote
❑ Ether
❑ Great Ball
❑ Net Ball
❑ Poison Barb
❑ Repel
❑ Super Potion

Hidden Items
❑ Honey ×3
❑ Super Potion

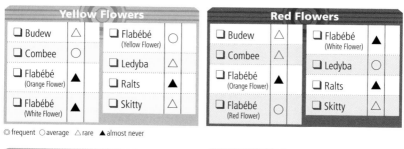

Yellow Flowers			
❑ Budew	△	❑ Flabébé (Yellow Flower)	◎
❑ Combee	◎	❑ Ledyba	△
❑ Flabébé (Orange Flower)	▲	❑ Ralts	▲
❑ Flabébé (White Flower)	▲	❑ Skitty	△

Red Flowers			
❑ Budew	△	❑ Flabébé (White Flower)	▲
❑ Combee	△	❑ Ledyba	◎
❑ Flabébé (Orange Flower)	▲	❑ Ralts	▲
❑ Flabébé (Red Flower)	◎	❑ Skitty	△

◎ frequent ◯ average △ rare ▲ almost never

Combee
`Bug` `Flying`
Ability: Honey Gather

Flabébé
`Fairy`
Ability: Flower Veil

STEP 1 Explore the geometric gardens

As promised, I'll tell you the official name! They're known as geometric gardens!

Romp through Route 4's simple hedge mazes to discover a number of worthwhile items. Gardeners you meet will challenge you to Pokémon battles, as will several others. You'll discover many more wild Pokémon in the flowers, too.

STEP 2 Battle the Roller Skaters

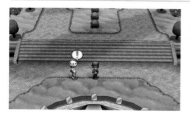

Stand in the way of the Roller Skaters that are circling the central fountain. They'll pause to battle you with their Pokémon. The extra prize money you win from these battles will come in handy in Lumiose City!

STEP 3 Meet Sina and Dexio

If you'd like, I'll show you the way to the lab. So, come along now!

Yes
No

Go to Route 4's north end, and you'll find two friendly faces waiting near the Lumiose City gate. They introduce themselves as Sino and Dexio, and tell you of a whole new type of Pokémon—the Fairy type! You're invited to follow them to Professor Sycamore's lab in Lumiose City.

Lumiose City (South)

Congratulations, you've arrived at the Kalos region's most famous city! Marvel at Lumiose's massive buildings and winding streets, but don't get lost in the excitement! Due to an odd blackout in the city's northern half, you're restricted to South Boulevard and a side street called Vernal Avenue for the time being.

Field Moves Needed

Items

- ❑ Lens Case
- ❑ Luxury Ball ×5
- ❑ Quick Ball ×3
- ❑ Quick Claw
- ❑ Timer Ball ×3
- ❑ Tiny Mushroom ×15
- ❑ TM27 Return
- ❑ TM54 False Swipe
- ❑ Venusaurite or
  Charizardite X (✘) or
  Charizardite Y (✔) or
  Blastoisinite
  (depending on Pokémon and game)

Poké Mart

TM78 Bulldoze	10,000
TM18 Rain Dance	50,000
TM76 Struggle Bug	10,000
TM11 Sunny Day	50,000
TM75 Swords Dance	10,000

Stone Emporium

Fire Stone	2,100
Leaf Stone	2,100
Water Stone	2,100

Herboriste

Energy Powder	500
Energy Root	800
Heal Powder	450
Revival Herb	2,800

Office Building

Estival Avenue

Shutterbug Café

Office Building

Café Soleil

Coiffure Clips

South Boulevard

Route 5
(to Camphrier Town)

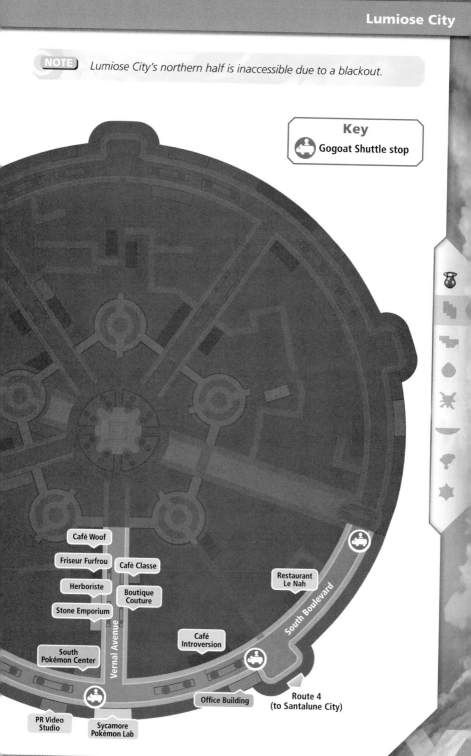

NOTE Lumiose City's northern half is inaccessible due to a blackout.

Key
Gogoat Shuttle stop

Café Woof

Friseur Furfrou

Café Classe

Herboriste

Boutique Couture

Stone Emporium

Vernal Avenue

Café Introversion

Restaurant Le Nah

South Boulevard

South Pokémon Center

PR Video Studio

Sycamore Pokémon Lab

Office Building

Route 4 (to Santalune City)

1 Receive TM27 Return

Here! This is the TM for Return.

As you pass through Lumiose City's southern entry gate, Sina and Dexio pause to hand you a new TM. This one can be used to teach Pokémon the move Return, which deals more damage when your friendship with your Pokémon is strong.

> **TIP** *Have Pokémon that you've spent time traveling and battling with learn Return. It can be a powerful move!*

2 Meet Sina outside the Sycamore Pokémon Lab

This building is the Sycamore Pokémon Lab! Let's go inside!

Lumiose City is really something. It's easy to become distracted while exploring it, but try to stay on course for the moment. Turn left and head down South Boulevard until you spot Sina standing in front of the Sycamore Pokémon Lab. Hurry inside as the professor awaits!

3 Battle Professor Sycamore

I'm Professor Sycamore! It's a pleasure to finally meet you!

Take the elevator up to the lab's third floor to meet the mysterious Professor Sycamore. Serena/Calem and Shauna soon arrive, too. The professor assesses your Pokédex, then asks to battle against you. It's a friendly test of skill, so prepare your Pokémon and show the professor what you've got!

Professor Sycamore's Pokémon

Bulbasaur
♂ Lv. 10 Grass Poison
Weak to: Fire Ice Flying Psychic

Squirtle
♂ Lv. 10 Water
Weak to: Grass Electric

Charmander
♂ Lv. 10 Fire
Weak to: Water Ground Rock

STEP 4 Choose a new Pokémon

The Fire-type Pokémon
Charmander

After besting the professor, you get to pick one of the Pokémon he used against you and have it join your party. They're all great choices, so take stock of your current Pokémon and consider picking one of a type that you don't already have.

Bulbasaur
Grass Poison
Ability: Overgrow

Charmander
Fire
Ability: Blaze

Squirtle
Water
Ability: Torrent

STEP 5 Receive a Mega Stone

If you're investigating Mega Evolution, why don't you check out Camphrier Town?

Professor Sycamore isn't done handing out gifts just yet. The good professor also hands you a powerful Mega Stone that holds the secret to making a Pokémon perform an awesome Mega Evolution during battle. The professor suggests you visit Camphrier Town in the hope of learning more about Mega Evolution, but there's still a lot to do in Lumiose City.

STEP 6 » Explore the Sycamore Pokémon Lab

Xavier put the TM54 in the TMs & HMs Pocket.

Now that you've met Professor Sycamore and scored a new Pokémon, take a moment to investigate his impressive lab. Speak to the female Scientist on 3F and you'll be rewarded with TM54 False Swipe if you've been diligent about finding lots of different Pokémon. Talk to the lab workers on the second floor to receive some Luxury Balls.

TIP *If you have a Rotom in your party, examine the cardboard boxes stacked around the room on 2F. They contain appliances that will allow it to change forms.*

STEP 7 » Meet Lysandre

I am Lysandre.

As you return to the lab's lobby, Sina introduces you to an arresting man named Lysandre, who says he wants to learn about Pokémon to build a better future. The meeting is brief and mysterious, and Lysandre soon departs. When your friends rejoin you, they discuss plans for how to enjoy the city life. Serena/Calem asks you for a rendezvous at a nearby café and dashes off.

STEP 8 » Join Shauna outside the PR Video Studio

You can make Trainer PR Videos here! It's called the PR Video Studio! ♪

Serena/Calem is waiting for you at Café Soleil, but you run into Shauna on the boulevard before you get there. Shauna is really excited about the nearby PR Video Studio and says that you can make Trainer PR Videos there. Sounds intriguing!

The signs near each building tell you their names. Stand near a sign and press Ⓐ to read it.

STEP
⑨ Make a Trainer PR Video

Creating a Trainer PR Video couldn't be easier. Just enter the PR Video Studio and speak to the clerk on the left. Choose a style from the available list, and you'll be whisked away to the recording studio to film your own unique Trainer PR Video. Afterward, you can choose to make your video viewable to Friends, Acquaintances, and Passersby on the PSS. You'll be able to change these settings later in the PSS Settings, if you ever change your mind.

TIPS

Use the PR Studio's fitting room to change your clothing prior to your shoot. You can also visit the green room on the left to change your look—adding decorative touches like makeup or even facial hair—anytime after shooting your first video.

Log on to any PC after filming a Trainer PR Video, and you'll be able to edit the video in all sorts of cool ways! See page 393 for more information.

STEP
⑩ Obtain the Lens Case

After shooting your Trainer PR Video, speak to the girl with pink hair near the set. She really liked your video, and she gives you a Lens Case to commemorate your first day on film. Spice up your appearance using different colors of contact lenses to change your eye color when you visit fitting rooms!

STEP 11 > Follow Serena/Calem into Café Soleil

Continue down South Boulevard until you spot Serena/Calem standing near a café. Serena/Calem calls out to you and asks you to come inside. Go ahead and follow her/him into the café.

STEP 12 > Meet Diantha and chat with Serena/Calem

Inside the café, you find none other than Lysandre speaking with a famous movie star named Diantha. Serena/Calem informs you that Lysandre is the head of Lysandre Labs, which created the Holo Caster, a video-messaging device you and your friends all use to reach one another. Lysandre and Diantha have an interesting conversation that provides further insight into Lysandre's dream of living in a beautiful, unchanging world.

STEP 13 > Swing by the beauty salon

A salon is located between Café Soleil and the Pokémon Center. If you're in the mood for a new 'do, head inside to change your hairstyle, hair color, or both. Of course, you'll have to pay for the service. If you're running low on prize money, head back to Route 4 or onward to Route 5 to earn some more pocket money by winning battles.

TIP *By doing a lot in Lumiose City, you will begin to find that people treat you a little differently. One such perk will be new hairstyles available to you in the beauty salon, so be sure to see everything that Lumiose has to offer.*

STEP
14 Explore more buildings around the city

Xavier obtained
a Quick Claw!

There are several more buildings to explore in Lumiose City, located along South Boulevard. Enter these unmarked buildings to speak to more of the city's residents. They give you more hints about Pokémon training and Evolution. One girl will give you a Quick Claw, and you can receive special Poké Balls from some generous fellows upstairs. In another building, try talking to the Roller Skater hanging out in the lobby.

TIP   *The Roller Skaters in Lumiose City can teach you a new trick to perform on your own Roller Skates, so it's not a bad idea to catch any that you find in the glittering metropolis!*

STEP
15 Get a taste for battle at Restaurant Le Nah

I'd like to dine
Tell me more
Another time

Welcome to Restaurant Le Nah.
Our flavors will never overwhelm your palate.

If you're in the mood for a Pokémon battle, backtrack east along South Boulevard, heading toward Route 4. Keep going, and you'll find a one-star restaurant on the north side of the street. Ensure that your party is well prepared, then enter and pay the fee to engage in Double Battles against chef Roger. You can win up to 15 Tiny Mushrooms if you beat the chef all three times in the number of turns he requests.

NOTES   *Double Battles are two-on-two affairs, which you haven't yet experienced. Type matchups become even more important in these battles. Keep them in mind—as well as which Pokémon will move first or last. Moves that can affect more than one opponent at a time are also a great help in these battles.*

Your Pokémon will have their health and PP restored between each battle, so there's no need to hold back when choosing moves.

Tiny Mushrooms can be sold for 250 apiece at Poké Marts, so battle wisely and you can end up earning a nice profit along with some valuable battle experience!

STEP
16 Check out Vernal Avenue

 A blackout in Lumiose City's northern half prevents you from exploring very far to the north, but you are able to visit a number of shops on Vernal Avenue, now that you've met Professor Sycamore.

 NOTE *The Boutique Couture looks like a great place to shop, but you have to be stylish to get past the front door! Maybe if you get to know Lumiose City, you'll radiate the right style vibes.*

STEP
17 Enter the Stone Emporium

 Be sure to visit the Stone Emporium on Vernal Avenue's west side. You'll find special stones for sale that can cause certain species of Pokémon to evolve. Purchase stones if you like, and then use them on the right Pokémon. Talk to the owner himself if you'd like to hear about his most select stock. He sometimes has some very special stones to offer you, though his prices aren't easy for many Trainers to handle! Maybe he'll cut you a little deal if you become famous in Kalos?

STEP
18 Say hello to the Herboriste

 Enter the building next to the Stone Emporium to visit the local Herboriste. Inside, you'll find potent herbs that can provide a benefit to your Pokémon during battle. Compared to other remedies, the herbs are quite affordable. However, they have a very bitter taste that your Pokémon won't enjoy!

Using herbs is cost effective, but they weaken the friendship between you and your Pokémon.

STEP
19 Visit the cafés

This café was set up by Furfrou admirers for Furfrou admirers and their beloved Furfrou!

Several cafés around Vernal Avenue and South Boulevard are teeming with patrons who are happy to share their knowledge of the region. Pop by every café to see what the locals have to say. Sprinkled across these two bustling streets are cafés for Furfrou enthusiasts, fashionistas, photography lovers, and even shy people who know about all kinds of communications features.

TIP *Talk to the Backpacker in the Shutterbug Café. If you have taken 1–14 pictures, you'll get a Wide Lens; for 15–29, a Scope Lens; for 30 or more, a Zoom Lens. You can take pictures at Photo Spots around Kalos. See page 387 for more information.*

STEP
20 Trim up your Furfrou

Furfrou is a favored Pokémon in the Kalos region, and people love to parade their Furfrou around as a point of pride. It has become quite the trend to have Furfrou groomed into fantastic styles, and you can already choose from three of them at Friseur Furfrou—and perhaps you'll discover others later! You can catch one of these frisky Pokémon on Route 5, so remember to come back when you do.

STEP
21 Visit the Pokémon Center

Hello, and welcome to the Pokémon Center. Would you like to rest your Pokémon?

After talking to Serena/Calem, you're able to leave Lumiose City and proceed to Camphrier Town. The route to Camphrier Town is filled with Trainers and wild Pokémon, so prepare your party by visiting Lumiose City's Pokémon Center. Rest your Pokémon and purchase items at the Poké Mart for the journey ahead.

22 Learn about Poké Miles

Speak with the PokéMileage representative within the Pokémon Center to trade your Poké Miles for prizes. You accumulate Poké Miles by trading Pokémon, passing by other players by StreetPass, or even just traveling around the Kalos region. Your Poké Miles can also be used on the PGL (Pokémon Global Link). To learn more, see page 404 and page 409.

TIP *Check your Trainer Card to see how many Poké Miles you've accumulated so far.*

23 Proceed to Route 5

After you've explored Lumiose City's southern half, head to Camphrier Town. Go west on South Boulevard till you reach the gate to Route 5. Tierno will call you on the Holo Caster to urge you to hurry. There are hordes of wild Pokémon to catch!

24 Meet Mr. Bonding

As you leave Lumiose City heading for Route 5, you're approached by a man named Mr. Bonding. He tells you about O-Powers, which can make your Pokémon stronger or help you earn more prize money. Many of the O-Powers he gives you—Attack Power and Defense Power—will bring you advantages in battle (see p. 72).

NOTES *O-Powers are activated using the PSS and will gain levels and become stronger the more you use them. So use them as often as you can!*

You can now use the Gogoat Shuttle in town.

Enhance Your Style in Lumiose City

Every little thing you do in Lumiose City adds to your style. Stylishness brings all kinds of rewards, such as meeting various characters, getting discounts, and unlocking facilities and fashions. See below for just a taste of what's on offer.

How to increase your stylishness

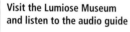

Slightly increases style

 Visit the Lumiose Museum and listen to the audio guide

Make a Trainer PR Video

Try your luck at the Loto-ID Center

Get your Furfrou styled at Friseur Furfrou and yourself at Coiffure Clips

Buy juice at the Juice Shoppe and Galettes at the Galette Stand

Take a Lumi Cab, Gogoat Shuttle, and train

Shop at the Herboriste, Stone Emporium, Poké Ball Boutique, and Boutique Couture

Have a meal at all of the restaurants in town

Take on the Battle Institute when it becomes available

Help out at Hotel Richissime

Chat with Alexa at Lumiose Press

Greatly increases style

Some rewards you can get for becoming stylish

Less Stylish

Unlock new hairstyles at Coiffure Clips

Gain access to Boutique Couture

Unlock new trims for your Furfrou at Friseur Furfrou

Unlock more effects for Trainer PR Videos

Unlock more juices at the Juice Shoppe

Get discounts on Galettes, in shops, and in restaurants

Get 50% off Lumi Cabs

Get the final O-Power from Mr. Bonding

More Stylish

TIP *The prices of Mega Stones at the Stone Emporium will also drop based on how stylish you are. They start at 1,000,000 each and go as low as 10,000. Wait until you're stylish enough to get the best bargain.*

Roller Skaters from across the Kalos region gather on this hilly path to demonstrate their best skills.

Route 5 (Versant Road)

This sloping path connects Lumiose City and Camphrier Town. It features a fun public skate park. Grinding along the many Roller Skate rails here leads you to a number of valuable items. Challenge some of the many Trainers around to help you hone your skills.

Field Moves Needed

Cut

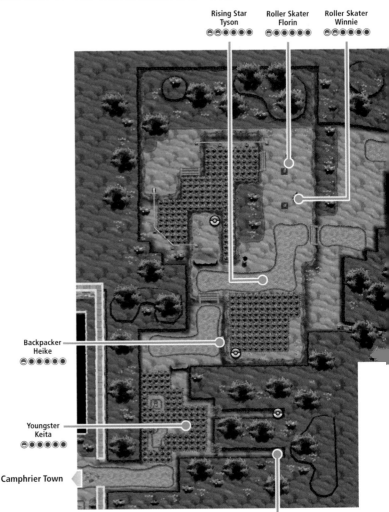

Rising Star Tyson

Roller Skater Florin

Roller Skater Winnie

Backpacker Heike

Youngster Keita

Camphrier Town

Youngster Anthony

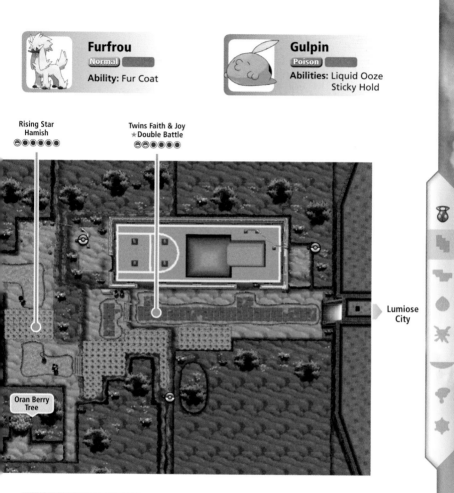

Furfrou
Normal
Ability: Fur Coat

Gulpin
Poison
Abilities: Liquid Ooze
Sticky Hold

Rising Star
Hamish
◉◉◉◉◉◉

Twins Faith & Joy
★Double Battle
◉◉◉◉◉◉

Lumiose
City

Oran Berry
Tree

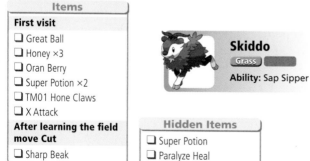

Items
First visit
❑ Great Ball
❑ Honey ×3
❑ Oran Berry
❑ Super Potion ×2
❑ TM01 Hone Claws
❑ X Attack
After learning the field move Cut
❑ Sharp Beak

Skiddo
Grass
Ability: Sap Sipper

Hidden Items
❑ Super Potion
❑ Paralyze Heal

121

Tall Grass		
❑ Abra	▲	
❑ Bunnelby	◎	
❑ Doduo	△	
❑ Furfrou	◎	
❑ Gulpin	△	
❑ Minun	▲	Y
❑ Pancham	△	
❑ Plusle	▲	X
❑ Skiddo	△	

Purple Flowers		
❑ Abra	▲	
❑ Bunnelby	△	
❑ Doduo	△	
❑ Furfrou	△	
❑ Gulpin	△	
❑ Minun	▲	Y
❑ Pancham	◎	
❑ Plusle	▲	X
❑ Skiddo	◎	

Horde Encounter		
❑ Gulpin ×5	◎	
❑ Minun ×4 Plusle ×1	△	Y
❑ Plusle ×4 Minun ×1	△	X
❑ Scraggy ×5	◎	

◎ frequent ◯ average △ rare ▲ almost never

STEP
① Meet Korrina and Lucario

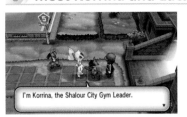

I'm Korrina, the Shalour City Gym Leader.

As you enter Route 5, you're suddenly approached by an intimidating-looking Pokémon named Lucario. After a few moments, Lucario's Trainer zips up on Roller Skates. She's far friendlier than stony Lucario and reveals that she is the Shalour City Gym Leader. Before skating off, Korrina hints that you'll likely run into her again before long.

STEP
② Hit the skate park

You can't miss the skate park as you stroll down Route 5. Why not slap on your Roller Skates and speed around for a bit? Skate onto the rail in the park's northeast corner, and you'll hop on top and grind over to a Super Potion.

STEP
③ Take on two Trainers at once in a Double Battle

A pair of Pokémon-loving Twins, Faith and Joy, draw you into a Double Battle just beyond the skate park. In this battle, the first two Pokémon in your party are pitted against the Twins' two Pokémon. Have your Pokémon work together to achieve victory!

TIPS *As always, feel free to switch out your Pokémon to ones that can better counter your opponents' types.*

Return to Restaurant Le Nah to practice Double Battles if you need a refresher.

STEP
④ Do a dance with Tierno

Trevor and Tierno are chatting just a bit farther ahead. The two are discussing Pokémon moves, and Tierno asks you to show him some of your best. Give him a dance lesson he won't soon forget!

Do your Pokémon know any sweet moves? Show me in a battle!

Vs. Tierno's Pokémon

Corphish
♂ Lv. 12 Water
Weak to: Grass Electric

STEP
5 Learn about Pokémon hordes

Tierno is impressed with your moves, and Trevor gives you a few tips about Pokémon hordes—and a Honey, which will attract them to you! Whenever lots of wild Pokémon gang up on your Pokémon, moves that can hit multiple targets become extremely effective.

 See page 32 in the Trainer's Handbook for more information about Pokémon hordes.

Some of your Pokémon likely already know moves that can affect more than one target at a time, like Leer and Tail Whip. These both lower the Defense of all opposing Pokémon. You can also get your hands on some attacks that will damage more than one target, by picking up the TMs for Bulldoze or Struggle Bug in the Pokémon Center back in Lumiose City on South Boulevard.

Bulldoze is a Ground-type move that inflicts damage and lowers opposing Pokémon's Speed stats. Struggle Bug is a Bug-type move that inflicts damage and lowers opposing Pokémon's Special Attack stats.

And remember to teach moves to Pokémon of the same type as the move for even more damage!

STEP
6 Ride the Roller Skate rails

Explore the rest of Route 5 after battling Tierno, and you'll notice several other sets of skate rails. Use your Roller Skates to grind along each one and reach special items. You'll need to build up a bit of speed in order to clear the kinks in the rails near the purple flowers. These rails lead to TM01 Hone Claws.

STEP
7 ▶ **Discover your first Berry**

One of the skate rails drops you off near a Berry tree. Collect an Oran Berry from the ground here. If you want to, you can give it to a Pokémon to hold. Snacking on an Oran Berry lets your Pokémon recover a little HP on its own if it's holding one during a battle. This doesn't take a turn, so it's a nice way to keep your competitive edge. You can even feed it to a Pokémon that's taken some damage, but you might want to hang on to it for now. After you reach Route 7, you'll be able to cultivate a Berry farm.

TIP *When you happen to acquire a Berry, consider hanging on to it so you can use it to grow more Berries in the Berry fields along Route 7.*

Camphrier Town

Few towns in the Kalos region are as old as Camphrier Town. Times have been better within its crumbling walls, but the townspeople are desperate to win you over and bring flocks of tourists back to their cobbled streets and empty castle keep.

Field Moves Needed

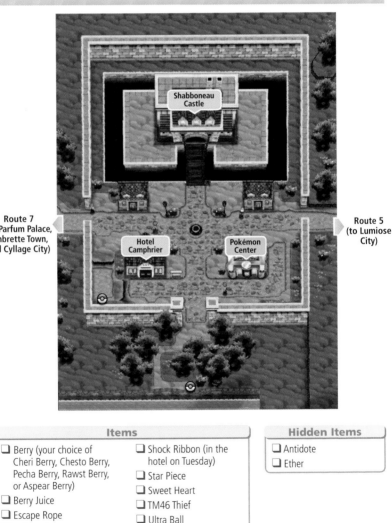

Shabboneau Castle

Route 7
(to Parfum Palace, Ambrette Town, and Cyllage City)

Route 5
(to Lumiose City)

Hotel Camphrier

Pokémon Center

Items

- ❑ Berry (your choice of Cheri Berry, Chesto Berry, Pecha Berry, Rawst Berry, or Aspear Berry)
- ❑ Berry Juice
- ❑ Escape Rope
- ❑ Full Heal
- ❑ Shock Ribbon (in the hotel on Tuesday)
- ❑ Star Piece
- ❑ Sweet Heart
- ❑ TM46 Thief
- ❑ Ultra Ball
- ❑ X Attack

Hidden Items

- ❑ Antidote
- ❑ Ether

STEP
① Swing by Cassius's house

Enter the very first cottage you see in Camphrier Town for a surprising dose of modern technology. A group of gifted computer buffs are keeping a powerful machine running here. Speak with Cassius, who runs the PC storage system, to learn that the contraption is actually the server on which your PC Boxes are stored! Cassius gladly tells you all about PC Boxes, and one of the girls gives you TM46 Thief just for stopping by.

NOTE *After meeting Cassius, you'll notice that the option on your PC screen has changed from "Someone's PC" to "Cassius's PC."*

You can access your PC Boxes by inspecting Cassius's server.

STEP
② Meet the Name Rater

Speak to the man in the suit in the Pokémon Center, and he'll introduce himself as the official Name Rater. This mysterious man gets a thrill out of critiquing the nicknames that you've given to your Pokémon. The Name Rater also has the power to change your Pokémon's nicknames if you like. What a guy!

STEP
③ Chat with the locals

Once you're done talking to the Name Rater, move on to talk to other locals around Camphrier Town. You never know who you will meet. Talk to everyone, and you'll receive lots of neat gifts, including an Ultra Ball, a Berry Juice, and a Sweet Heart.

STEP
④ Score a Star Piece

Walk the grassy path that stretches south beyond the town's wall, and you'll discover a Star Piece at the end. This valuable item can be sold for some quick prize money at stores, giving you extra funds for Poké Mart items and other purchases.

STEP
⑤ Check in at Hotel Camphrier

Take a moment to investigate Hotel Camphrier, which lies just west of the Pokémon Center. This impressive establishment may be short-staffed, but a Rising Star in the lobby will hand you a valuable Full Heal.

> **TIP** *If you visit this hotel on a Tuesday, you can get a Shock Ribbon from a traveler who is passing through.*

STEP
⑥ Meet up with Mr. Bonding again

While exploring the hotel, sprint upstairs to find none other than Mr. Bonding waiting in one of the second-floor rooms. The friendly fellow grants you a new O-Power: Sp. Atk Power, and recounts the advantages that O-Powers can bestow.

STEP
⑦ Show off a Pokémon and get a Berry

A man in the cottage near Camphrier Town's west gate will give you a Berry of your choice, provided that you can show him the type of Pokémon he's interested in seeing. If you don't have the right type of Pokémon in your party, use the PC at the Pokémon Center to swap one in. You can also get a Sweet Heart here from a real sweetheart of a girl.

STEP
⑧ Visit Shabboneau Castle

This castle, chateau if you will, was a manor house of a noble family.

Your final stop is Shabboneau Castle, which stands at the north end of town. Cross the drawbridge and head inside to find Shauna speaking with the castle caretaker. Unfortunately, the man has no idea what Mega Evolution might be, despite Professor Sycamore hoping that you'd find out more here. Before you can question him further, the castle caretaker is called away to some sort of crisis on Route 7.

STEP
⑨ Search the castle, then head to Route 7

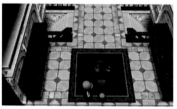

You might not have learned anything new about Mega Evolution, but your trip to Shabboneau Castle isn't a total loss. Go upstairs to find a valuable Escape Rope on the castle's second floor. This handy item lets you instantly escape back to the entrance of any cave or dungeon.

Route 7 (Rivière Walk)

Your first visit to this scenic path is brief indeed, for a massive, snoozing Snorlax is blocking the bridge. Still, you can spend a little time cultivating Berry trees at the southern farm. After you remove the Snorlax roadblock, you'll find Fighting- and Ground-type Pokémon very valuable while battling Route 7's many Trainers.

Field Moves Needed

Cut

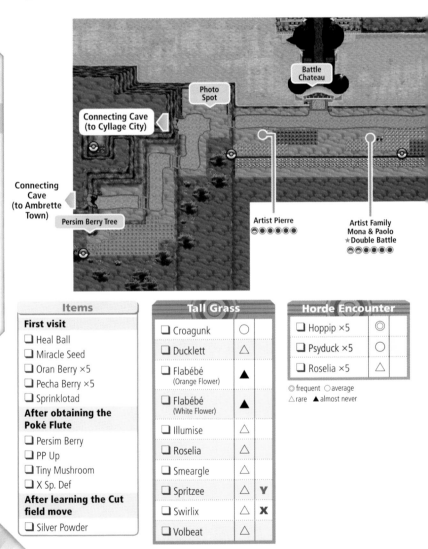

Battle Chateau

Photo Spot

Connecting Cave (to Cyllage City)

Connecting Cave (to Ambrette Town)

Persim Berry Tree

Artist Pierre
◉◉◉◉◉◉

Artist Family Mona & Paolo
★Double Battle
◉◉◉◉◉◉

Items
First visit
❑ Heal Ball
❑ Miracle Seed
❑ Oran Berry ×5
❑ Pecha Berry ×5
❑ Sprinklotad
After obtaining the Poké Flute
❑ Persim Berry
❑ PP Up
❑ Tiny Mushroom
❑ X Sp. Def
After learning the Cut field move
❑ Silver Powder

Tall Grass		
❑ Croagunk	○	
❑ Ducklett	△	
❑ Flabébé (Orange Flower)	▲	
❑ Flabébé (White Flower)	▲	
❑ Illumise	△	
❑ Roselia	△	
❑ Smeargle	△	
❑ Spritzee	△	**Y**
❑ Swirlix	△	**X**
❑ Volbeat	△	

Horde Encounter		
❑ Hoppip ×5	◎	
❑ Psyduck ×5	○	
❑ Roselia ×5	△	

◎ frequent ○ average
△ rare ▲ almost never

Spritzee Y
`Fairy`
Ability: Healer

Swirlix X
`Fairy`
Ability: Sweet Veil

Route 6
(to Parfum Palace)

Camphrier
Town

Berry
Fields

Pokémon
Day Care

Artist Georgia
◉●●●●●

Yellow Flowers		
❑ Croagunk	▲	
❑ Ducklett	△	
❑ Flabébé (Orange Flower)	▲	
❑ Flabébé (White Flower)	▲	
❑ Flabébé (Yellow Flower)	○	
❑ Illumise	△	
❑ Roselia	△	
❑ Smeargle	△	
❑ Spritzee	△	Y
❑ Swirlix	△	X
❑ Volbeat	△	

Purple Flowers		
❑ Croagunk	▲	
❑ Ducklett	△	
❑ Flabébé (Blue Flower)	○	
❑ Flabébé (Orange Flower)	▲	
❑ Flabébé (White Flower)	▲	
❑ Illumise	△	
❑ Roselia	△	
❑ Smeargle	△	
❑ Spritzee	△	Y
❑ Swirlix	△	X
❑ Volbeat	△	

STEP
1 Find the castle caretaker

Look! It's practically a mountain, right? It's blocking the road completely.

Sprint west along Route 7, and it won't be long before you run into the castle caretaker. The man needs a hand, for a monstrous Snorlax has fallen asleep right on Route 7's bridge! The path is completely blocked, and only the Poké Flute will wake this snoozing Pokémon.

STEP
2 Visit the Berry fields

I know this is an unexpected request, but I need you to take care of my Berry field!

The Poké Flute is kept at Parfum Palace, which lies beyond Route 6 to the north. Before you speed over there, take a moment to visit the Berry fields to the south. The friendly farmer you find there needs help tending his fields!

Learn more about Berry farming on page 382.

STEP
3 Consider making some Mulch

Yes
No

Do you want to compost some Berries to make Mulch?

The Berry farmer hands you five Oran Berries, five Pecha Berries, and a watering tool called a Sprinklotad. You can simply plant the Berries and water them if you like, or you can use the nearby composter to make Mulch out of some of your Berries first. Mulch can help your Berry trees yield greater crops—or even surprising ones.

STEP
4 Plant some Berries

Yes
No

The soil is dry... Would you like to water it?

After making some Mulch, go ahead and start planting your Berries. The first step is to spread Mulch if you've made some. Mulch can help your Berries grow, so it pays to use it. First inspect a patch of soft soil to spread the Mulch, then plant a Berry. Examine the soil afterward to see if it needs watering. Try to keep your soil nice and watered!

TIPS *You can get more tips about planting Berries by visiting the farmer in his home in the northeast corner of the field.*

You don't need to plant all of your Berries. Feel free to give some to your Pokémon if you'd like to make use of them sooner rather than later.

STEP
5 Go to Parfum Palace on Route 6

Now that you've gotten your hands dirty in the Berry fields, you'd best hurry off to Parfum Palace. Travel north along Route 6 to get there. After you obtain the Poké Flute in Parfum Palace (p. 141), return to this section and continue with the remaining steps.

AFTER VISITING PARFUM PALACE:
Use the Poké Flute to wake Snorlax

After you've retrieved the Poké Flute from Parfum Palace, return to the slumbering Snorlax. Hand the castle caretaker the Poké Flute, which only he can play. You'll have to battle Snorlax after it wakes, so make sure your party is prepared!

AFTER VISITING PARFUM PALACE:
Catch or defeat Snorlax

The Poké Flute does its work, but Snorlax isn't happy about being awoken. You must battle the wild Snorlax to scare it off, or you may try to catch it with a Poké Ball. Be advised that Snorlax will greatly enhance its defenses during the battle, making it tough to topple.

Catch Snorlax!

Lv. 15 Normal

Abilities: Immunity
Thick Fat

Moves:
Tackle
Defense Curl
Amnesia
Lick

It's probably a good idea to save the game before you challenge Snorlax. Even if you work hard to chip away at its HP, Snorlax can recover effectively with its held item, a Sitrus Berry. What's more, it can use Defense Curl and Amnesia. These moves raise Snorlax's Defense and Sp. Defense stats respectively. To mow down its HP as quickly as possible, try Fighting-type moves.

AFTER VISITING PARFUM PALACE:

❋❯ Check out the Pokémon Day Care

With Snorlax out of the way, you're free to explore the rest of Route 7. The Pokémon Day Care is just ahead, and your friends Trevor and Tierno are excited to check it out.

AFTER VISITING PARFUM PALACE:

❋❯ Leave two Pokémon at the Pokémon Day Care

Join your friends inside the Pokémon Day Care and consider leaving a couple of Pokémon here to play. If you leave two Pokémon at the Pokémon Day Care together, sometimes a Pokémon Egg will be found when you return to pick them up! Use the PC inside the Pokémon Day Care to access all of the Pokémon you've caught so far. The service isn't free, though, and you'll have to pay when you pick your Pokémon up.

The Pokémon Day Care specializes in raising Pokémon for busy Trainers. If you leave a Pokémon there for a while and then take it back, you'll probably find that it's at a higher level.

The man who stands just outside the Pokémon Day Care gives hints on how well your Pokémon are getting along. If the man says they like playing together, then your chances of finding an Egg are better. See the Trainer's Handbook section (p. 46) for more information regarding Eggs and the Pokémon Day Care.

AFTER VISITING PARFUM PALACE:

Visit the Battle Chateau

It's called the Battle Chateau, and it's famous for being a place where Trainers

Trevor calls out to you farther down the road, asking if you're familiar with another nearby building called the Battle Chateau. Here you can test your battle skills against noble Trainers who seek to become the region's best. Sounds like a good place to hone your skills!

The Battle Chateau is one of the places in the Kalos region where you can return as many times as you like to battle other Trainers. Most Trainers you encounter on routes will only challenge you the first time you meet them, and you may begin to miss the challenge of taking on another trained Pokémon team. It's also worth remembering that your Pokémon get slightly more Exp. Points for battles against other Trainers than they do in battles against wild Pokémon. Use these facilities well to challenge yourself and gain some experience—and maybe even prizes!

AFTER VISITING PARFUM PALACE:

Battle other Trainers in the Battle Chateau

Trainers with noble titles can do battle against other Trainers with titles in the nobility here

Enter the Battle Chateau to learn more about it. You are given the lowly rank of Baron or Baroness and must battle other Trainers in the Chateau to increase your rank. Battling Trainers in the Chateau is not only fun, but also profitable. You may also find that some of the biggest VIPs in Kalos show up when you reach the highest ranks of the nobility. Spend some time in the Chateau and see if you can increase your rank! Learn more on page 399.

AFTER VISITING PARFUM PALACE:
⚙ Learn about Writs

If you have the funds to spare, consider issuing the Writ of Invitation at the Battle Chateau. This will entice more Trainers to challenge you at the Battle Chateau, helping you increase your rank faster. Note that Writs you issue will expire at midnight, so don't issue one unless you're planning to devote some time to battling at the Chateau.

AFTER VISITING PARFUM PALACE:
⚙ Multi Battle with your friends

Serena/Calem is waiting just past the Battle Chateau, hoping to find some friends who are up for a Multi Battle. Agree to the friendly match, and you'll join forces with Serena/Calem to battle against Trevor and Tierno. A good play is to wipe out Tierno's Corphish first because he doesn't have any other Pokémon to send out.

Serena/Calem's Pokémon

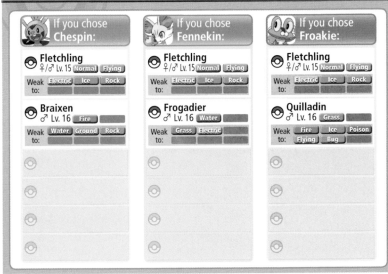

If you chose Chespin:	If you chose Fennekin:	If you chose Froakie:
Fletchling ♀/♂ Lv. 15 Normal Flying	**Fletchling** ♀/♂ Lv. 15 Normal Flying	**Fletchling** ♀/♂ Lv. 15 Normal Flying
Weak to: Electric Ice Rock	Weak to: Electric Ice Rock	Weak to: Electric Ice Rock
Braixen ♂ Lv. 16 Fire	**Frogadier** ♂ Lv. 16 Water	**Quilladin** ♂ Lv. 16 Grass
Weak to: Water Ground Rock	Weak to: Grass Electric	Weak to: Fire Ice Poison Flying Bug

Vs. Tierno's Pokémon

Corphish
♂ Lv. 16 Water
Weak to: Grass Electric

Vs. Trevor's Pokémon

Pikachu
♂ Lv. 14 Electric
Weak to: Ground

Flabébé
♀ Lv. 14 Fairy
Weak to: Poison Steel

AFTER VISITING PARFUM PALACE:

⚙ Cut through the prickly thorns

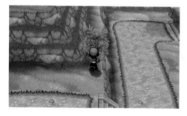

Make a thorough search of Route 7 to find valuable items. Teach one of your Pokémon the HM01 Cut that you discovered in Parfum Palace's vast courtyard, and you'll quickly slash through the prickly thorns between the Connecting Cave's two entrances to reach an item.

TIP *If you're up for a little backtracking, you can use Cut to get through more prickly thorns at Route 3 (p. 94), Route 5 (p. 120), and Route 22 (p. 102) to find additional items.*

⚙️ Gather items, and then enter the Connecting Cave

Connecting Cave Ahead
This is the shortcut to Ambrette Town.

Return to Camphrier Town if you need to stock up on items. Next, travel back to Route 7's west end and enter the second cave you encounter, the southeast entrance to the Connecting Cave. This leads toward Route 8 and Ambrette Town, the next destination on your journey. Go to page 146 to dive into this dark cave.

When you enter the Connecting Cave, a Scientist will heal your Pokémon, so there is no need to heal them in Camphrier Town.

Healing Pokémon in the field

It can sometimes be a long road between cities and towns. When you're facing many opponents, it can be hard to keep all your Pokémon healthy. Here are the main ways to keep your team going down the road!

Using items to heal your Pokémon

The easiest way to heal your Pokémon is to use items. You can buy items like Potions at Pokémon Centers in every town and city across the region. More powerful items become available as you earn more Gym Badges (see p. 410).

Using Berries to heal your Pokémon

With access to the Berry fields, an endless supply of healing Berries lies at your fingertips! Some Berries heal more HP than others, so farm your fields wisely. You'll soon have an abundance of Berries to use on your Pokémon, and you won't have to spend a thing!

Using moves to heal your Pokémon

Some Pokémon can learn moves that restore HP. While many moves can be used in battle to restore the user's own HP, some moves can also be used in the field to restore HP to another party Pokémon. Take advantage of these moves, like Soft-Boiled and Milk Drink.

Using an O-Power to heal your Pokémon

Your handy O-Powers can be used for straight-up healing for free, and without visiting a Pokémon Center. In just a few seconds, the HP Restoring Power will add HP to your lead Pokémon!

Route 6 (Palais Lane)

Route 6 is a deceptively complex area that runs between Route 7 and Parfum Palace. While traveling toward the palace, you can only sprint straight down the main road. However, when traveling back from the palace, you can explore a pair of side paths to the west and east, which feature lots of hidden goodies and tough Pokémon Trainers.

Field Moves
Needed

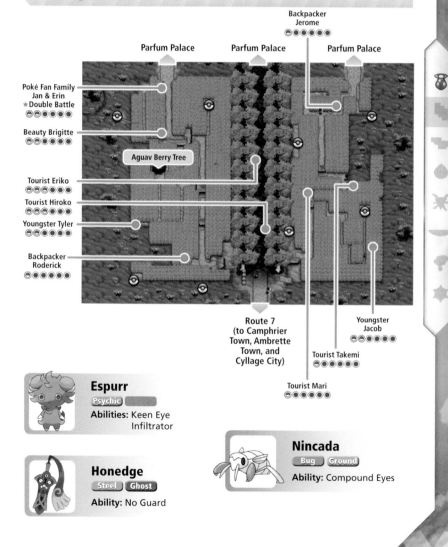

Backpacker
Jerome

Parfum Palace   Parfum Palace   Parfum Palace

Poké Fan Family
Jan & Erin
★Double Battle

Beauty Brigitte

Aguav Berry Tree

Tourist Eriko

Tourist Hiroko

Youngster Tyler

Backpacker
Roderick

Route 7
(to Camphrier
Town, Ambrette
Town, and
Cyllage City)

Youngster
Jacob

Tourist Takemi

Tourist Mari

Espurr
Psychic
Abilities: Keen Eye
Infiltrator

Honedge
Steel Ghost
Ability: No Guard

Nincada
Bug Ground
Ability: Compound Eyes

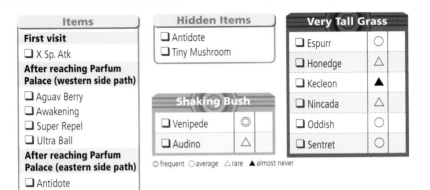

Items					
Hidden Items			**Very Tall Grass**		

Items

First visit
- ☐ X Sp. Atk

After reaching Parfum Palace (western side path)
- ☐ Aguav Berry
- ☐ Awakening
- ☐ Super Repel
- ☐ Ultra Ball

After reaching Parfum Palace (eastern side path)
- ☐ Antidote
- ☐ Paralyze Heal
- ☐ TM09 Venoshock
- ☐ X Speed

Hidden Items
- ☐ Antidote
- ☐ Tiny Mushroom

Shaking Bush	
☐ Venipede	◎
☐ Audino	△

Very Tall Grass	
☐ Espurr	○
☐ Honedge	△
☐ Kecleon	▲
☐ Nincada	△
☐ Oddish	○
☐ Sentret	○

◎ frequent ○ average △ rare ▲ almost never

STEP 1 — Travel to Parfum Palace

As you enter Route 6, go west and snag an X Sp. Atk from the nearby grassy path. Return to the main road and sprint north, heading for Parfum Palace. Seemingly innocent Tourists will test your battle skills as you advance toward the palace, so be ready to fight!

AFTER VISITING PARFUM PALACE:

✿ Explore Route 6's side paths

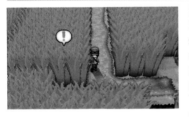

It's not long till you reach Parfum Palace. If you like, take one of the two southern side paths back to Route 6 and explore the rest of the area. You'll find many items of value, and the very tall grass hides plenty of tough Pokémon Trainers who are itching for battle (or perhaps simply from allergies).

Search the very tall grass thoroughly to encounter hidden Pokémon. Also, watch out for the hidden Pokémon Trainers—as soon as they see you, they will challenge you!

Was that a bush you just saw shaking? That's right—there might be Pokémon lurking in more places than just the very tall grass that stretches to the sides of this path. If you walk by a shaking bush, a Pokémon might just leap out and attack!

Parfum Palace

This magnificent palace is truly a sight to behold. Tourists flock from all over the region just to gaze at its majestic architecture. It is here that the Poké Flute is said to be kept, but a crisis at the palace must be resolved before the Poké Flute can be obtained.

Field Moves Needed

Entrance

Photo Spot

Route 6
(to Camphrier Town,
Ambrette Town, and
Cyllage City)

1F Small Room 1

1F Small Room 2

Rest your Pokémon here

1F Center

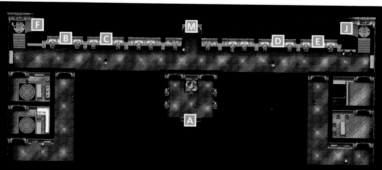

1F Small Room 3

1F Small Room 4

2F Left

2F Right

2F Small Room 1

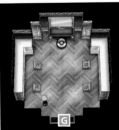

2F Small Room 2

2F Small Room 3

2F Small Room 4

2F Balcony

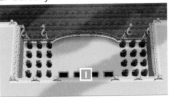

Courtyard

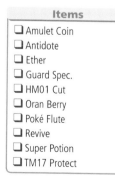

Items
❑ Amulet Coin
❑ Antidote
❑ Ether
❑ Guard Spec.
❑ HM01 Cut
❑ Oran Berry
❑ Poké Flute
❑ Revive
❑ Super Potion
❑ TM17 Protect

Hidden Items
❑ X Sp. Atk
❑ Rare Candy
❑ Pretty Wing

STEP 1 Enter the palace

You've got to be kidding!
It costs money to go inside?

As it turns out, entering Parfum Palace isn't cheap. You must pay 1,000 in cold hard cash just to get past the front gate. Shauna joins you at this point, remarking that this must be how the rich get richer.

TIP *If you don't have the money, you will still be allowed to enter. Perhaps the palace's inhabitants aren't all as bad as they seem?*

STEP 2 Help the palace's owner find his lost Furfrou

My beloved little Furfrou has disappeared!

Inside the palace, you and Shauna find the palace's owner in distress. His beloved Furfrou has gone missing, and he can't find it anywhere. It doesn't seem like he will listen to any of your questions about the Poké Flute while he is in such a panic, so you might as well help him look for his poor lost Pokémon if you ever hope to continue your journey.

STEP 3 Search Parfum Palace

Xavier found an Amulet Coin!

The palace is a wonder of classic architectural design. Speak to everyone inside to learn more about the royal family's tumultuous past. Enter one of the bedrooms to find a luxurious bed in which you can sleep to rest your Pokémon party. The upstairs library contains a valuable Amulet Coin. There are many other items to be found around the grounds as well.

TIP *Be sure to search the grounds, both in front of the gate and in the sprawling gardens behind the palace, for several valuable items— including HM01 Cut.*

④ Catch the palace owner's Furfrou

Go to the courtyard's northwestern hedge maze to find the missing Furfrou. You must work with Shauna to catch the little one. Approach the Furfrou, and it will flee. Tell Shauna to wait at the spot where you previously found Furfrou. Keep it up until you finally trap the missing Furfrou at the northern dead end.

Stuck running in circles?

If you're having trouble getting that frisky Furfrou pinned in place, here is a helpful guide. When you start, Furfrou should be standing in the center of the garden. Have Shauna wait at point A and from there, you will head east and then north to point B. Furfrou will panic, seeing no clear way to the exit, and run further into the garden. Then go back to collect Shauna and have her stand at point B this time. Head west to point C then head north. With you approaching from the south and Shauna blocking the east, Furfrou will run itself right into the dead end deep in the gardens.

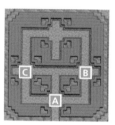

⑤ Watch the fireworks and receive the Poké Flute

Parfum Palace's owner couldn't be happier about having his poor Furfrou returned to him. He insists that you go to his palace's balcony to watch a celebratory firework display. Head back into the palace and go upstairs to find the balcony, then enjoy the show with Shauna. Afterward, you're lent the Poké Flute as a reward for all your help, and you get TM17 Protect to keep for yourself. Nicely done!

 TIP — *Now that you have the Poké Flute, it is time to head back to Route 7 (p. 130) and rouse Snorlax. But don't forget to explore the rest of Route 6 as you go!*

Connecting Cave (Zubat Roost)

The Connecting Cave is a dark and eerie place filled with frightening Pokémon hordes. Fortunately, it isn't very large, and there's a nice Scientist who offers to rest your Pokémon party at any time. You can explore more of the cave after you defeat the Gym Leader in Cyllage City.

Field Moves Needed

Strength

Pokémon Breeder Mercy

Cyllage City

Route 7 (to Parfum Palace and Camphrier Town)

Route 8 (to Ambrette Town and Cyllage City)

Rest your Pokémon here

Route 7 (to Parfum Palace and Camphrier Town)

Meditite
Fighting Psychic
Ability: Pure Power

Whismur
Normal
Ability: Soundproof

Items
After learning the field move Strength
❑ TM21 Frustration
❑ TM40 Aerial Ace

Cave		
❑ Axew	△	
❑ Meditite	○	
❑ Whismur	○	
❑ Zubat	○	

Horde Encounter		
❑ Axew ×5	△	
❑ Whismur ×5	◎	
❑ Zubat ×5	○	

◎ frequent ○ average
△ rare ▲ almost never

STEP
1 Cut through the cave

Your first visit to the Connecting Cave is a quick one. Sprint straight through, heading for the west exit to Route 8. Ambrette Town isn't very far! If you feel like sticking around and catching some new Pokémon, though, don't miss the chance to have the Scientist heal your team so they are ready for all those hordes!

AFTER EARNING THE CLIFF BADGE:
Use the field move Strength to explore more of the cave

Snorlax used Strength!

After you obtain HM04 Strength in Cyllage City and earn the Cliff Badge, have one of your Pokémon assist you by using Strength, allowing you to shove the cave's massive blocks out of your way. Now you can explore the entire cave and claim some special goodies!

AFTER EARNING THE CLIFF BADGE:
Collect a few more TMs to use

Xavier obtained
TM21 Frustration!

Talk to the steaming Backpacker stuck in a dead end to get TM21 Frustration, but don't forget to look for items as well. Behind the boulder farthest west in the cave is another TM waiting for you on the floor. Finally, be sure to drop the southern boulder into place so that you'll be able to make your way quickly back through the cave in future.

TIP *Using Strength will allow you to move even large boulders. You will find huge square boulders, like the one pictured above, littered across the Kalos region. They are often located near pesky holes that prevent you from reaching other locations. If you drop these boulders into the holes, you'll create a nice level surface that you can walk across. Getting the right boulders into the right holes is sometimes a tricky business, though. If you've gotten your boulders stuck in a corner and can't work your way out, exit the area. When you enter the area again, the boulders will generally be back in their original locations.*

Route 8 (Muraille Coast)

This sizable route features high, rocky cliffs that overlook a sandy shoreline. You'll emerge on the cliffs after passing through the Connecting Cave. By passing through the Ambrette Aquarium, you can explore Route 8's lower beach. However, much of Route 8's beach can't be explored until after you've accomplished an important task at Glittering Cave.

Field Moves Needed

Rock Smash   Surf

Strength

Cyllage City

Connecting Cave (to Parfum Palace and Camphrier Town)

Swimmer ♂
Estaban

Swimmer ♀
Marissa

Swimmer ♂
Ramses

Fisherman
Shad

Rising Star
Paulette

Rising Star
Rhys

Sky Trainer
Aveza
★ Sky Battle

Swimmer ♀
Genevieve

Fisherman
Wharton

Black
Belt Cadoc

Sky Trainer
Colm
★ Sky Battle

Mago Berry Tree

Sky Trainer
Howe
★ Sky Battle

Ambrette
Town

Ambrette
Town

Items

First visit
- ❑ HP Up
- ❑ Leaf Stone
- ❑ Heart Scale

After passing through the Ambrette Aquarium (lower shore items)
- ❑ Mago Berry

After clearing Glittering Cave
- ❑ Dowsing Machine

After learning the field move Strength
- ❑ Water Stone

After learning the field move Surf
- ❑ TM19 Roost

Hidden Items

- ❑ Escape Rope
- ❑ Heart Scale
- ❑ Pearl
- ❑ Stardust
- ❑ Super Potion
- ❑ Ultra Ball

After learning the field move Surf
- ❑ Heart Scale

Binacle
Rock Water
Abilities: Tough Claws / Sniper

Claucher X
Water
Ability: Mega Launcher

Skrelp Y
Poison Water
Abilities: Poison Point / Poison Touch

Tall Grass

❑ Absol	△	
❑ Bagon	▲	
❑ Drifloon	○	
❑ Inkay	△	
❑ Mienfoo	△	
❑ Seviper	△	
❑ Spoink	○	
❑ Zangoose	△	

Yellow Flowers

❑ Absol	○	
❑ Bagon	▲	
❑ Drifloon	△	
❑ Inkay	△	
❑ Meinfoo	○	
❑ Seviper	△	
❑ Spoink	△	
❑ Zangoose	△	

Horde Encounter

❑ Seviper ×4 Zangoose ×1	○	Y
❑ Taillow ×5	△	
❑ Wingull ×5	◎	
❑ Zangoose ×4 Seviper ×1	○	X

Cracked Rock

❑ Binacle	○
❑ Dwebble	◎

Water Surface

❑ Tentacool	◎
❑ Wailmer	○

Fishing

Old Rod

❑ Luvdisc	◎	

Good Rod

❑ Clauncher	◎	X
❑ Shellder	○	Y
❑ Skrelp	◎	Y
❑ Staryu	○	X

Super Rod

❑ Clawitzer	○	X
❑ Cloyster	▲	Y
❑ Dragalge	○	Y
❑ Qwilfish	◎	
❑ Starmie	▲	X

◎ frequent ○ average △ rare ▲ almost never

STEP
1 Get your Pokédex powered up

A pair of familiar faces greet you as you begin exploring Route 8. It's Professor Sycamore's special assistants—Sina and Dexio! Your journey has led you to the Kalos region's western coast, and so the two deem you worthy of having your Pokédex powered up. Now you can record new Pokémon species in the Coastal Kalos Pokédex!

STEP
2 Hop across the stepping stones

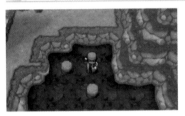

Plunder Route 8's rocky terrain as you make your way south toward Ambrette Town. Pick your way over the ledges with care, or you may have to backtrack to get all of the items to be found. You'll need to hop across some stepping stones in order to reach the town. Start at the north end and hop southward to cross this simple obstacle. Ambrette Town is just ahead!

TIP *Hop eastward across the stepping stones to reach a Leaf Stone.*

STEP
3 Try a Sky Battle

While hopping across the stepping stones (starting from the north end), land on one of the east stones to move within range of a Sky Trainer. If you have at least one flying or levitating Pokémon with you, the Sky Trainer will be happy to take you on in battle. Only flying or levitating Pokémon can participate in these challenging fights.

TIPS *There are two more Sky Trainers to be found on Route 8. Seek them out if you enjoy a good Sky Battle!*

See the Trainer's Handbook section (p. 31) for more details on Sky Battles.

STEP
④ Meet Serena/Calem

First, we should go to the Fossil Lab and have them tell us about Fossils.

When you approach the stairs that lead down into Ambrette Town, your friendly rival Serena/Calem will run up to you and suggest that you check out the Fossil Lab in town. Head down the stairs to see it, and all that Ambrette Town has to offer (p. 153).

AFTER VISITING THE GLITTERING CAVE:
⊛ Explore the shoreline

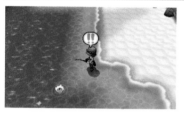

After you've fully explored Ambrette Town, pass through the Ambrette Aquarium to reach Route 8's western shoreline. There are more items to find around here, and you can use the Old Rod from the man in the aquarium to fish up wild Pokémon from the sea.

TIP *Open your Bag and register the Old Rod so that you may easily access it by pressing Ⓨ. When you get a bite, be quick to press Ⓐ and reel it in!*

AFTER VISITING THE GLITTERING CAVE:
⊛ Smash rocks for fun and profit

Yes
No

Would you like to use Rock Smash?

There are many small, cracked rocks to smash around Route 8. Be sure to break each one and see what you find. If you're drawn into battle, try to catch the wild Pokémon that emerge from the cracked rocks.

Obtain the Dowsing Machine

The first time you visit Route 8's sandy shore, a woman who has lost a precious Fossil won't let you explore very far to the north. After you clear Glittering Cave, the woman not only lets you pass, but also gives you a valuable item called the Dowsing Machine. Now you can search for buried treasure all over the Kalos region!

Do a little Dowsing

Put the Dowsing Machine to use right away and start combing the beach for buried goodies. Simply walk around with the Dowsing Machine out and pay attention when its beams of colored light begin to shine. The beams will point toward nearby buried treasure, and they change from blue to green to amber as you draw near. When the beams finally cross and turn red, you've hit pay dirt! Press Ⓐ to see what you've discovered.

Join in another Sky Battle

As you make your way northward along Route 8's sandy beach, a Trainer on a high perch will call down to you and invite you to challenge her in a Sky Battle. Remember: you can only participate in these exciting fights if your party contains Pokémon that can fly or levitate. Whether or not you choose to battle, Cyllage City is just ahead. That's your next stop!

TIP *To battle Sky Trainer Aveza, find her location on the map of Route 8. She is standing high on the cliffs, which you cannot reach—but if you stand on the shore just below her, she'll call down to you.*

Ambrette Town

This dusty town features a number of important facilities, including a Pokémon Center, an aquarium, and a laboratory where Pokémon Fossils are studied and restored. Passing through the Ambrette Aquarium lets you explore Route 8's southern shoreline, while heading through Ambrette Town's east gate will take you to Route 9.

Field Moves Needed

Rock Smash

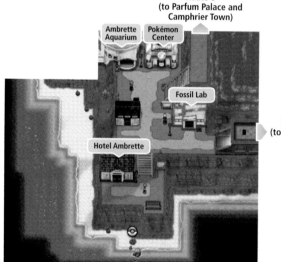

Route 8
(to Parfum Palace and Camphrier Town)

Ambrette Aquarium

Pokémon Center

Fossil Lab

Route 9
(to Glittering Cave)

Hotel Ambrette

Items

First visit
- ❑ Alert Ribbon
- ❑ Health Wing
- ❑ Old Rod
- ❑ Pearl
- ❑ Rocky Helmet
- ❑ TM94 Rock Smash
- ❑ TM96 Nature Power

After returning from Glittering Cave
- ❑ Aerodactylite

Trade Items
- ❑ Dive Ball (trade for Poké Ball)

Hidden Items
- ❑ Rare Candy
- ❑ X Attack

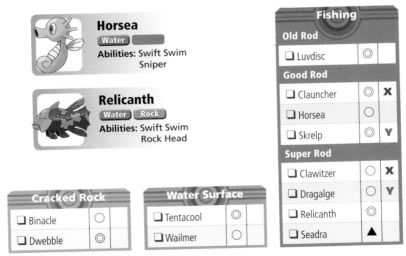

Horsea

Water

Abilities: Swift Swim
Sniper

Relicanth

Water   Rock

Abilities: Swift Swim
Rock Head

Fishing		
Old Rod		
❏ Luvdisc	◎	
Good Rod		
❏ Clauncher	◎	X
❏ Horsea	○	
❏ Skrelp	◎	Y
Super Rod		
❏ Clawitzer	○	X
❏ Dragalge	○	Y
❏ Relicanth	◎	
❏ Seadra	▲	

Cracked Rock		
❏ Binacle	○	
❏ Dwebble	◎	

Water Surface		
❏ Tentacool	◎	
❏ Wailmer	○	

◎ frequent ○ average △ rare ▲ almost never

STEP 1 >> Obtain TM94 Rock Smash

Here, Trainer! Use this TM!
It's Rock Smash!

As you enter Ambrette Town, pause for a moment to speak to the person near the Pokémon Center. They give you TM94 Rock Smash, a very useful field move that lets you smash through small, cracked boulders. This will open up all kinds of new routes for you to explore!

TIP *Rock Smash can be used on the small, cracked rocks you sometimes find on routes and in towns. When you smash one of these rocks, you may find an item, you may be attacked by a Pokémon, or the rock may simply crumble and disappear. Rocks will reappear if you exit and reenter an area, though, in case you are in the mood for more smashing!*

STEP 2 >> Find a Heart Scale

Xavier found a Heart Scale!

In Ambrette Town, after you've rested your weary Pokémon, walk along the narrow space on the Pokémon Center's east side. You will reach a thin ledge back at Route 8 that holds a Heart Scale. What a find!

STEP 3 Trade a Poké Ball for a Dive Ball

A man near the Fossil Lab will give you a valuable Dive Ball, provided that you part with a normal Poké Ball in trade. It's a great deal for you, so go ahead and make it! The man will offer you similar trades each day, if you ask him.

STEP 4 Visit the Fossil Lab

Serena/Calem is anxious to visit the Fossil Lab, so make it your next stop. Unfortunately, the lab workers can't shed much light on the mystery of Mega Evolution. However, they are able to point you in a new direction, hinting that you might find some answers by locating their field assistant in Glittering Cave to the east.

STEP 5 Meet Mr. Bonding at Hotel Ambrette

You know where you need to go next, but there's more to explore in Ambrette Town. Visit Hotel Ambrette next to find Mr. Bonding waiting on the top floor. This time, the kindly gent gives you an O-Power called Sp. Def Power. You can also get TM96 Nature Power in the lobby, so remember to be friendly to other travelers.

 If you stop in the hotel on a Monday, you may get an Alert Ribbon for your head Pokémon, thanks to a generous traveler.

STEP
6 Get a Health Wing

A Trainer in the small house west of the Fossil Lab will give you a Health Wing if you can show her a Pokémon with the kind of Speed she wants to see. She'll give you one a day, as long as you can show her a speedy Pokémon to her liking.

STEP
7 Visit the Ambrette Aquarium and grab an Old Rod

Your next stop is the Ambrette Aquarium, which is located up north, near the Pokémon Center. Go inside, head downstairs, and then speak with a generous man to receive an Old Rod. This special item lets you fish up Pokémon from any body of water, including the ocean. You can't complete your Kalos Coastal Pokédex without it!

NOTE *You'll be able to acquire different fishing rods throughout the game, enabling you to catch different Water-type Pokémon that swim in the Kalos region's bodies of water. Each time you get a better rod, revisit previous locations to see which new and rare Pokémon you may be able to catch!*

STEP
8 Plunder the sandy shore far below the town

Exit the Ambrette Aquarium through its lower doorway to reach the sandy beaches beside the sea. Go down the stairs and head south to explore the town's coastline. Use the TM94 Rock Smash you received in Ambrette Town to shatter each of the small, cracked rocks you encounter. The rocks may contain Pokémon that won't be happy about having their homes destroyed or cough up some useful items.

9 » Head for Route 9 and receive a Rocky Helmet

It doesn't take long to fully explore the sandy shores by Ambrette Town, and you can't explore very much of Route 8's coastline at the moment, for a woman in distress has lost a Fossil and won't let you pass until she finds it. Return to Ambrette Town and proceed to Route 9, chatting with the folks in the town's east gate to receive a Rocky Helmet.

 If you'd like to try another Sky Battle on your way to Glittering Cave, make sure to bring at least one flying or levitating Pokémon with you.

AFTER VISITING THE GLITTERING CAVE:
✪ » Revisit the Fossil Lab for some restoration

After you've conquered Glittering Cave, return to Ambrette Town and revisit the Fossil Lab. Speak with the assistant who now stands at the counter, and he'll restore the Pokémon Fossil you received in Glittering Cave and hand you a Pokémon! You can also receive a special Mega Stone by talking to one of the lab workers on the right.

AFTER VISITING THE GLITTERING CAVE:
✪ » Return to Route 8 by way of the Ambrette Aquarium

You're all done here in Ambrette Town. Make a quick pit stop at the Pokémon Center to rest your Pokémon and purchase items, and then head through the aquarium's lower door and proceed to Route 8's sandy beach.

 Ensure that your party features Fighting-, Ground-, and Steel-type Pokémon, as these will be most valuable to you in the upcoming battle against the Cyllage City Gym Leader. Also, consider bringing a flying or levitating Pokémon with you if you'd like to try another Sky Battle along Route 8, or a Grass- or Electric-type Pokémon if you'd like to take on the many Water types that populate this sandy coastline.

Route 9 (Spikes Passage)

If you've always wanted to ride on a Rhyhorn, now's your chance! This rough route features rocky terrain that only a thick-skinned Rhyhorn can cross. Fortunately, the resident Rhyhorn is used to being ridden, having participated in many a Rhyhorn race in its younger days.

Field Moves Needed

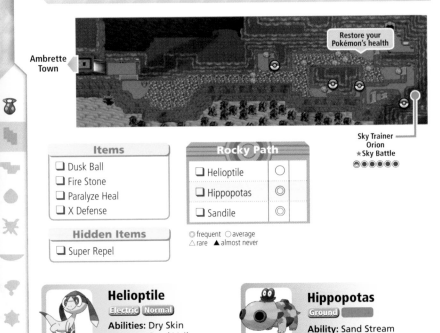

Ambrette Town

Restore your Pokémon's health

Sky Trainer Orion
★Sky Battle

Items

- ☐ Dusk Ball
- ☐ Fire Stone
- ☐ Paralyze Heal
- ☐ X Defense

Hidden Items

- ☐ Super Repel

Rocky Path

☐ Helioptile	◎
☐ Hippopotas	◎
☐ Sandile	◎

◎ frequent ◯ average
△ rare ▲ almost never

Helioptile
Electric **Normal**
Abilities: Dry Skin
Sand Veil

Hippopotas
Ground
Ability: Sand Stream

STEP
1 Ride the friendly Rhyhorn

You can't get very far on foot here at Route 9, for the rough trail is too painful to walk across. Fortunately, there's a Rhyhorn waiting right near the entry. Hop onto the Pokémon's back and ride the Rhyhorn toward Glittering Cave.

STEP

2 Smash some rocks, scale some steps, grab some goodies

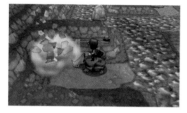

Large rocks block your path as you advance toward Glittering Cave. Ride the Rhyhorn right up to one, and then press Ⓐ to smash the rock to bits. Be sure to destroy the rocks that block off steps. Then press Ⓑ to dismount and climb the stairs. You'll be rewarded for your hard work when you find useful items at the end of your ascent.

 Walk along the narrow ledge near the second set of steps to reach a Fire Stone.

STEP

3 Test your skills in a Sky Battle

With my rubber flying suit, I can completely shrug off Electric-type moves!

Before entering Glittering Cave, sprint up a double flight of steps to move within range of a Sky Trainer who stands on a high ledge. The Sky Trainer will invite you to try a Sky Battle if there are any flying or levitating Pokémon in your party.

STEP

4 Rest your Pokémon before entering Glittering Cave

Hail, Trainer. Allow me to restore your Pokémon to full health.

A Pokémon Ranger in her customary red stands near the entrance to Glittering Cave. Speak with her, and she'll rest your Pokémon party—free of charge! Glittering Cave is filled with wild Pokémon, so take full advantage of this kind woman's assistance.

TIP *If you haven't caught an Electric-type Pokémon already, try getting a Helioptile on your team! Electric types are super effective against all the Water-type Pokémon you are likely to encounter as you continue to travel along Kalos's west coast.*

Glittering Cave

This deep, dark cave is filled with twists and turns, and of course, lots of wild Pokémon. But fear not, you have a map to guide you through! The workers at the Fossil Lab in Ambrette Town told you that one of their colleagues has been searching for Fossils here. Perhaps this person knows more about Mega Evolution...

Field Moves Needed

Rock Smash

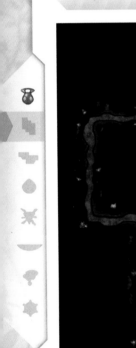

A

Entrance

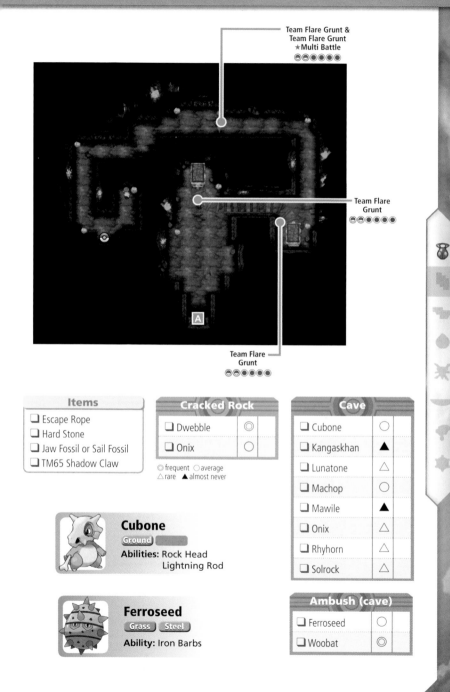

Team Flare Grunt &
Team Flare Grunt
★Multi Battle
◉◉◉◉◉◉

Team Flare
Grunt
◉◉◉◉◉◉

Team Flare
Grunt
◉◉◉◉◉◉

Items
- ❑ Escape Rope
- ❑ Hard Stone
- ❑ Jaw Fossil or Sail Fossil
- ❑ TM65 Shadow Claw

Cracked Rock

❑ Dwebble	◎
❑ Onix	○

◎ frequent ○ average
△ rare ▲ almost never

Cave

❑ Cubone	○	
❑ Kangaskhan	▲	
❑ Lunatone	△	
❑ Machop	○	
❑ Mawile	▲	
❑ Onix	△	
❑ Rhyhorn	△	
❑ Solrock	△	

Ambush (cave)

❑ Ferroseed	○	
❑ Woobat	◎	

Cubone
Ground

Abilities: Rock Head
Lightning Rod

Ferroseed
Grass Steel

Ability: Iron Barbs

Glittering Cave

STEP 1 » Navigate the cave's first set of tunnels

Glittering Cave's first set of tunnels is quite dark, and it's easy to become lost if you're not careful. If you're in a rush, simply run straight through these first tunnels without taking any of the side turns, and you'll soon arrive at the second set of tunnels. But beware: every time you hit a patch of darkness, a wild Pokémon will attack.

 If you see a green stone on the walls of the tunnels, keep going that way!

STEP 2 » Search the cave's first set of tunnels for items

Of course, if you're feeling adventurous, there's no reason not to search the first set of tunnels thoroughly. Simply turn off the route at every junction, and you'll discover valuable items off the beaten path.

- Take the second junction to discover a Hard Stone.
- Turn off the path at the third junction to discover TM65 Shadow Claw.

STEP 3 » Battle the Team Flare Grunts

Glittering Cave's second set of tunnels is much easier to navigate, but features even more danger. Several members of a stylish yet snobby group called Team Flare are searching for Fossils, and they don't take kindly to your presence in Glittering Cave. Be ready to battle these Team Flare Grunts as you continue your search for the Fossil Lab assistant.

Team Flare's goal is to make it so we're the only ones who are happy!

STEP
④ Join Serena/Calem in a Multi Battle against Team Flare

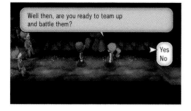

Well then, are you ready to team up and battle them?

Yes
No

Eventually, a pair of Team Flare Grunts will block your path. Serena/Calem catches up with you at this point and offers to help you clear the feisty fashionistas from your path. You're given the chance to prepare your Pokémon before the Multi Battle begins, so take advantage of this time and put your best brawler at the front of your party.

Serena/Calem's Pokémon

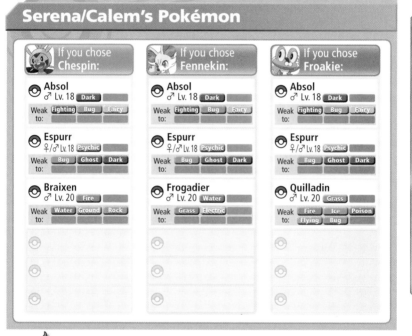

If you chose Chespin:

Absol ♂ Lv. 18 [Dark]
Weak to: [Fighting] [Bug] [Fairy]

Espurr ♀/♂ Lv. 18 [Psychic]
Weak to: [Bug] [Ghost] [Dark]

Braixen ♂ Lv. 20 [Fire]
Weak to: [Water] [Ground] [Rock]

If you chose Fennekin:

Absol ♂ Lv. 18 [Dark]
Weak to: [Fighting] [Bug] [Fairy]

Espurr ♀/♂ Lv. 18 [Psychic]
Weak to: [Bug] [Ghost] [Dark]

Frogadier ♂ Lv. 20 [Water]
Weak to: [Grass] [Electric]

If you chose Froakie:

Absol ♂ Lv. 18 [Dark]
Weak to: [Fighting] [Bug] [Fairy]

Espurr ♀/♂ Lv. 18 [Psychic]
Weak to: [Bug] [Ghost] [Dark]

Quilladin ♂ Lv. 20 [Grass]
Weak to: [Fire] [Ice] [Poison] [Flying] [Bug]

Vs. Team Flare's Pokémon

Scraggy ♂ Lv. 20 [Dark] [Fighting]
Weak to: [4×][Fairy] [Fighting] [Flying]

Vs. Team Flare's Pokémon

Croagunk
♀ Lv. 20 [Poison] [Fighting]
Weak [4x] [Psychic] [Ground] [Flying]
to:

STEP 5 » Locate the Fossil Lab assistant

You two are very lucky!
I just now found two Fossils!

The Fossil Lab assistant you seek is conducting research just beyond the site of the Multi Battle. Speak to the assistant, and he'll let you take one of the Fossils he's just found. You may choose either the Jaw Fossil or the Sail Fossil. The choice you make will determine the Pokémon you'll receive when the Fossil is restored back at the lab.

NOTE *If you choose the Jaw Fossil, you'll get a powerful Rock- and Dragon-type Pokémon called Tyrunt when you return to the Fossil Lab. If you pick the Sail Fossil, you'll receive the Rock- and Ice-type Amaura.*

STEP 6 » Explore the cave's second set of tunnels

Would you like to use Rock Smash?
► Yes
No

More goodies can be found in the Glittering Cave's second set of tunnels, provided you've taught one of your Pokémon the field move Rock Smash. Shatter every cracked rock you see to discover items, but beware of wild Pokémon that occasionally pop out!

STEP
7 Use an Escape Rope to exit Glittering Cave

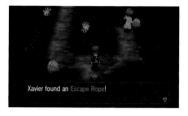

Xavier found an Escape Rope!

The Fossil Lab in Ambrette Town is your next stop, but it's a long trek back to fresh air. Fortunately, there's an Escape Rope on the ground close by. If you're in a hurry, use this item to return instantly to Glittering Cave's entrance and hasten your trip back to Ambrette Town (p. 153).

 See the Ambrette Town section (p. 153) for details on what to do after you return to the Fossil Lab.

A city nestled between the cliffs and the sea, overlooked by steep Bicycle racecourses.

Cyllage City

This coastal city features a special shop that sells Bicycles. Pick one up and cruise around the paved course that winds up through the east cliffs. The Cyllage City Gym is found near the summit, and another Gym Leader is ready to take on all comers.

Field Moves Needed

Surf

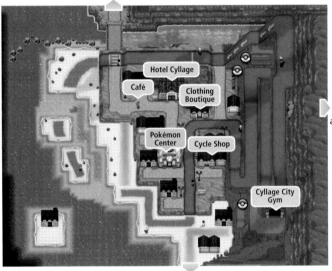

Route 10
(to Geosenge Town)

Hotel Cyllage

Café

Clothing Boutique

Connecting Cave
(to Parfum Palace and Camphrier Town)

Pokémon Center

Cycle Shop

Cyllage City Gym

Route 8
(to Ambrette Town)

Items
❑ Bicycle
❑ Destiny Knot
❑ HM04 Strength
❑ Persim Berries ×3
❑ Whipped Dream (**X**) or Sachet (**Y**)
❑ Snooze Ribbon
❑ Super Potion
❑ TM39 Rock Tomb
❑ TM44 Rest
❑ TM88 Sleep Talk
❑ X Defense
❑ X Sp. Atk

Hidden Items
❑ Ether
❑ Protein
❑ X Speed
After learning Surf
❑ Pearl

Poké Mart	
Dusk Ball	1,000
Nest Ball	1,000
Net Ball	1,000

Soda Vendor	
Soda Pop	300

Steelix
Steel Ground
Abilities: Rock Head
Sturdy

Trade
❑ Steelix (trade for Luvdisc)

Cracked Rock		
❑ Binacle	◯	Y
❑ Dwebble	◎	
❑ Onix	◎	X

Water Surface		
❑ Tentacool	◎	
❑ Wailmer	◯	

◎ frequent ◯ average
△ rare ▲ almost never

Fishing		
Old Rod		
❑ Luvdisc	◎	
Good Rod		
❑ Clauncher	◎	X
❑ Horsea	◯	
❑ Skrelp	◎	Y
Super Rod		
❑ Clawitzer	◯	X
❑ Dragalge	◯	Y
❑ Relicanth	◎	
❑ Seadra	▲	

STEP
1 Visit the Pokémon Center and trade Pokémon with Farris

As you enter Cyllage City, go north a bit to find the local Pokémon Center. Speak to a man named Farris in the Pokémon Center, and he'll offer to trade you his Steelix for a Luvdisc. If you don't have a Luvdisc, you can fish one up from the sea using the Old Rod you acquired in the Ambrette Aquarium. It's a good trade to make, since Luvdisc are common and Steelix can be extremely effective in the upcoming battle against the Gym Leader.

 Don't forget to smash cracked rocks on the beach next to the city and use your Dowsing Machine to locate buried items!

STEP
2 Ride off with a Bicycle

There's a Bicycle shop just across the street from the Pokémon Center. Head inside to speak with the shop owner. He'll give you a free Bicycle if you answer his question correctly. The correct answer is, "Of course!" Bicycles really do come in more than one color in the Kalos region!

STEP 3 Chat with the locals and get a Pokémon massage

Would you like me to massage your Machop?

Now that you've got some wheels, speed around the city and speak with every resident you meet. One kind person will offer to massage one of your Pokémon for you, free of charge. Massages are great because they make your Pokémon happy, which in turn increases your friendship with them.

TIP *You can return to the Pokémon masseuse for another massage each day.*

STEP 4 Take a quiz and win yourself some Berries

Fantastic answer! Here's a prize for you!

Another resident will ask you to take a quiz. If you pass, you'll receive three valuable Persim Berries. Don't worry if you guess wrong—you can keep trying!

STEP 5 Buy some Soda Pop

₱ 24,490

I'll take one.
I'll take a dozen!
I'll pass.

Could I tempt you with some super-refreshing Soda Pop? Only ₱300 a bottle! How about it?

A woman on the street just north of the Bicycle shop sells Soda Pop. These refreshing beverages provide your Pokémon with a quick pick-me-up, restoring 60 HP when consumed. The price is right, so go ahead and stock up.

STEP 6 Visit the boutique and café

The café is known for this special juice.

Cyllage City features both a boutique and a café. Update your attire at the boutique if you like, or do a little mingling with the folks at the café. The café patrons just love showing off their Pokémon and will give you a look at their favorites when you talk to them.

STEP
7 >> Check in to Hotel Cyllage

Welcome to Hotel Cyllage.

Be sure to visit Hotel Cyllage, as the kind folks there will give you several valuable items. Mr. Bonding is also waiting in his usual room (upstairs to the east) and will grant you a new O-Power—Prize Money Power.

NOTE *Visit on a Saturday and you can get a Snooze Ribbon for your lead Pokémon here at the hotel!*

STEP
8 >> Venture up the hill and gain HM04 Strength

I feel bad that you missed it. Here--allow me to give you this Strength HM in consolation.

Head up the east hill along the paved road. As you near the first bend, the local Gym Leader, Grant, pays you a visit. Unfortunately, the Bicycle race has just ended, but Grant does hand you a consolation prize—HM04 Strength. When used in the field, this move allows Pokémon to shove large boulders out of your way, but it can't be used in this fashion until you defeat Grant and obtain the Cyllage City Gym Badge.

STEP
9 >> Enter the Cyllage City Gym

When you've finished sightseeing around Cyllage City, it's time to check out the local Gym. Ensure your Pokémon party is well rested and ready for the challenges to come, then ride your Bicycle up the east hill and enter the Gym.

TIP *Once you get Surf, come back and visit the little house in the bay to get a Charti Berry from the Preschooler there.*

Cyllage City Gym Battle

Gym Battle Tips

✓ Bring lots of Super Potions and items that heal status conditions
✓ Use Fighting-, Ground-, and Steel-type Pokémon

Front view

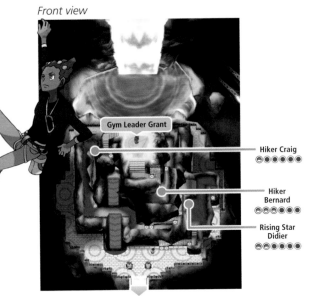

Gym Leader Grant

Hiker Craig
◉◉◉◉◉◉

Hiker
Bernard
◉◉◉◉◉◉

Rising Star
Didier
◉◉◉◉◉◉

Entrance

Rear view   Entrance

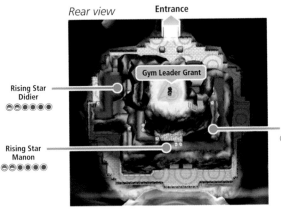

Gym Leader Grant

Rising Star
Didier
◉◉◉◉◉◉

Hiker Craig
◉◉◉◉◉◉

Rising Star
Manon
◉◉◉◉◉◉

Cyllage City Gym Leader

Grant

Rock-type Pokémon User

Use Fighting-, Ground-, and Steel-type moves to deal massive damage

Scale the rock walls, climbing ever higher until you reach Gym Leader Grant at the summit. You'll battle several Trainers along the way, but a sneaky shortcut can help you avoid several Trainers if you ignore the wall in front of you when you enter the Gym. Instead, head to the right. Go around the side of the stone pillar and begin your climb there, bearing left whenever you have the chance. Remember, you can always exit the Gym and rest your Pokémon at the Pokémon Center.

Like all of the Cyllage City Gym's Trainers, Grant uses Pokémon that are at least part Rock type. Rock types are vulnerable to Water-, Grass-, Fighting-, Ground-, and Steel-type moves, although secondary types make things more complicated. Still, with so many weaknesses to exploit, you shouldn't have much trouble taking on this king of the hill!

Grant's Pokémon

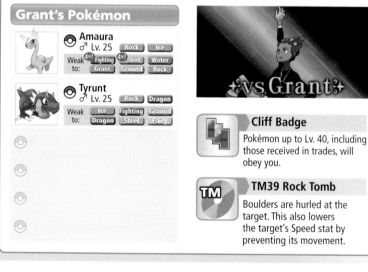

Amaura ♂ Lv. 25 — Rock / Ice
Weak to: Fighting (4x), Steel (4x), Water, Grass, Ground, Rock

Tyrunt ♂ Lv. 25 — Rock / Dragon
Weak to: Ice, Fighting, Ground, Dragon, Steel, Fairy

Cliff Badge
Pokémon up to Lv. 40, including those received in trades, will obey you.

TM39 Rock Tomb
Boulders are hurled at the target. This also lowers the target's Speed stat by preventing its movement.

NOTE *Now that you have your second Gym Badge, you can get Hyper Potions, Super Repels, and Revives at Poké Marts. Revives allow you to revive a fainted Pokémon, so it's always good to have a few!*

STEP 10 — Use the Strength field move to explore more of the Connecting Cave

After you defeat the Gym Leader Grant and receive the Cliff Badge, you're able to take full advantage of HM04 Strength. Teach the move to one of your Pokémon, then continue biking uphill to discover an entrance to the Connecting Cave you visited some time ago. Armed with the Strength field move, you can now shove the giant boulders out of your path within the cave and reach additional items (see p. 147).

STEP 11 — Rest up, then venture onward to Route 10

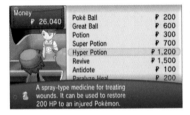

After so much battling at the Cyllage City Gym, you'll likely need to rest your Pokémon. Now that you've obtained the Cliff Badge, you can purchase additional items at Cyllage City's Poké Mart. Have a look at their new wares and consider making some purchases before venturing northward to Route 10.

Getting around Kalos

Kalos was made to be explored, and you now have four different ways to get around: walking, dashing, using Roller Skates, or riding a Bicycle. Your Bicycle is the fastest of all these options, although it doesn't provide all the fun of doing tricks with Roller Skates. And you'll still want to forego Bicycle and Roller Skates at times and get back on your own two feet, because you can't use handy items like your Dowsing Machine while on a set of wheels!

Countless stones line this mysterious path in such numbers and arrays that it seems overwhelming.

Route 10 (Menhir Trail)

This trail is famous throughout the Kalos region for its mind-boggling array of standing stones. No one knows exactly how or why these enigmatic stones have been arranged here, but many who visit this revered site recount tales of feeling some sort of mysterious energy.

Field Moves Needed

Strength

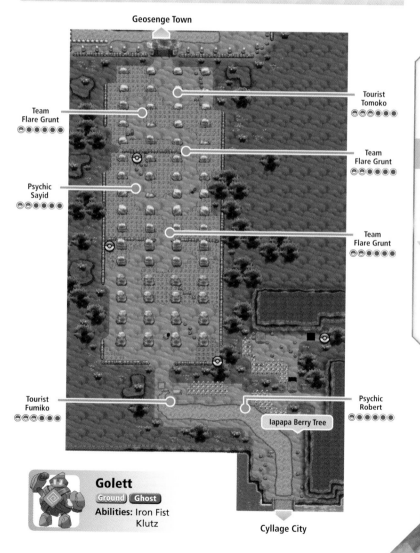

Geosenge Town

Tourist Tomoko

Team Flare Grunt

Team Flare Grunt

Psychic Sayid

Team Flare Grunt

Tourist Fumiko

Psychic Robert

Iapapa Berry Tree

Golett

Ground Ghost

Abilities: Iron Fist
Klutz

Cyllage City

Items

- ❑ Iapapa Berry
- ❑ Mind Plate
- ❑ Thunder Stone
- ❑ X Accuracy

**After learning the
Strength field move**

- ❑ TM73 Thunder Wave

Hidden Items

- ❑ Burn Heal
- ❑ Paralyze Heal
- ❑ Revive

Tall Grass		
❑ Eevee	▲	
❑ Electrike	△	Y
❑ Emolga	▲	
❑ Golett	○	
❑ Hawlucha	○	
❑ Houndour	△	✗
❑ Sigilyph	○	
❑ Snubbull	△	

Yellow Flowers		
❑ Eevee	○	
❑ Electrike	○	Y
❑ Emolga	▲	
❑ Golett	△	
❑ Hawlucha	▲	
❑ Houndour	○	✗
❑ Sigilyph	△	
❑ Snubbull	○	

◎ frequent ○ average
△ rare ▲ almost never

Horde Encounter		
❑ Electrike ×5	△	Y
❑ Houndour ×5	△	✗
❑ Nosepass ×5	◎	
❑ Yanma ×5	○	

STEP 1 ▸ Shove boulders to reach a TM

If one of your Pokémon knows HM04 Strength, put it to use as you enter Route 10 by shoving a large boulder into a hole so that you may explore a small, flowery clearing. Maneuver another boulder around some small stones and plug another hole to reach TM73 Thunder Wave.

TIP *Shove the second boulder as follows to reach the TM: down ×3, right, up, right ×2, up ×2, right ×3, up, right ×5.*

STEP
2 › Team Flare makes its stylish appearance

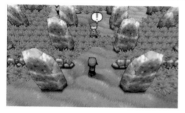

Traveling Trainers will engage you as you advance along Route 10, but the real threats are the Team Flare Grunts you encounter near the standing stones. These guys are still sore over their recent losses to you back at the Glittering Cave, and they're a bit tougher this time around. Use your Pokémon's best moves to take them out in style!

STEP
3 › Don't forget to dowse for items

Those standing stones sure are strange, but don't let them distract you from scouring the grounds for items. The Dowsing Machine can help you track down a few buried goodies you'd otherwise miss on your way to Geosenge Town.

Geosenge Town

A town lined with mysterious stones and encircled by strange ruins of old.

Geosenge Town

This old town has a rich past, but much of its history is shrouded in mystery. Legends tell of incredible power being channeled by the unusual stones that populate the landscape, and people travel from all over the region to marvel at them. Unfortunately, few facts regarding their mysterious purpose have survived the test of time.

Field Moves Needed

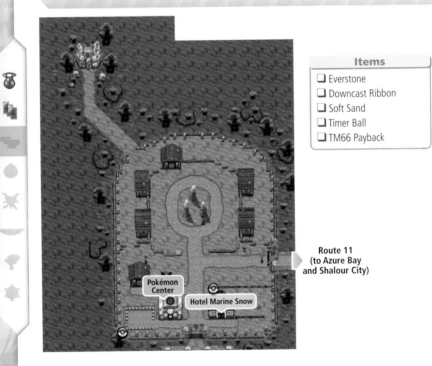

Items
- ☐ Everstone
- ☐ Downcast Ribbon
- ☐ Soft Sand
- ☐ Timer Ball
- ☐ TM66 Payback

Pokémon Center

Hotel Marine Snow

Route 11 (to Azure Bay and Shalour City)

STEP 1 Rest your Pokémon and get a TM

If you have a Pokémon that is pretty slow, give this one a try!

Team Flare likely did a number on your Pokémon as you traveled along Route 10. Rest your party at the Pokémon Center. If you speak with the man on the left, he'll dish out TM66 Payback, which slower Pokémon will find quite useful.

STEP
2 » Do some bonding at Hotel Marine Snow

Let's get started, shall we? It's bonding time!

Cross the street and enter Hotel Marine Snow to find Mr. Bonding in his room upstairs. The gentleman works his familiar magic, and you soon receive the Speed Power O-Power.

TIP   *If you visit the center room on the second floor on Wednesday, a traveler will give you a Downcast Ribbon.*

STEP
3 » Receive an Everstone

Xavier obtained an Everstone!

Go into the house on the west side of town and get an Everstone from the Scientist there. Everstones prevent Pokémon from evolving. Be sure to enter all the houses in town to get hints on your journey!

STEP
4 » Team Flare! It's everywhere!

Geosenge Town is the town of stones! ♪

Go north to find a member of Team Flare admiring Geosenge Town's mystical stones. Excited, he runs off in search of something. Pursue the Team Flare member to the northwest corner of town, following him to a dead end. Where could he have gone?

STEP
5 » Examine the standing stones, and then speak to the guide

Hey, you! If you want to know more about the stones, come to the Hotel!

If you haven't yet marveled at the giant stones in the center of town, take a look for a moment. Then go south to find a Pokémon Ranger. She'll tell you much about the history of Geosenge Town's mysterious stones if you follow her to Hotel Marine Snow.

STEP
6 Head for Route 11 and battle Leader Korrina

After exploring all of Geosenge Town and thoroughly questioning the locals, it's time to move on. Head east to Route 11, but beware: Leader Korrina makes a reappearance before you can even make it between the standing stones. You are thrust into battle against her two Lucario companions!

Vs. Korrina's Pokémon

Lucario	Lucario	
♂ Lv. 25 Fighting Steel	♂ Lv. 25 Fighting Steel	
Weak to: Fire Fighting Ground	Weak to: Fire Fighting Ground	

Route 11 (Miroir Way)

This short trail leads into the mountains east of Geosenge Town, and must be traveled on your way to Shalour City. The mysterious crystals that line the path radiate a soft energy and are rumored to hold valuable secrets. Taking a closer look at some of these shiny treasures with your Dowsing Machine will reap rewards.

Field Moves Needed

Cut

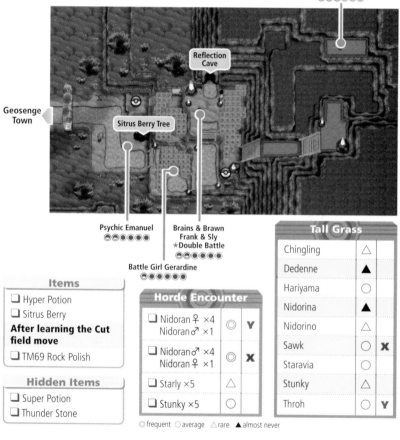

Sky Trainer Yvette
★Sky Battle
◉◉◉◉◉◉

Reflection Cave

Geosenge Town

Sitrus Berry Tree

Psychic Emanuel
◉◉◉◉◉◉

Brains & Brawn
Frank & Sly
★Double Battle
◉◉◉◉◉◉

Battle Girl Gerardine
◉◉◉◉◉

Items

- ❑ Hyper Potion
- ❑ Sitrus Berry

After learning the Cut field move

- ❑ TM69 Rock Polish

Hidden Items

- ❑ Super Potion
- ❑ Thunder Stone

Horde Encounter

❑ Nidoran ♀ ×4 Nidoran ♂ ×1	◎	Y
❑ Nidoran ♂ ×4 Nidoran ♀ ×1	◎	X
❑ Starly ×5	△	
❑ Stunky ×5	○	

Tall Grass

Chingling	△	
Dedenne	▲	
Hariyama	○	
Nidorina	▲	
Nidorino	△	
Sawk	○	X
Staravia	○	
Stunky	△	
Throh	○	Y

◎ frequent ○ average △ rare ▲ almost never

Dedenne

Electric Fairy

Abilities: Cheek Pouch
Pickup

Stunky

Poison Dark

Abilities: Stench
Aftermath

STEP 1 » Receive a Holo Clip from Professor Sycamore

Sycamore: Hello there! Looks like you've almost made it to Shalour City!

Route 11 isn't very long, and Professor Sycamore contacts you via the Holo Caster as you near the entrance to the Reflection Cave. The canny professor informs you that Shalour City is just ahead, and advises you to speak to the Mega Evolution guru when you arrive. Sounds like a plan!

STEP 2 » Cut through thorns, and then slide to reach a TM

After speaking to the professor, turn left and hack through the nearby prickly thorns by using the Cut field move. Slide down the slope beyond to reach TM69 Rock Polish.

> **TIP** *Don't forget to use your Dowsing Machine! Route 11's mysterious crystals hide a couple of worthy items.*

STEP 3 » Defeat a pair of Trainers in a Double Battle

The Reflection Cave is just ahead, but you must face a pair of Trainers in a Double Battle before you may enter. Ensure that your Pokémon are healthy and ready for battle before you approach.

STEP 4 » Try a tough Sky Battle before entering the cave

This suit has been specially designed to reduce wind resistance! Off I go!

Before you enter the Reflection Cave, consider scaling Route 11's east steps to reach a Sky Trainer. This is a challenge because her Emolga is resistant to Flying-type moves—and will do supereffective damage against your Flying types with its Electric attacks!

Reflection Cave

This sizable cave is home to hordes of wild Pokémon. This, coupled with its remarkably reflective walls, has lured many a Trainer and traveler to probe its dark depths.

Field Moves Needed

Strength

1F

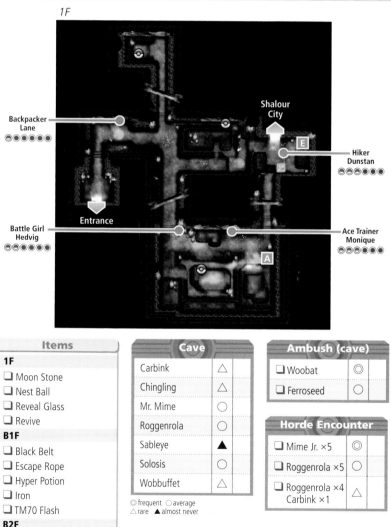

Backpacker Lane ⊚⊚⊚⊚⊚⊚

Shalour City

Hiker Dunstan ⊚⊚⊚⊚⊚⊚

E

Battle Girl Hedvig ⊚⊚⊚⊚⊚⊚

Entrance

Ace Trainer Monique ⊚⊚⊚⊚⊚⊚

A

Items

1F
- ☐ Moon Stone
- ☐ Nest Ball
- ☐ Reveal Glass
- ☐ Revive

B1F
- ☐ Black Belt
- ☐ Escape Rope
- ☐ Hyper Potion
- ☐ Iron
- ☐ TM70 Flash

B2F
- ☐ Earth Plate

Connecting Cave
- ☐ TM74 Gyro Ball

Cave

Carbink	△	
Chingling	△	
Mr. Mime	○	
Roggenrola	○	
Sableye	▲	
Solosis	○	
Wobbuffet	△	

◎ frequent ○ average
△ rare ▲ almost never

Ambush (cave)

☐ Woobat	◎	
☐ Ferroseed	○	

Horde Encounter

☐ Mime Jr. ×5	◎	
☐ Roggenrola ×5	○	
☐ Roggenrola ×4 Carbink ×1	△	

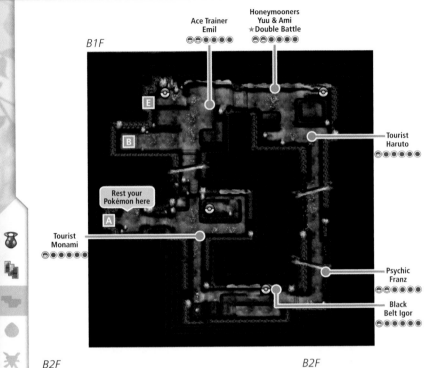

B1F

Ace Trainer
Emil

Honeymooners
Yuu & Ami
★Double Battle

E

B

Tourist
Haruto

Rest your
Pokémon here

A

Tourist
Monami

Psychic
Franz

Black
Belt Igor

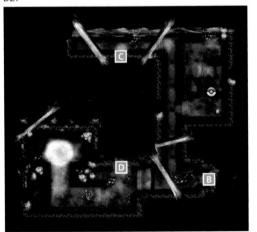

B2F

C

D

B

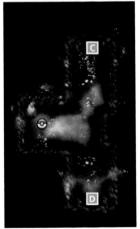

B2F

C

D

Wobbuffet
Psychic

Ability: Shadow Tag

Mime Jr.
Psychic Fairy

Abilities: Soundproof
Filter

STEP
1 Battle through the first floor

Reflection Cave certainly lives up to its name. Gaze into mirrorlike walls to spy concealed items and environmental objects as you make your way eastward, heading for the stairs that lead down to the first basement floor.

> **TIP** *Did you see some dust falling from the crumbling cave roof? To avoid additional battles with wild Pokémon that lurk high up on the ceiling, go around the circular shadows you see on the cave floor below you. But then again, you never know if stepping into the circular shadows will allow you to see and possibly catch Pokémon like Woobat and Ferroseed.*

STEP
2 Meet up with Tierno and receive TM70 Flash

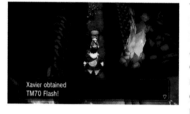

Xavier obtained
TM70 Flash!

Take the stairs down to the first basement floor. You'll meet a Pokémon Breeder who will heal your Pokémon at the foot of the stairs. Rest up and continue onward, and you'll eventually meet up with your friend Tierno. He gives you a new TM that can help reduce the number of random wild Pokémon encounters you'll face as you explore the rest of the cave.

> **TIP** *Using Flash does more than reduce the number of wild Pokémon that leap out at you in the darkness of the cave. It will also increase your field of view, so you can see more of the cave at once. This comes in mighty handy for avoiding dead-end passageways.*

STEP 3 » Exit to Shalour City or delve deeper into the cave

The first basement floor features two sets of exit stairs: one that leads back up to the first floor, and another that leads down to the second basement level. If you're done with this place, head upstairs to make your way out to Shalour City.

TIPS *Use the Strength field move to shove back the boulder you find on the cave's first floor, and you'll be able to breeze through Reflection Cave with greater ease during future visits.*

If you have Tornadus, Thundurus, or Landorus in your party you can receive the Reveal Glass from the Scientist by the entrance.

STEP 4 » Find TM74 Gyro Ball

Xavier found
TM74 Gyro Ball!

True adventurers will want to head down to the second basement level to find additional items. Go north and find an Earth Plate. Peer into the north reflective wall to spy a doorway in the parallel wall to the south. Go through the doorway to reach another short chamber, where you'll discover TM74 Gyro Ball. Continue south and go through another entrance.

Shalour City

The imposing Tower of Mastery keeps a silent vigil over this serene city, where the Mega Evolution guru makes his home. Here you will finally begin to unlock the secrets of Mega Evolution. In addition, the local Gym features numerous challenges for you to overcome in pursuit of the Kalos region's third Badge.

Field Moves Needed

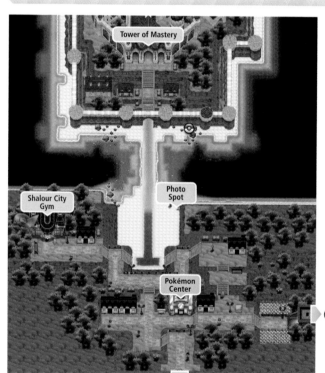

Tower of Mastery

Shalour City Gym

Photo Spot

Pokémon Center

Route 12 (to Azure Bay and Coumarine City)

Reflection Cave

Chinchou
Water Electric
Abilities: Volt Absorb
Illuminate

Poké Mart	
TM28 Dig	10,000
TM07 Hail	50,000
TM84 Poison Jab	10,000
TM20 Safeguard	30,000
TM37 Sandstorm	50,000

Items

First visit
- ❑ Eviolite
- ❑ Footprint Ribbon
- ❑ Intriguing Stone
- ❑ Max Ether
- ❑ Soothe Bell
- ❑ Stardusts ×5

After earning the Rumble Badge
- ❑ Mega Ring
- ❑ TM47 Low Sweep
- ❑ TM98 Power-Up Punch
- ❑ HM03 Surf

Hidden Items
- ❑ Max Repel
- ❑ Stardust
- ❑ X Sp. Atk

Trade Items
- ❑ Leppa Berry (trade for Sitrus Berry)
- ❑ Sun Stone (trade for Intriguing Stone)

Fishing		
Old Rod		
❑ Luvdisc	◎	
Good Rod		
❑ Chinchou	○	
❑ Remoraid	◎	
Super Rod		
❑ Alomomola	◎	
❑ Lanturn	▲	
❑ Octillery	○	

Water Surface		
❑ Mantyke	△	
❑ Tentacool	◎	

◎ frequent ○ average △ rare ▲ almost never

STEP
1 » Bump into Mr. Bonding at the Pokémon Center

You'll find a familiar face in Shalour City's Pokémon Center: Mr. Bonding! This guy sure gets around. This time, Mr. Bonding graciously grants you the Critical Power O-Power.

STEP
2 » Lend a lady a hand and get handed some Stardusts

Would you help me get some luggage that's too high for me to reach?

After resting your Pokémon, begin exploring Shalour City and speaking to its residents. Inside one home, a woman needs help from a Flying- or Psychic-type Pokémon to get some luggage down from a shelf. If you have such a Pokémon in your party, offer to help the woman, and your good deed will be rewarded with not one but five Stardusts!

 Have you raised your Pokémon a whole lot? If you have a Pokémon in your party that you have raised at least 30 levels since you received it, you can also get the Footprint Ribbon in this house.

STEP
3 Earn an Eviolite and a Soothe Bell

Two other locals will weigh your progress in the Kalos region and reward you with items if you've done well so far. One is curious about your friendship bond with a Pokémon, while another wishes to inspect your Coastal Kalos Pokédex. Impress these two people, and you'll score some worthy rewards. If you've seen 40 Pokémon or more in the Coastal Kalos area, visit the house east of the Pokémon Center and you'll receive an Eviolite. If you have a Pokémon that you're friendly with, visit the house to the west and receive a Soothe Bell.

TIP *Not sure how friendly your Pokémon are feeling toward you? Remember that there's a woman in Santalune City who can tell you how close you are to your Pokémon. If you don't feel like going back that far, though, think about which Pokémon you have spent the most time with. Walking together and battling together makes your Pokémon more friendly toward you.*

STEP
4 Have a chat with Trevor and Tierno

Tierno and Trevor catch up with you as you go north along the central path. The two are excited to be so close to the Mega Evolution guru and believe that he can be found in the Tower of Mastery to the north. That's your next stop!

STEP
5 Head for the Tower of Mastery

Finish searching Shalour City, using the Dowsing Machine to locate hidden items. When you're ready, proceed north toward the Tower of Mastery. Tierno calls out to you as you advance on the tower and gives you an Intriguing Stone. He's so generous!

⑥ Meet the Mega Evolution guru

Mega Evolution is a transformation of Pokémon that were thought to be unable to evolve any further! ▼

At long last, the answers you seek regarding Mega Evolution are at hand. Enter the Tower of Mastery to speak with the Mega Evolution guru, who also happens to be Gym Leader Korrina's grandfather. The wise man imparts much knowledge, and soon the secrets of Mega Evolution are revealed.

STEP
⑦ Battle with Serena/Calem for the Mega Ring

Are you ready?

Yes
No

You will need the Mega Ring to perform Mega Evolution, but the guru only has one Mega Ring to bestow. You must therefore battle Serena or Calem for the right to wear this awesome item. This is an important battle, so give it all you've got!

Vs. Serena/Calem's Pokémon

If you chose Chespin:

Meowstic
♀/♂ Lv. 28 Psychic
Weak to: Bug Ghost Dark

Absol
♂ Lv. 28 Dark
Weak to: Fighting Bug Fairy

Braixen
♂ Lv. 30 Fire
Weak to: Water Ground Rock

If you chose Fennekin:

Meowstic
♀/♂ Lv. 28 Psychic
Weak to: Bug Ghost Dark

Absol
♂ Lv. 28 Dark
Weak to: Fighting Bug Fairy

Frogadier
♂ Lv. 30 Water
Weak to: Grass Electric

If you chose Froakie:

Meowstic
♀/♂ Lv. 28 Psychic
Weak to: Bug Ghost Dark

Absol
♂ Lv. 28 Dark
Weak to: Fighting Bug Fairy

Quilladin
♂ Lv. 30 Grass
Weak to: Fire Ice Poison Flying Bug

STEP
8 **Rest your party, and then challenge Korrina at the Gym**

Well done! You've bested Serena or Calem and have earned the right to wear the Mega Ring. It isn't yours quite yet, however, for you still need to defeat the local Gym Leader, Korrina, here in Shalour City. Prepare your Pokémon and then head for the Gym.

Shalour City Gym Battle

Gym Battle Tips

✓ Bring lots of HP recovery items and status condition healers

✓ Use Flying-, Psychic-, and Fairy-type Pokémon

Roller Skater Rolanda*

Roller Skater Kate*

Roller Skater Shun*

Gym Leader Korrina

Roller Skater Dash*

Entrance

*These Roller Skaters are constantly on the move, so engage them in battle wherever you catch up with them.

Korrina

Fighting-type Pokémon User

Use Flying-, Psychic-, and Fairy-type moves to deal massive damage

You must battle all four Trainers within the Shalour City Gym in order to open the way to the Gym's central platform, where Korrina awaits. Skate up to each Trainer in turn, getting close enough to them that they stop to engage you in battle. After you have defeated the four Trainers, you'll be able to grind on the assembled skate rail and reach the central platform, where Korrina makes her grand appearance.

You've battled Korrina before, but this time she lets her Lucario rest while sending other Fighting-type Pokémon against you. Korrina's Pokémon are vulnerable to Flying-, Psychic-, and Fairy-type moves, and many of their moves are not very effective against Flying- and Psychic-type Pokémon. Beware—Korrina will heal her weary Pokémon with a Hyper Potion if you allow her the chance. Finish them off quickly with powerful moves!

Korrina's Pokémon

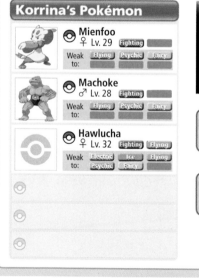

Mienfoo ♀ Lv. 29 `Fighting`
Weak to: `Flying` `Psychic` `Fairy`

Machoke ♂ Lv. 28 `Fighting`
Weak to: `Flying` `Psychic` `Fairy`

Hawlucha ♀ Lv. 32 `Fighting` `Flying`
Weak to: `Electric` `Ice` `Flying` `Psychic` `Fairy`

✧vs Korrina✧

Rumble Badge

Pokémon up to Lv. 50, including those received in trades, will obey you.

TM98 Power-Up Punch

Striking opponents over and over makes the user's fists harder. Hitting a target raises the Attack stat.

Now that you have your three Gym Badges, you can buy Full Heals, Max Repels, and Ultra Balls at any Poké Mart around the region!

STEP
⑨ ⟩ **With the Rumble Badge in hand, return to the Tower of Mastery**

Oh! Korrina, I mean the Mega Evolution successor, is waiting for you at the top of the tower!

You've defeated Korrina and earned the right to carry the Rumble Badge, but you still need to claim the Mega Ring. Korrina invites you to join her in one last battle atop the Tower of Mastery. Return there without delay.

STEP
⑩ ⟩ **Explore the Tower of Mastery**

So do you know the Mega Evolution guru's real name? It's Gurkinn!

Now that you have full access to the Tower of Mastery, you can speak with the people who reside here to learn more about the history of Mega Evolution. One person will even tell you the Mega Evolution guru's real name: Gurkinn! Another person inside the tower will hand you TM47 Low Sweep.

STEP
⑪ ⟩ **Battle Korrina at the top of the Tower of Mastery**

A Lucario-on-Lucario battle! It will be nothing short of riveting.

Korrina waits at the tower's apex and gives you the Mega Ring. Now you can Mega Evolve your Pokémon! In a surprise twist, one of her Lucario decides to join you and fight against the other Lucario. Both Lucario are holding Mega Stones, so use Mega Evolution right away by tapping the glowing Mega Evolution button at the bottom of the Touch Screen. After that, unleash the Power-Up Punch move to defeat the opposing Lucario with ease.

> **TIP** *Korrina offers to let you take Lucario with you, since it seems to have grown attached to you. If you choose not to take it with you now, you can always come back and let it join you later.*

STEP
⑫ Receive HM03 Surf on your way to Route 12

Xavier obtained
HM03 Surf!

Now that you've obtained both the Rumble Badge and Mega Ring, it's time to move on. Revisit the Pokémon Center one more time, then proceed east onto Route 12. Before you get there, Serena/Calem catches up to you and gives you a vital item: HM03 Surf. Now you can surf along the surface of water and fully explore aquatic areas!

TIPS

Once you have HM03 Surf, feel free to revisit areas like Route 8 to explore their waters. Consider waiting until you've earned the next Gym Badge, though. At that point, you'll be able to use Fly to return to any Pokémon Center you've previously visited, which will speed up your backtracking efforts.

Before you leave town, visit the Hiker on the east side of town who blocked the stairs earlier in your visit. If you give him your Intriguing Stone, he will give you a Sun Stone in return.

Route 12 (Fourrage Road)

Route 12 runs between Shalour City and Coumarine City, with Azure Bay lying within surfing distance to the north. This sizable path features many hidden items, though most of them can be discovered only by using field moves such as Cut and Surf. Pop by the Baa de Mer Ranch and ride a Skiddo, and you'll find even more hidden goodies.

Field Moves Needed
Cut Surf

Swimmer ♂
Alessandro

Azure Bay

Baa de Mer Ranch

Shalour City

Aspear Berry Tree

Coumarine City

Backpacker Joren

Pokémon Breeder Amala

Fisherman Murray

Youngster Aidan

Pokémon Breeder Foster

Items
❑ Aspear Berry
❑ Leftovers
❑ Sachet
❑ Shiny Stone
❑ TM45 Attract
❑ Whipped Dream

Hidden Items
❑ Honey
❑ Ice Heal
❑ Net Ball
❑ Water Stone

Exeggcute
Grass Psychic
Ability: Chlorophyll

Lapras
Water Ice
Abilities: Water Absorb
Shell Armor

Miltank
Normal
Abilities: Thick Fat
Scrappy

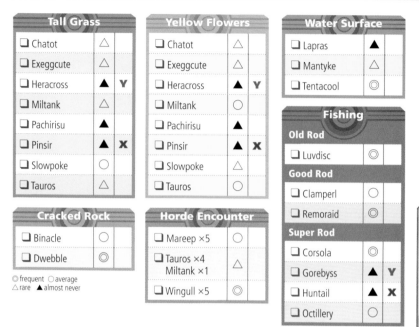

Tall Grass		
❑ Chatot	△	
❑ Exeggcute	△	
❑ Heracross	▲	Y
❑ Miltank	△	
❑ Pachirisu	▲	
❑ Pinsir	▲	X
❑ Slowpoke	○	
❑ Tauros	△	

Yellow Flowers		
❑ Chatot	△	
❑ Exeggcute	△	
❑ Heracross	▲	Y
❑ Miltank	○	
❑ Pachirisu	▲	
❑ Pinsir	▲	X
❑ Slowpoke	△	
❑ Tauros	○	

Water Surface		
❑ Lapras	▲	
❑ Mantyke	△	
❑ Tentacool	◎	

Fishing		
Old Rod		
❑ Luvdisc	◎	
Good Rod		
❑ Clamperl	○	
❑ Remoraid	◎	
Super Rod		
❑ Corsola	◎	
❑ Gorebyss	▲	Y
❑ Huntail	▲	X
❑ Octillery	○	

Cracked Rock		
❑ Binacle	○	
❑ Dwebble	◎	

◎ frequent ○ average
△ rare ▲ almost never

Horde Encounter		
❑ Mareep ×5	○	
❑ Tauros ×4 Miltank ×1	△	
❑ Wingull ×5	◎	

STEP 1 ▶ Obtain Lapras

Speak to the Pokémon Breeder just past the gate, and he'll tell you a story about the Lapras that saved his life. He wants you to take this Lapras with you on your travels. It is a rare Water- and Ice-type Pokémon, so go ahead and accept the generous offer. If you don't have space in your party right now, return to the Pokémon Center in Shalour City to make room for this worthy newcomer.

STEP 2 ▶ Surf across the sea

Deep water presents an impassable obstacle just ahead, so it's fortunate indeed that Serena/Calem recently gave you HM03 Surf. Teach this move to any capable Pokémon in your party, then approach the water and press Ⓐ to surf across it. Beware: wild Pokémon and Swimmers will engage you as you surf!

3 Visit the Baa de Mer Ranch and score a TM

Beyond the water lies a Skiddo ranch. Stroll into the Baa de Mer Ranch and enter the cottage near the Skiddo pen. Speak to the child inside the cottage to receive TM45 Attract. This unique move can make Pokémon of the opposite gender largely ineffective against your Pokémon in battle.

STEP
4 Ride a Skiddo and reach more treats

Go back outside and approach one of the roaming Skiddo in the nearby pen. You'll find that you can hop on a Skiddo's back and ride it around. Skiddo can leap low ledges, which helps you reach a couple of items that you otherwise couldn't get to.

TIP *Jump the broken fence to the east to escape the pen and explore more of Route 12 by way of Skiddo.*

STEP
5 Surf across Azure Bay

If you're up for a bit of exploration, use Surf to sail across every corner of the wide expanse of Azure Bay. There are many items, Pokémon, and Trainers awaiting you in these crystal-blue waters. But if your Pokémon are weary from the journey, feel free to rush onward to Coumarine City (p. 200) and return to Azure Bay at a later time.

TIP *While out on the water, visit the small beach to the west to collect the last hidden item on Route 12.*

The deep blue ocean off Kalos's coast, where Pokémon from distant lands are said to visit.

Azure Bay

This large, aquatic area is a favorite vacation spot for Swimmers around the Kalos region. Though it isn't a mandatory destination on your journey, it's worth surfing north from Route 12's eastern beach and exploring Azure Bay before you enter Coumarine City. You'll find all sorts of treasures hidden on the bay's many isles.

Field Moves Needed

Surf

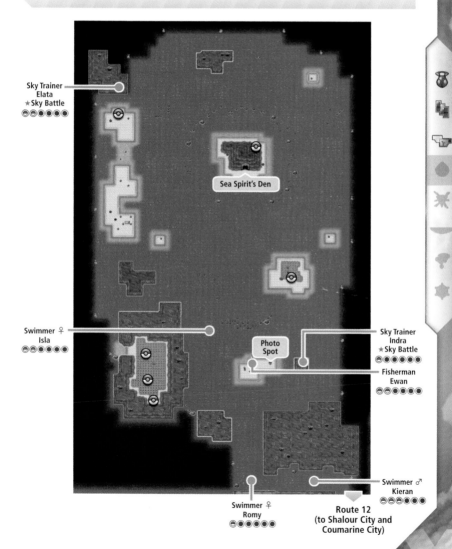

Sky Trainer
Elata
★Sky Battle

Sea Spirit's Den

Swimmer ♀
Isla

Sky Trainer
Indra
★Sky Battle

Photo
Spot

Fisherman
Ewan

Swimmer ♂
Kieran

Swimmer ♀
Romy

Route 12
(to Shalour City and
Coumarine City)

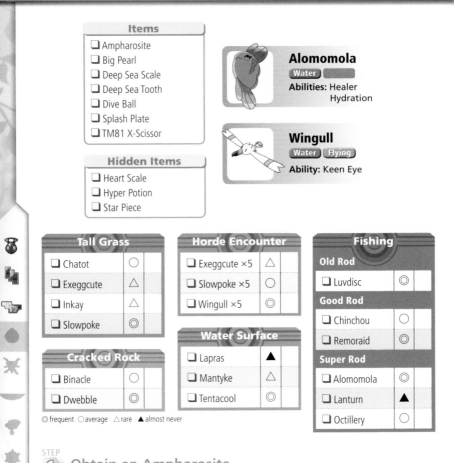

Items

- ❑ Ampharosite
- ❑ Big Pearl
- ❑ Deep Sea Scale
- ❑ Deep Sea Tooth
- ❑ Dive Ball
- ❑ Splash Plate
- ❑ TM81 X-Scissor

Hidden Items

- ❑ Heart Scale
- ❑ Hyper Potion
- ❑ Star Piece

Alomomola

Water

Abilities: Healer
Hydration

Wingull

Water Flying

Ability: Keen Eye

Tall Grass		
❑ Chatot	○	
❑ Exeggcute	△	
❑ Inkay	△	
❑ Slowpoke	◎	

Cracked Rock		
❑ Binacle	○	
❑ Dwebble	◎	

Horde Encounter		
❑ Exeggcute ×5	△	
❑ Slowpoke ×5	○	
❑ Wingull ×5	◎	

Water Surface		
❑ Lapras	▲	
❑ Mantyke	△	
❑ Tentacool	◎	

Fishing		
Old Rod		
❑ Luvdisc	◎	
Good Rod		
❑ Chinchou	○	
❑ Remoraid	◎	
Super Rod		
❑ Alomomola	◎	
❑ Lanturn	▲	
❑ Octillery	○	

◎ frequent ○ average △ rare ▲ almost never

STEP 1 ❯ Obtain an Ampharosite

Surf the briny blue waters until you reach a small, sandy isle. Speak to the old man here to receive a new type of Mega Stone. This one is intended for Ampharos, which can be evolved from the Mareep that you can catch on Route 12.

 Snap another photograph to remember your journey at the photo spot here.

STEP
2 » Take on Sky Trainers

Go to the sandy isle's east shore, near the photo spot, and a Sky Trainer on a grassy isle to the east will ask if you'd like to battle. Take stock of your party and see if you have any flying or levitating Pokémon that are ready for a challenge.

NOTE *There is one more Sky Trainer waiting for you out across the great blue expanse of Azure Bay. In the northwest corner of the bay is Sky Trainer Elata, and she'll challenge you if you stand at the tip of the last sandy islet in that corner of the map.*

STEP
3 » Explore the great bay

Azure Bay is huge and has many other isles that you can explore. Spend some time surfing the sea, and see if you can discover all of its secrets. Use your Dowsing Machine whenever you reach dry land, and keep an eye out for that other Sky Trainer who'd like to help you improve.

NOTE *The Sea Spirit's Den lies to the north, but it's empty. There's nothing for you to do there at present.*

TIP *If you're in a rush, use a Repel to prevent random encounters as you surf around Azure Bay.*

Coumarine City

This scenic city uses a monorail system to merge both bay and bluff. Coumarine City's lower bay area features an impressive pier where expensive boats are docked. Hop on the monorail and ride up into the mountains to visit the city's other half, where you'll find breathtaking views of the surrounding landscape, along with a Pokémon Center and Pokémon Gym.

Field Moves Needed

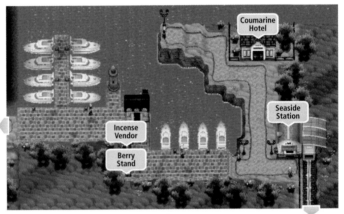

Route 12 (to Shalour City)

Coumarine Hotel

Seaside Station

Incense Vendor

Berry Stand

To lower Coumarine City

To upper Coumarine City

Coumarine City Gym

Pokémon Center

Hillcrest Station

Route 13 (to Kalos Power Plant and Lumiose City)

Items

Lower bay area

❑ Careless Ribbon (in the hotel on Thursday)
❑ Good Rod
❑ HM02 Fly
❑ Lucky Egg
❑ Silk Scarf
❑ Smile Ribbon (in the hotel on Sunday)
❑ TM62 Acrobatics
❑ TM63 Embargo
❑ TM92 Trick Room
❑ TM100 Confide

Upper mountain area

❑ Black Sludge
❑ Metronome
❑ Poké Toy
❑ Sky Plate
❑ TM86 Grass Knot

Hidden Items

Lower bay area

❑ Awakening
❑ Elixir

Upper mountain area

❑ Max Repel

Berry Stand

❑ Aspear Berry
❑ Cheri Berry
❑ Chesto Berry
❑ Pecha Berry
❑ Rawst Berry

Incense Vendor

Full Incense	9,600
Lax Incense	9,600
Luck Incense	9,600
Odd Incense	9,600
Pure Incense	9,600
Rock Incense	9,600
Rose Incense	9,600
Sea Incense	9,600
Wave Incense	9,600

STEP 1 » Receive a Holo Clip from Serena/Calem

Serena: Xavier. I challenge you to a battle in front of the Gym!

As you enter Coumarine City, Serena/Calem contacts you via Holo Caster. She/he is itching for a fight and challenges you to a battle outside the city's Gym. You'd better find the local Pokémon Center and make sure your Pokémon are ready to go!

STEP 2 » Receive a Silk Scarf

I used to buy Silk Scarves all the time for my wife...

Enter the house on the pier to speak to an elderly couple. The old woman is a bit rude, but the old man gives you a Silk Scarf to make up for her remark. It's a great item for Pokémon that use Normal-type moves.

STEP
3 » Shop for some incense

An industrious man tends a small stand on the pier, from which he peddles an interesting variety of incenses. Some of them are quite potent, and it's worth taking a look at his goods.

> I've traveled around the world and collected many different kinds of incense!

TIP *Feel free to claim the Berry from the vacant stand to the south. Another random Berry (an Aspear Berry, Cheri Berry, Chesto Berry, Pecha Berry, or Rawst Berry) will be placed here each day for you to take.*

STEP
4 » Reel in a Good Rod

> Here you are: one Good Rod! Go take it for a spin, all right?

A friendly fisherman strolls the pier and will offer you a Good Rod if you talk to him. You won't lose your Old Rod, so there's no reason not to take the fisherman up on his kind offer. The Good Rod can reach deeper depths than the Old Rod when you go fishing for new Pokémon.

STEP
5 » Visit the Coumarine Hotel

> Since you're so friendly with your Pokémon, I'm going to give you this Lucky Egg!

Ignore the Seaside Station for the moment and follow the path north to reach the Coumarine Hotel. If you're very friendly with your party's lead Pokémon (and why shouldn't you be?), then a girl in the lobby will give you a precious Lucky Egg. Give this to a Pokémon that needs a little help leveling up.

NOTE *If your visit occurs on Thursday, a traveller in the middle room upstairs will give your lead Pokémon a Careless Ribbon. And if it's Sunday, she will bestow upon you a Smile Ribbon. She sure must love Coumarine City! And with its different views—one on the seaside and one high above on the bluffs—there's something for everyone to enjoy.*

STEP
6 Meet the Game Director

You might expect Mr. Bonding to be waiting for you in the Coumarine Hotel's upstairs room, but this is not the case. Instead, you find the Game Director in the room where Mr. Bonding usually appears. The Game Director seems interested in talking to you after you've filled in more of your Pokédex. You'll have to return later and see what he's about.

STEP
7 Ace a quiz and gain a TM

Follow the path to its end at the lookout west of the Hotel Coumarine, and you'll meet a girl who's eager to test your knowledge of TMs. Answer the girl's question correctly and you'll get one of four moves as a prize! Return to the girl each day and play her game again until she has given you all four TMs.

NOTE *This Veteran can give you the TMs for Acrobatics, Embargo, Trick Room, and Confide. These are all moves used by wise strategists, so learn the effects of each with care!*

STEP
8 Enter Seaside Station and get ready to Fly!

You've fully explored this half of the city, so it's time to enter Seaside Station and travel to the city's other half. Some familiar faces greet you inside the station—it's Professor Sycamore and famous movie star Diantha! The good professor congratulates you on obtaining everything you need for Mega Evolution and gives you HM02 Fly. This powerful move will come in handy at the Pokémon Gym!

9 Ride the monorail to Coumarine City's other half

The famous movie star Diantha speaks with you inside the station, and she hints that she'd like to challenge you to a Pokémon battle the next time you meet. You're moving up in the world! For now, speak to the woman behind the counter to book a monorail ride to Coumarine City's other half. When you arrive at Hillcrest Station, talk to a man inside the station to receive a Metronome.

10 Visit the Pokémon Center

Swing by the Pokémon Center next, which is right outside Hillcrest Station. You'll meet Mr. Bonding inside the Pokémon Center, and he will bestow upon you the Befriending Power O-Power.

11 Talk to the locals and receive a few more items

Before entering the Pokémon Gym, score a few more items by talking with the locals around this half of Coumarine City. Play a guessing game with a lady in her home to receive a Poké Toy.

> **TIPS** *Talk to the Psychic in the same house where you receive a Poké Toy to hear a nostalgic tune from the past.*

> *Consider taking a brief peek ahead and entering the gate that connects Coumarine City to Route 13. You don't need to go all the way out onto the route yet, but talk to the Punk Guy you find in the gate and he will give you a Black Sludge. This item will restore HP to a Poison-type Pokémon every turn. Poison-type moves are super effective against two of the three Pokémon that the Coumarine City Gym Leader uses, and Poison types are resistant to Grass-type moves. If you've got one trained up, it could be a huge advantage in the coming battles, so consider adding it to your party and have it hold Black Sludge.*

⑫ Battle Serena/Calem outside the Pokémon Gym

So, could you show me Mega Evolution?

As promised, Serena/Calem meets you outside the Pokémon Gym, hoping you'll show off your newfound power of Mega Evolution in a battle. Wipe out your rival in style, then rest up at the Pokémon Center before entering the Gym.

Vs. Serena/Calem's Pokémon

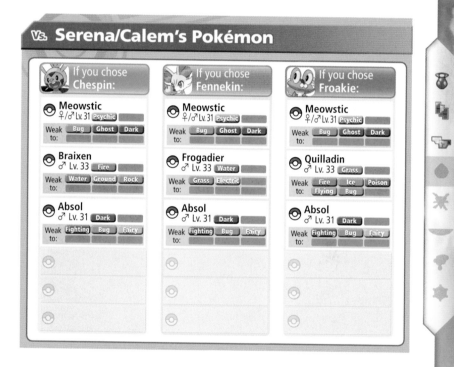

If you chose Chespin:

Meowstic
♀/♂ Lv. 31 Psychic
Weak to: Bug Ghost Dark

Braixen
♂ Lv. 33 Fire
Weak to: Water Ground Rock

Absol
♂ Lv. 31 Dark
Weak to: Fighting Bug Fairy

If you chose Fennekin:

Meowstic
♀/♂ Lv. 31 Psychic
Weak to: Bug Ghost Dark

Frogadier
♂ Lv. 33 Water
Weak to: Grass Electric

Absol
♂ Lv. 31 Dark
Weak to: Fighting Bug Fairy

If you chose Froakie:

Meowstic
♀/♂ Lv. 31 Psychic
Weak to: Bug Ghost Dark

Quilladin
♂ Lv. 33 Grass
Weak to: Fire Ice Poison Flying Bug

Absol
♂ Lv. 31 Dark
Weak to: Fighting Bug Fairy

Coumarine City Gym Battle

Gym Battle Tips

✓ Bring lots of Super Potions and items that heal status conditions

✓ Use Fire-, Ice-, Poison-, Flying-, and Bug-type Pokémon

This verdant Pokémon Gym is made up of many levels, and the Gym Leader Ramos awaits you at the very top.

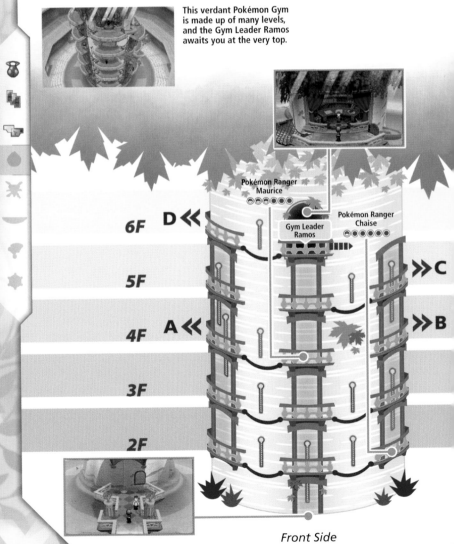

Pokémon Ranger
Maurice

Pokémon Ranger
Chaise

Gym Leader
Ramos

6F **D ≪**

5F **≫ C**

4F **A ≪** **≫ B**

3F

2F

Front Side

Step on the footprint-shaped marks on each balcony and press Ⓐ. You will jump up and grab hold of a rope to either climb or swing across voids.

Use ropes to climb up and down between the balconies as you work your way up to the top of the tree.

When you leap out into the void between balconies, you will automatically catch hold of the rope and swing across to the next landing spot.

C ≪

B ≪

≫ D

≫ A

Pokémon Ranger
Brooke
◉◉◉◉◉◉

Pokémon Ranger
Twiggy
◉◉◉◉◉◉

Back Side

Coumarine City Gym Leader

Ramos

Grass-type Pokémon User

Use Fire-, Ice-, Poison-, Flying-, and Bug-type moves to deal massive damage

You're about to get a workout here at the Coumarine City Gym. To reach Ramos at the top of the tower, you'll need to climb a number of ropes. Just approach a rope and press Ⓐ to climb it. Other ropes let you swing across gaps. Keep climbing until you at last reach Ramos.

Ramos has a strong fondness for all things flora and fauna, and as such, he favors Grass-type Pokémon. His Pokémon are vulnerable to a variety of moves, and the HM02 Fly that Professor Sycamore recently gave you is an excellent move to employ.

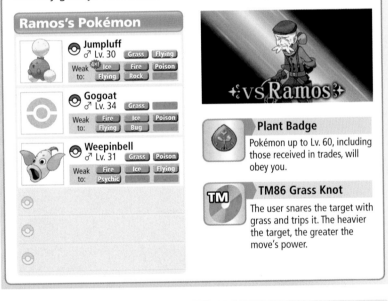

Ramos's Pokémon

Jumpluff ♂ Lv. 30 `Grass` `Flying`
Weak to: `Ice` `Fire` `Poison` `Flying` `Rock` **4x!**

Gogoat ♂ Lv. 34 `Grass`
Weak to: `Fire` `Ice` `Poison` `Flying` `Bug`

Weepinbell ♂ Lv. 31 `Grass` `Poison`
Weak to: `Fire` `Ice` `Flying` `Psychic`

Plant Badge
Pokémon up to Lv. 60, including those received in trades, will obey you.

TM86 Grass Knot
The user snares the target with grass and trips it. The heavier the target, the greater the move's power.

NOTE *You're halfway to challenging the Pokémon League! With four Gym Badges, the left clerk at Poké Marts will now sell you Max Potions!*

13 Get a move on, along with a Holo Clip from Lysandre

With that power, you can steer
your future in a better direction!

Nice work, you've earned your fourth Gym Badge! Coumarine City's been a hoot, but it's time to move along. Head south toward the gate to Route 13, and you'll receive a Holo Clip from Lysandre as you go. He's excited that you've learned how to use Mega Evolution and hopes that you'll use this power to help shape a better world.

14 Receive the Mountain Kalos Pokédex

So I'm going to take this opportunity
and power up your Pokédex again.

As you pass through the gate to Route 13, you get a surprise visit from Professor Sycamore's assistants, Sina and Dexio. The duo divulges that a problem at the Kalos Power Plant has shut the gate connecting Route 13 to Lumiose City. More importantly, the pair powers up your Pokédex yet again. With the Mountain Kalos Pokédex in your possession, you can now make a record of every Pokémon in the entire Kalos region! With it in hand, continue south to Route 13!

All of Kalos's Pokémon lie at your fingertips!

You finally have unlocked all three parts of the Kalos Regional Pokédex: the Central Kalos Pokédex, the Coastal Kalos Pokédex, and the Mountain Kalos Pokédex. Each of these three sections contains 150 Pokémon that must be seen in order for that section to be considered complete. That means that there are at least 450 Pokémon to be seen in the Kalos Regional Pokédex—and you'll have to actually catch them all if you want to be able to see their full Pokédex entries, including their Habitat information!

The Central Kalos Pokédex

This Pokédex covers the heart of Kalos, an area rich with greenery and blooming flowers. There are many forests, grassy routes, and gardens in the center of this beautiful region, and many of the Pokémon found here seem perfectly at home in this natural setting.

The Coastal Kalos Pokédex

This Pokédex includes the balmy, coastal regions that stretch along Kalos's west coast. Many Water-type Pokémon are included in this Pokédex, which covers the sea that stretches out in all its glittering splendor beneath the blue skies of this half of Kalos.

The Mountain Kalos Pokédex

This Pokédex features the Pokémon that inhabit the rockier and mountainous reaches that make up the northern and eastern parts of the Kalos region. This is a place of crisp, autumnal breezes and icy peaks, and you will find some tough Pokémon to battle here.

Route 13 (Lumiose Badlands)

This inhospitable area provides a sharp contrast to the lovely vistas you were recently enjoying at Coumarine City. Many Ground-type Pokémon tunnel beneath the red clay of these parched badlands, and they're quite aggressive and will pursue you as you explore. Perhaps their behavior has something to do with the problems at the nearby Kalos Power Plant...

Field Moves Needed

Rock Smash

Dugtrio

Ground

Abilities: Sand Veil
Arena Trap

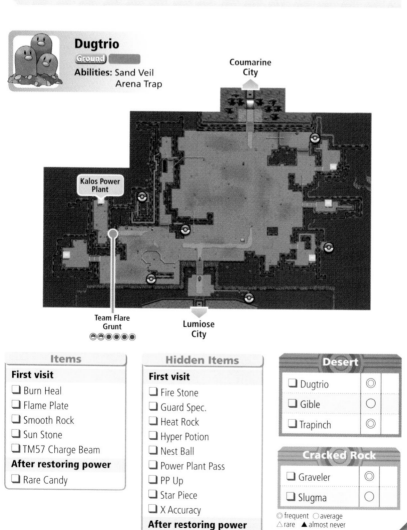

Coumarine City

Kalos Power Plant

Team Flare Grunt

Lumiose City

Items

First visit
- ❑ Burn Heal
- ❑ Flame Plate
- ❑ Smooth Rock
- ❑ Sun Stone
- ❑ TM57 Charge Beam

After restoring power
- ❑ Rare Candy

Hidden Items

First visit
- ❑ Fire Stone
- ❑ Guard Spec.
- ❑ Heat Rock
- ❑ Hyper Potion
- ❑ Nest Ball
- ❑ Power Plant Pass
- ❑ PP Up
- ❑ Star Piece
- ❑ X Accuracy

After restoring power
- ❑ Stardust

Desert

❑ Dugtrio	◎	
❑ Gible	○	
❑ Trapinch	◎	

Cracked Rock

❑ Graveler	◎	
❑ Slugma	○	

◎ frequent ○ average
△ rare ▲ almost never

STEP
①▶ Brave the badlands

Route 13's harsh landscape may not feature tall grass, but many wild Pokémon tunnel around beneath the cracked clay. If these wild Pokémon catch you, you're in for a fight! Still, it's worth giving the badlands a thorough search because so many helpful items can be found here.

TIPS *Repels won't keep these wild Pokémon at bay. However, if a wild Pokémon is about to catch you, try standing still for a moment. It may lose interest and disappear.*

Remember: you need speed to grind across skate rails that feature kinks. When the wind is blowing strongly, you'll find it nearly impossible to skate against it, but weather is inconstant in Kalos. Try again later when the wind dies down.

Use the Rock Smash field move to destroy the badlands' small, cracked rocks and explore more of the area.

STEP
②▶ Locate the Power Plant Pass

Many hidden items can be found around Route 13, and one of them is an item that you need to find. Follow your Dowsing Machine to the large boulder near the metal bridge to the west, which is guarded by a Team Flare Grunt. Locate the Power Plant Pass by inspecting this large boulder.

STEP
③▶ Battle the Team Flare Grunt, and then enter the Power Plant

After locating the Power Plant Pass, approach the nearby Team Flare Grunt to engage him in battle. After you beat the Grunt, move past him and enter the door to start exploring the Kalos Power Plant (p. 214).

AFTER RESTORING THE POWER:

⚙ Go south to reach Lumiose City

After you've cleared the Kalos Power Plant and restored power to the city, travel south to reach Lumiose. You'll meet a strange individual along the way, but the mysterious and oversized traveler doesn't say much before heading into Lumiose City (p. 218). Perhaps your paths will cross again.

> **TIP** *Use Rock Smash to demolish the cracked rocks to the east to discover a few more items before entering Lumiose City.*

Kalos Power Plant

This advanced power facility is a marvel of modern technology. It supplies clean, efficient energy to Lumiose City, but a recent string of blackouts indicates that something has gone awry here.

Field Moves Needed

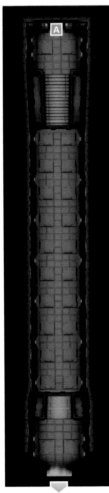

Route 13
(to Lumiose City and Coumarine City)

Team Flare Grunt

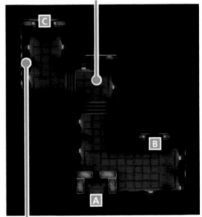

Team Flare Grunt

Items		Fresh Water Seller	
First visit		**First visit**	
❑ Zap Plate		Fresh Water	300
After restoring power		**After restoring power**	
❑ Full Restore ×2		Fresh Water	100
❑ Magnet			
❑ TM43 Flame Charge			

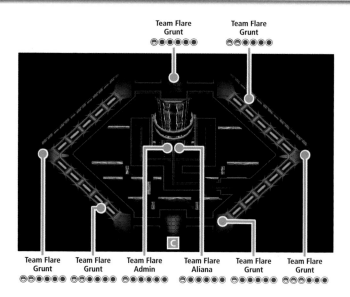

Team Flare
Grunt
◉◉◉◉◉◉

Team Flare
Grunt
◉◉◉◉◉◉

Team Flare
Grunt
◉◉◉◉◉◉

Team Flare
Grunt
◉◉◉◉◉◉

Team Flare
Admin
◉◉◉◉◉◉

Team Flare
Aliana
◉◉◉◉◉◉

Team Flare
Grunt
◉◉◉◉◉◉

Team Flare
Grunt
◉◉◉◉◉◉

STEP
1 Explore the Kalos Power Plant

Only authorized personnel are allowed in here!

Team Flare is clearly up to something at the Kalos Power Plant, because it's not long before you're approached by another well-groomed Grunt. Defeat this pest in battle to learn that Team Flare is stealing power from the plant for their own selfish purposes.

STEP
2 Find a Zap Plate and some Fresh Water

How 'bout some Fresh Water?

Enter a small room on the right to find the Kalos Power Plant's workers. They've all been cooped up in this room to prevent them from meddling with Team Flare's scheme. Speak to one man to purchase some HP-restoring Fresh Water, and find a Zap Plate in the far nook.

STEP 3 Fight your way to the Kalos Power Plant's center

The Kalos Power Plant's central chamber is filled with Team Flare Grunts. Whatever they are up to, they must be stopped! Work your way around the outer walkway, battling a number of Grunts as you go.

STEP 4 Defeat the Team Flare Admin and Aliana

Beware: two powerful Team Flare associates are up to something at the center of the plant. First you must face the Team Flare Admin, and then a Scientist working for Team Flare called Aliana. These are tough fights, but you have a chance to heal your Pokémon between battles.

Vs. Team Flare Admin's Pokémon

Houndoom
♂ Lv. 36 Dark Fire
Weak to: Water Fighting Ground Rock

Vs. Team Flare Aliana's Pokémon

Mightyena
♀ Lv. 38 Dark
Weak to: Fighting Bug Fairy

STEP
5 Meet the defenders of Kalos

You chased off that mysterious bunch before we could even get here?

Defeating both the Team Flare Admin and Aliana brings the Kalos Power Plant back to full functionality. Soon after, two masked strangers arrive on the scene. They were coming to investigate the Kalos Power Plant as well, but you beat them to it. The duo are impressed and hand you a couple of Full Restores before they leave.

STEP
6 Snag a TM on your way out of the Kalos Power Plant

Xavier obtained
TM43 Flame Charge!

As you make your way out of the Kalos Power Plant, take a moment to check in on the employees of the power plant in the side room. One of them will reward your heroism with TM43 Flame Charge, and another will give you a Magnet. Also, the Fresh Water seller will now cut you a deal on his refreshing beverages. What a guy!

Lumiose City (Center)

It's been a long journey, but you've come full circle. You're back at Lumiose City! Much more of this teeming metropolis can be explored now that you've restored the flow of energy from the Kalos Power Plant. When you're ready to claim your next Badge, you'll find a new Gym Leader awaiting all comers atop the Prism Tower.

Field Moves Needed

Prism Tower as seen from Estival Avenue.

Route 13 (to Coumarine City)

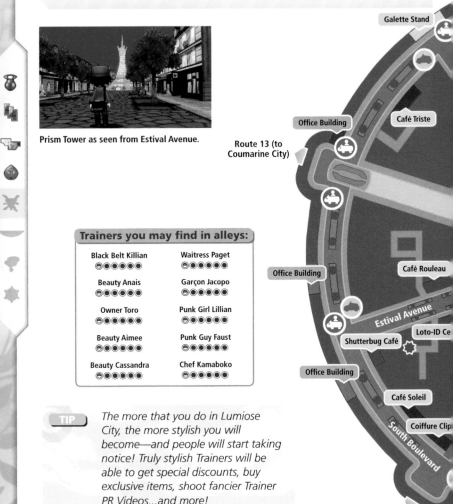

Trainers you may find in alleys:

Black Belt Killian ●●●●●●	Waitress Paget ●●●●●●
Beauty Anais ●●●●●●	Garçon Jacopo ●●●●●●
Owner Toro ●●●●●●	Punk Girl Lillian ●●●●●●
Beauty Aimee ●●●●●●	Punk Guy Faust ●●●●●●
Beauty Cassandra ●●●●●●	Chef Kamaboko ●●●●●●

TIP *The more that you do in Lumiose City, the more stylish you will become—and people will start taking notice! Truly stylish Trainers will be able to get special discounts, buy exclusive items, shoot fancier Trainer PR Videos...and more!*

Route 5 (to Camphrier Town)

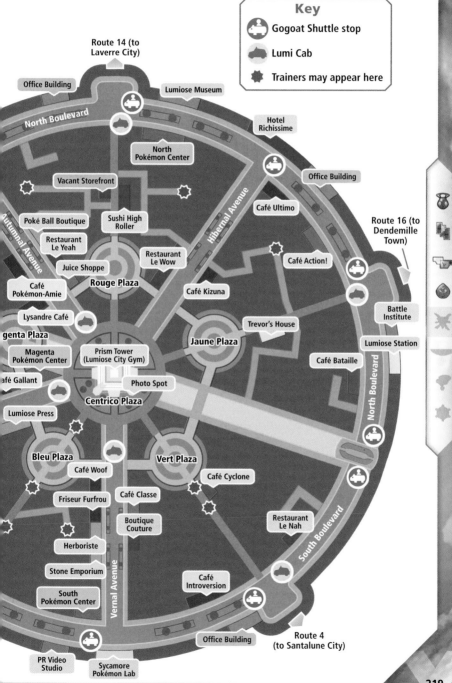

Key
- Gogoat Shuttle stop
- Lumi Cab
- Trainers may appear here

Route 14 (to Laverre City)

Office Building

North Boulevard

Lumiose Museum

Hotel Richissime

North Pokémon Center

Vacant Storefront

Office Building

Café Ultimo

Route 16 (to Dendemille Town)

Poké Ball Boutique

Sushi High Roller

Restaurant Le Yeah

Café Action!

Hibernal Avenue

Restaurant Le Wow

Juice Shoppe

Rouge Plaza

Café Kizuna

Battle Institute

Autumnal Avenue

Café Pokémon-Amie

Trevor's House

Lumiose Station

Lysandre Café

Jaune Plaza

Magenta Plaza

Magenta Pokémon Center

Prism Tower (Lumiose City Gym)

Café Bataille

Café Gallant

Photo Spot

North Boulevard

Lumiose Press

Centrico Plaza

Bleu Plaza

Café Woof

Vert Plaza

Café Cyclone

Friseur Furfrou

Café Classe

Herboriste

Boutique Couture

Restaurant Le Nah

South Boulevard

Stone Emporium

Vernal Avenue

Café Introversion

South Pokémon Center

PR Video Studio

Sycamore Pokémon Lab

Office Building

Route 4 (to Santalune City)

Items

- ❑ Expert Belt
- ❑ King's Rock
- ❑ Luxury Ball ×1 or Heal Ball ×3
- ❑ Prism Scale
- ❑ Protein
- ❑ Star Piece
- ❑ TM24 Thunderbolt
- ❑ TM49 Echoed Voice
- ❑ TM82 Dragon Tail

Lumiose Galette Stand (North Boulevard)

Galette	100

Stone Emporium (Vernal Avenue)

Venusaurite or Charizardite X (**X**) or Charizardite Y (**Y**) or Blastoisinite	Varies
Fire Stone	2,100
Leaf Stone	2,100
Water Stone	2,100

Poké Mart (North Boulevard Pokémon Center)

Heal Ball	300
Nest Ball	1,000
Net Ball	1,000

Herboriste (Vernal Avenue)

Energy Powder	500
Energy Root	800
Heal Powder	450
Revival Herb	2,800

Poké Ball Boutique (Autumnal Avenue)

Dive Ball	1,000
Dusk Ball	1,000
Heal Ball	300
Luxury Ball	1,000
Nest Ball	1,000
Net Ball	1,000
Premier Ball	200
Quick Ball	1,000
Repeat Ball	1,000
Timer Ball	1,000

Poké Mart (South Boulevard Pokémon Center)

TM78 Bulldoze	10,000
TM18 Rain Dance	50,000
TM76 Struggle Bug	10,000
TM11 Sunny Day	50,000
TM75 Swords Dance	10,000

Juice Shoppe (Autumnal Avenue)

Premium Berry Juice	Varies
Fresh Berry Juice	Varies

STEP

1 ›› Have a chat with Shauna

They're gonna light the tower!

As you stroll through the Route 13 gate and enter Lumiose City, your good friend Shauna catches up to you. She's thrilled that the city's power has been restored and eager to watch the relighting of the Prism Tower.

STEP
2 Watch Prism Tower's lighting be restored

Prism Tower stands in the center of Lumiose City. Shauna won't let you do much exploring until you watch the lighting of the tower with her, so head for Centrico Plaza without delay. When you arrive, the local Gym Leader, Clemont, turns on the lights, and Prism Tower begins to shine.

STEP
3 Visit the Pokémon Center near Magenta Plaza

You passed a Pokémon Center on your way to Prism Tower. Head back the way you came after the lighting to visit the Pokémon Center and prepare for the upcoming Gym Battle. But there's still much more of the city to explore before you tackle the Lumiose City Gym!

STEP
4 Check out Lysandre Café

Visit Lysandre Café near Magenta Plaza. It's the red building with the stylish Team Flare member standing nearby. There isn't much to do here, but you can at least get a taste for Lysandre's type of hangout.

TIP   *There are two rings that run around Lumiose City. The outer ring is divided into North Boulevard and South Boulevard. The inner ring is a single loop that connects all of the plazas and avenues in the city.*

STEP
5 ▶ Explore the avenues and plazas

Autumnal Avenue is right near the Lysandre Café and features many intriguing shops and cafés, as do Lumiose City's other three avenues. Plazas lie between the avenues, and you can discover a few more interesting shops in the narrow alleys that connect the plazas with the avenues and the city's outer ring. Spend some time exploring these side streets and seeing all they have to offer.

TIPS

Speak to everyone you meet for valuable gossip and information. Some residents might even give you special gifts—such as the kid in Autumnal Avenue's Poké Ball Boutique.

Don't forget to talk to Roller Skaters around town to learn new skate tricks: the parallel swizzle, drift-and-dash, backflip, and the 360. You may already have learned some of the tricks by yourself, but it's nice to chat with fellow Roller Skaters!

Now that you've been diligently farming your Berries, you should have plenty to use at the Juice Shoppe. Have the young lady make you fresh juices each day to help your Pokémon grow stronger.

You may want to seek out Mr. Bonding (p. 225) before you go on a real shopping spree. He will grant you Bargain Power on this visit, which gives you a special discount when you shop!

Avenue Shops and Destinations

Vernal Avenue

- Boutique Couture
- Café Classe
- Café Woof
- Friseur Furfrou
- Herboriste
- Stone Emporium

Estival Avenue

- Café Gallant
- Café Rouleau
- Loto-ID Center
- Lumiose Press

Autumnal Avenue

- Café Pokémon-Amie
- Juice Shoppe
- Poké Ball Boutique
- Restaurant Le Yeah

Hibernal Avenue

- Café Kizuna
- Restaurant Le Wow

Plaza Shops and Destinations
(includes connecting alleys)

Bleu Plaza
- (Nothing)

Jaune Plaza
- Trevor's house

Magenta Plaza
- Lysandre Café
- Pokémon Center

Rouge Plaza
- Sushi High Roller
- Vacant Storefront

Vert Plaza
- Café Cyclone

STEP
6 ▶ Seek out city battles

While exploring Lumiose City's many nooks and crannies, keep an eye out for Trainers standing in narrow alleys. These Trainers will be happy to battle you right there in the city if you talk to them. Test your skills against these tough customers, and revisit a Pokémon Center to rest up as often as needed.

TIP *Can't get enough battling? Visit the restaurants around Lumiose City to participate in a challenging series of special battles, like Double and Triple Battles. You'll find the restaurants on South Boulevard, Autumnal Avenue, Hibernal Avenue, and in an alley off Rouge Plaza. The more stars a restaurant has, the harder it will be to tackle. In fact, the most exclusive restaurants won't let anyone less than a Champion in! See the Trainer's Handbook section (p. 28) for tips and info on all battle types.*

STEP
7 ▶ Swing down to South Boulevard

Hello! Welcome to the Lumiose Transportation Office. ▼

South Boulevard is still rocking the same shops as before, but you may be able to enjoy them more fully now. Why not make a circuit and see?

Plus, you can now explore Estival Avenue, which features a number of shops and cafés that were blocked off on your first visit to Lumiose.

TIP *The Lumiose Transportation Office on South Boulevard offers information about various transportation options in Lumiose City. Just talk to the receptionist to learn how they work.*

South Boulevard Shops and Destinations

- Café Introversion
- Café Soleil
- Coiffure Clips
- Lumiose Transportation Office

- Pokémon Center
- PR Video Studio
- Restaurant Le Nah
- Route 4 Gate
- Route 5 Gate

- Shutterbug Café
- Sycamore Pokémon Lab
- Office buildings ×2

STEP 8 Hail a taxi to get around quickly

There's no need to journey around Lumiose City on foot. Now that the blackout has been resolved, the Lumi Cabs are up and running again! And you can still use the Gogoat Shuttle when you're low on cash.

- Lumi Cabs can take you directly to many spots in the city, but they can be expensive, depending on how far you need to travel. Talk to any cab driver to view a full list of destinations. They'll get cheaper the more stylish you become.

- Gogoat Shuttles are fun and affordable, but they'll only take you to a handful of stops around North and South Boulevards. Inspect a Gogoat signpost to see where you can go from that stop.

TIP *Don't have the cash to pay for your cab? The driver won't take that too kindly and he'll challenge you to a Pokémon battle! If you win, you may be able to get a free ride out of it—but if you lose, you may just get a one-way trip to the nearest Pokémon Center.*

STEP 9 Explore North Boulevard

North Boulevard features many interesting destinations, including the Lumiose Museum, Hotel Richissime, and the Battle Institute. There are some cool things to do up here, and the following steps tell you what you need to know about all of them.

North Boulevard Shops and Destinations

- Battle Institute
- Café Action!
- Café Bataille
- Café Triste
- Café Ultimo
- Hotel Richissime
- Lumiose Galette Stand
- Lumiose Museum
- Lumiose Station
- Pokémon Center
- Route 13 Gate
- Route 14 Gate
- Route 16 Gate
- Office buildings ×3

STEP 10 Stop at the Galette Stand

Speak to the girl who tends the small stand at North Boulevard's west end, and she'll offer to sell you Lumiose Galettes for just 100 per treat. These tasty snacks will heal all of a Pokémon's status conditions, making them a fantastic bargain. They sometimes sell out because of this, so hit the stand right after a fresh batch is baked—at 9:00 A.M., 3:00 P.M., and 9:00 P.M.

STEP 11 Visit the Lumiose Museum

The Lumiose Museum is a monument to fine art and culture. Some of the most impressive works from around the regions are displayed here. Pay a small fee, and you'll be treated to descriptions of each work as you explore the museum. Be sure to speak to all of the people here, because one of them will give you TM82 Dragon Tail.

STEP 12 Gawk at Hotel Richissime

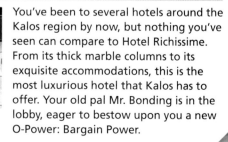

You've been to several hotels around the Kalos region by now, but nothing you've seen can compare to Hotel Richissime. From its thick marble columns to its exquisite accommodations, this is the most luxurious hotel that Kalos has to offer. Your old pal Mr. Bonding is in the lobby, eager to bestow upon you a new O-Power: Bargain Power.

STEP
13 Try some part-time work

A place as big as Hotel Richissime can always use a little extra help. Speak to the receptionist, and she'll offer to hire you for some part-time work. You can perform three part-time jobs each day, and the better your performance, the more prize money you'll make.

Room service: Remember every detail of the order(s) and relay them back to the kitchen staff.

Making beds: Race around one of the hotel's floors and make every bed as fast as you can.

Lost and found: Carefully search the room for the missing item(s). You can't see them, so go slow and press Ⓐ to search after every step. Do your best not to accidentally crush what you're looking for!

TIP *Be prepared to spend lots of prize money if you check into Hotel Richissime. Sure, it's a gorgeous place and all, but your Pokémon can get healthy at any of Lumiose City's three Pokémon Centers.*

STEP
14 Score a TM on the hotel's top floor

Take the elevator up to Hotel Richissime's top floor, and speak to the Lady in one of the suites' lavish bathrooms. She's thrilled at hearing the sound of her own voice echo off the bathroom walls and gives you TM49 Echo Voice as a present just for stopping by.

TIP *Did you swing by Autumnal Avenue opposite the Galette Stand yet? You'll find the Poké Ball Boutique there. If you talk to a young Schoolgirl inside, she will give you some special Poké Balls. You can also get juices made at the Juice Shoppe, which will make your Pokémon friendlier or stronger!*

STEP
15 Visit office buildings

I'm sure someone like you could use this Prism Scale and really accessorize!

North Boulevard features three unmarked buildings along its path. There isn't much to do in the west building due to a photo shoot that's taking place. If you visit the middle office building and ride the elevator up to the second floor, you'll meet an unusual character. Speak to the child on the east office building's top floor, and you'll receive a Prism Scale to help you accessorize.

> **TIP** *Show off a Pokémon with the Aroma Veil, Flower Veil, or Sweet Veil Ability to a Scientist in the lobby of an unmarked building, and you will get a Star Piece. The Fighting Dojo has also set up shop in one of these buildings! Can you find it—and the handy items awaiting you there?*

STEP
16 Check out the Battle Institute and Lumiose Station

It's probably still too early for you to try any of the Battle Tests here.

You can't do much at the Battle Institute or Lumiose Station yet, but it's worth having a look at them. The Battle Institute is a place where a Champion can put his or her battling skills to the ultimate test, but you need to become the Champion of the Kalos region before you can utilize it. Lumiose Station's high-speed trains can whisk travelers away to a distant city, but they aren't in service at the moment.

STEP
17 Go to Centrico Plaza and enter Prism Tower

Prism Tower is the very symbol of Lumiose City, and it doubles as the city's Pokémon Gym. Gym Leader Clemont, the genius inventor of the Super Training system (among other things), awaits all visitors at the tower's top. This is the most challenging Pokémon Gym you've faced to date, so be ready for some shocking clashes!

Lumiose City Gym Battle

Gym Battle Tips

✓ Bring lots of items that heal status conditions, like Lumiose Galettes
✓ Use Ground-type Pokémon to nullify the effects of Electric-type moves
✓ Use Ice- or Rock-type moves against Emolga

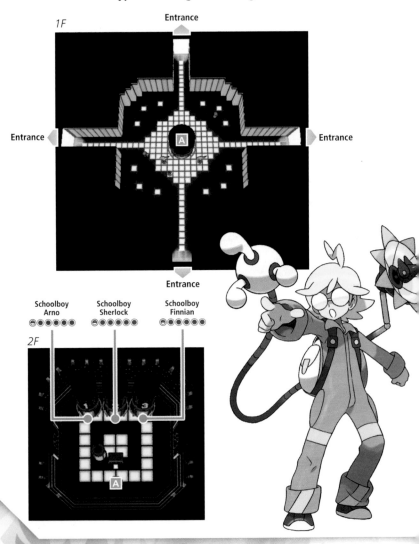

1F

Entrance

Entrance

Entrance

Entrance

Schoolboy
Arno

Schoolboy
Sherlock

Schoolboy
Finnian

2F

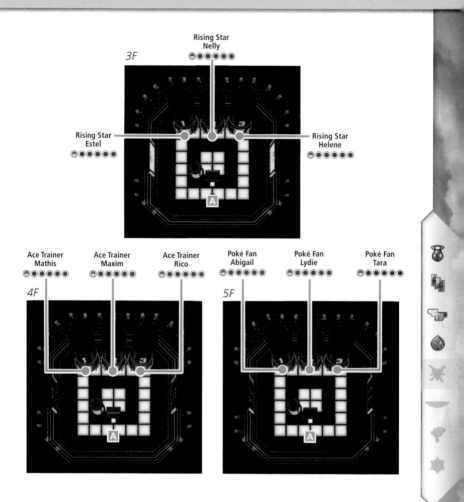

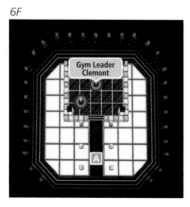

Lumiose City Gym Leader

Clemont

Electric-type Pokémon User

Use Ground-type moves to deal massive damage

Prism Tower features six floors, and you must climb them one by one. On each floor, Gym Leader Clemont's little sister, Bonnie, will quiz you about Pokémon. Give the right answer, and you'll be free to move up to the next floor—after a battle, of course. For each wrong answer, you'll have to face additional Trainers on your way to the big showdown. Depending on your knowledge of Pokémon, you may face anywhere from four to 12 Trainers before at last reaching Leader Clemont. If you're in a rush, the correct answers to each of Bonnie's questions are on the bottom of the page.

Clemont is a tough customer, bringing three powerful Pokémon against you. His first, Emolga, has the Volt Switch move, which lets it deal damage and then switch out for another of Clemont's Pokémon in one smooth maneuver. Ground-type Pokémon are your best options in this battle due to their natural resistance to Electric-type moves, but be aware that Ground-type moves won't affect Clemont's first Pokémon, Emolga. A Ground- and Rock-type Pokémon, like Geodude or Rhyhorn will serve you well against it. Did you catch any along Route 13 or in Glittering Cave?

Clemont's Pokémon

Emolga
♂ Lv. 35 `Electric` `Flying`
Weak to: `Ice` `Rock`

Magneton
Lv. 35 `Electric` `Steel`
Weak to: `4x!` `Ground` `Fire` `Fighting`

Heliolisk
♂ Lv. 37 `Electric` `Normal`
Weak to: `Fighting` `Ground`

 Voltage Badge

Pokémon up to Lv. 70, including those received in trades, will obey you.

TM **TM24 Thunderbolt**

A strong electric blast crashes down on the target. This may also leave the target with paralysis.

The answers to the quizzes are: Pikachu (#3), Fletchling (#1), Panpour (#3), Vivillon (#2)

STEP 18 — Now that you have the Voltage Badge, get a Holo Clip from Professor Sycamore and arrange a meeting

I wanted to talk to you for a little bit. Could you come to Lysandre Café?

As you exit Prism Tower, Voltage Badge in hand, you'll receive a Holo Clip from Professor Sycamore. He invites you to meet him at Lysandre Café, located in the alley between Magenta Plaza and Autumnal Avenue, not far from the Pokémon Center. Use a Lumi Cab to locate Lysandre Café if you're having trouble finding it on foot.

STEP 19 — Visit Lysandre Café and receive a King's Rock

I would like to congratulate you as well.

When you arrive at Lysandre Café, Professor Sycamore and Lysandre are discussing Mega Evolution. Lysandre goes into more detail about his passion for beauty, and he reveals that he is related to a powerful king who ruled Kalos 3,000 years ago. Professor Sycamore thinks Lysandre is a great man, and Lysandre gives you a valuable King's Rock before taking his leave.

STEP 20 — Receive a Holo Clip from Trevor and head for Route 14

I just wanted to let you know we're all going to meet on Route 14.

Trevor contacts you via the Holo Caster after you exit the café. He and the rest of your friends are planning to meet at Route 14. There's lots more adventure to be had in the Kalos region, so visit a Pokémon Center and rest your Pokémon before setting off for Route 14. Since you have five Gym Badges now, you can buy Full Restores at any Pokémon Center. A Full Restore is a medicine that can fully restore the HP of a single Pokémon and heal any status conditions it has. What a wonderful medicine!

The lush trees and boggy swamps of this trail give off an eerie vibe, even in broad daylight.

Route 14 (Laverre Nature Trail)

Route 14 is a long, foreboding path filled with wild Pokémon. It stretches between Lumiose City to the south and Laverre City to the north. Along with the trail's thick, murky marshes, a playground and a spooky house are the route's most notable features.

Field Moves Needed

Cut Surf

Laverre City

Scary House

Roseli Berry tree

Fairy Tale Girl Imogen

Pokémon Ranger Reed

Hex Maniac Anina

Pokémon Ranger Nash

Pokémon Ranger Melina

Lumiose City

Items
- ❏ Big Mushroom
- ❏ Cleanse Tag
- ❏ Damp Rock
- ❏ Hyper Potion
- ❏ Rare Candy
- ❏ Roseli Berry
- ❏ Spell Tag
- ❏ TM06 Toxic
- ❏ TM61 Will-O-Wisp

Hidden Items
- ❏ Revive
- ❏ Super Potion
- ❏ Tiny Mushroom

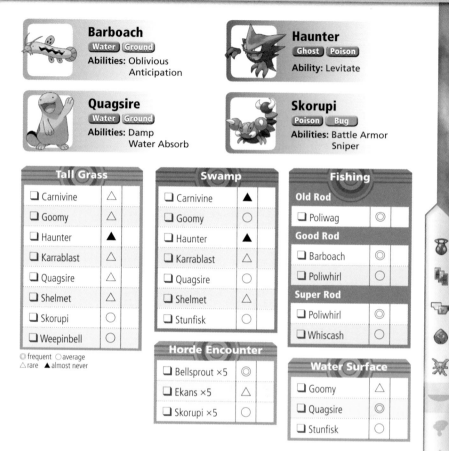

Barboach
Water Ground
Abilities: Oblivious
Anticipation

Haunter
Ghost Poison
Ability: Levitate

Quagsire
Water Ground
Abilities: Damp
Water Absorb

Skorupi
Poison Bug
Abilities: Battle Armor
Sniper

Tall Grass		
❑ Carnivine	△	
❑ Goomy	△	
❑ Haunter	▲	
❑ Karrablast	△	
❑ Quagsire	△	
❑ Shelmet	△	
❑ Skorupi	○	
❑ Weepinbell	○	

◎ frequent ○ average
△ rare ▲ almost never

Swamp		
❑ Carnivine	▲	
❑ Goomy	○	
❑ Haunter	▲	
❑ Karrablast	△	
❑ Quagsire	○	
❑ Shelmet	△	
❑ Stunfisk	○	

Horde Encounter		
❑ Bellsprout ×5	◎	
❑ Ekans ×5	△	
❑ Skorupi ×5	○	

Fishing		
Old Rod		
❑ Poliwag	◎	
Good Rod		
❑ Barboach	◎	
❑ Poliwhirl	○	
Super Rod		
❑ Poliwhirl	◎	
❑ Whiscash	○	

Water Surface		
❑ Goomy	△	
❑ Quagsire	◎	
❑ Stunfisk	○	

STEP
1
Meet your friends and have a battle with Serena/Calem

Now it's my turn!

Trevor and Serena/Calem are waiting for you just outside the Lumiose City gate. Trevor wishes to compare his Mountain Kalos Pokédex with yours, while Serena/Calem wants to test you again in another friendly Pokémon battle.

TIP

Take the time to poke around this deserted playground before rushing ahead. The equipment is diverting, but there are also items to be found here.

Vs. Serena/Calem's Pokémon

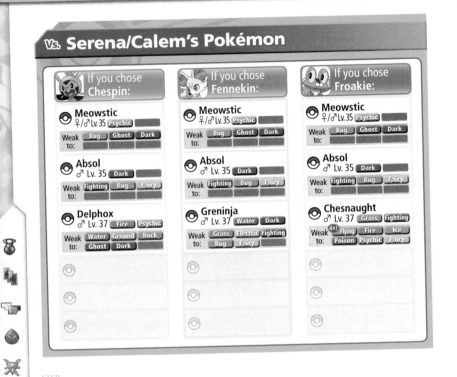

If you chose Chespin:

Meowstic
♀/♂ Lv. 35 `Psychic`
Weak to: `Bug` `Ghost` `Dark`

Absol
♂ Lv. 35 `Dark`
Weak to: `Fighting` `Bug` `Fairy`

Delphox
♂ Lv. 37 `Fire` `Psychic`
Weak to: `Water` `Ground` `Rock` `Ghost` `Dark`

If you chose Fennekin:

Meowstic
♀/♂ Lv. 35 `Psychic`
Weak to: `Bug` `Ghost` `Dark`

Absol
♂ Lv. 35 `Dark`
Weak to: `Fighting` `Bug` `Fairy`

Greninja
♂ Lv. 37 `Water` `Dark`
Weak to: `Grass` `Electric` `Fighting` `Bug` `Fairy`

If you chose Froakie:

Meowstic
♀/♂ Lv. 35 `Psychic`
Weak to: `Bug` `Ghost` `Dark`

Absol
♂ Lv. 35 `Dark`
Weak to: `Fighting` `Bug` `Fairy`

Chesnaught
♂ Lv. 37 `Grass` `Fighting`
Weak to: `4x!` `Flying` `Fire` `Ice` `Poison` `Psychic` `Fairy`

STEP 2 » Explore the forest

After the battle, your friends hurry off to check out a scary house that's rumored to be along this route. Begin exploring the area, searching for items with the Dowsing Machine and battling Trainers. Beware of the swamps, for you'll be drawn into battle against wild Pokémon while you explore the cheerless depths.

TIPS

Use the Surf field move to cross the deep swamp waters.

Get a TM from one of the Hex Maniacs lurking in the boggy swamp.

STEP
③ Check out the scary house, then head for Laverre City

And I saw the faint outline of a man huddling in the corner of the room.

As you near the route's north end, Shauna appears and tells you to follow her to the scary house. Inside, a very unusual man tells a spooky tale. Whether or not you tip the man afterward, you and your friends all hurry outside, eager to reach Laverre City. Finish exploring the forest on your way north to friendlier surroundings.

TIP *Make sure you collect all the items that lurk within the tall grass and boggy marshes. The paths branch and sinkholes in the swamp may try to deter you, but soldier on to find that Roseli Berry tree in the northeast corner! Roseli Berries are new to the Kalos region and if you give one to a Pokémon to hold, it will lessen the damage taken from a supereffective Fairy-type attack. Having one to hold might help keep your Fighting-, Dragon-, or Dark-type Pokémon in the game for more battles. It's also one of the ingredients used to make Ultra Rare Soda at the Juice Shoppe in Lumiose City, a special drink that will raise your Pokémon's level quite a bit!*

Laverre City

This small city features quaint homes that surround a massive tree. While it may not be what you'd call an ideal vacation spot, there's much for you to accomplish here—like learning battle-combo moves from the resident Move Tutor and earning your sixth Gym Badge.

Field Moves Needed

Poké Ball Factory

Pokémon Fan Club

Café

Laverre City Gym

Move Tutor's House

Boutique

Pokémon Center

Route 15 (to Dendemille Town)

Route 14 (to Lumiose City)

Poliwag

Water

Abilities: Water Absorb
Damp

Poliwhirl

Water

Abilities: Water Absorb
Damp

Items
❑ Effort Ribbon
❑ Ether
❑ Gengarite
❑ Poké Doll
❑ TM99 Dazzling Gleam
❑ TM41 Torment

Hidden Items
❑ Leaf Stone
❑ Tiny Mushroom
❑ Ultra Ball

Poké Mart	
Calcium	9,800
Carbos	9,800
HP Up	9,800
Iron	9,800
Protein	9,800
Zinc	9,800

Fishing		
Old Rod		
❑ Poliwag	◎	
Good Rod		
❑ Basculin (Blue-Striped Form)	◎	X
❑ Basculin (Red-Striped Form)	◎	Y
❑ Poliwhirl	○	
Super Rod		
❑ Basculin (Blue-Striped Form)	○	Y
❑ Basculin (Red-Striped Form)	○	X
❑ Poliwhirl	◎	

◎ frequent ○ average
△ rare ▲ almost never

STEP
1 Meet Mr. Bonding at the Pokémon Center

Let's get started, shall we?
It's bonding time!

Route 14 was a tough road to follow, so visit Laverre City's Pokémon Center to rest your weary Pokémon. Mr. Bonding is there and will grant you the Encounter Power O-Power if you take a moment to speak to him.

STEP
2 Show off large and tiny Pokémon for prizes

Tiny Pokémon are the most interesting!

One of Laverre City's youths will hand you TM41 Torment just for speaking with him, but two other locals aren't so easily impressed. They'll give you items only if you can show them Pokémon of certain requested sizes. One wants to see a really tiny Pokémon, while the other wants to see a really big one. Use the Pokémon Center's PC to put such Pokémon in your party, and then speak to these two again to receive a Poké Doll from each person. You can rack up more prizes from these two each day by showing them more Pokémon of extreme sizes.

STEP
③ **Show some effort, get a Ribbon**

Xavier received an Effort Ribbon!

Some friendly townsfolk want to give you things for free! The head of the Kalos region's Pokémon Fan Club will give you an Effort Ribbon if any of your Pokémon are Fully Trained Pokémon. If you haven't been using Super Training (p. 372), get on it or you might miss out on this Ribbon! The Pokémon Breeder in the same house can also tell you how friendly your Pokémon are toward you!

NOTE *Did you happen to see a Haunter on your way through Route 14? If you did, or if you've encountered any of the Pokémon in its evolutionary line, the Hex Maniac on the west side of town also has something to share with you.*

STEP
④ **Teach your Pokémon some battle-combo moves**

Yes
No

Want me to teach it a battle-combo move?

Visit the home of the Move Tutor in the house east of the Pokémon Gym, and he'll teach your Pokémon special battle-combo moves. These moves are extremely powerful, and they become even more impressive when used together on the same turn during Double or Triple Battles. The Move Tutor can teach these moves to the Pokémon that you receive from Pokémon Professors, like the first Pokémon partner you chose in Aquacorde Town and the Pokémon you received when you met Professor Sycamore for the first time in Lumiose City.

The First New Pokémon Type in 13 Years: Your Guide to the Fairy Type!

The last time that new types were added to the Pokémon series was the addition of Dark and Steel types in *Pokémon Gold Version* and *Pokémon Silver Version*. Now the Fairy type has arrived on the scene, giving a new type to some old favorites and helping to balance out the type matchups among Pokémon. The Dragon type had become a real powerhouse, and the Fairy type will be your best friend in taking Dragon-type Pokémon down! Continue reading for an analysis of the strengths and weaknesses of the new Fairy-type Pokémon!

Fairy types are super effective against Fighting, Dragon, and Dark types

These popular types can often deal great damage in battles, but it's probably not the best idea to bring them out against Fairy types! Fairies can be thought of as "light" and "magic" and everything that stands opposed to these powerful types, so Fairy-type attacks will pierce right through the defenses of Fighting-, Dragon-, and Dark-type Pokémon.

Fairy types are not very effective against Fire, Poison, and Steel types

Fairy types are weak to both Poison and Steel types, so it's not much of a surprise that their attacks do little damage to such opponents. Poison- and Steel-type Pokémon are good choices to face most Fairy-type Pokémon. Fire types will also take less damage from Fairy-type moves, and while they are not always super effective against Fairy types, Pokémon that may have more than one type—like Valerie's Mawile—will get a chance to show off how hot their fighting spirit burns.

Fairy types take massive damage from Poison and Steel types

Poison types may have been easy to overlook in past games. Although poisoning an opponent can be a great strategy and allows for continual damage from a single attack, until now Poison-type moves were only super effective against Grass-type Pokémon. But Poison is also super effective against Fairy types, so it's time to have fun with all of those venomous old favorites! It's also time to call on your steely-eyed comrades. The Steel type, super effective against Rock and Ice types, is now also super effective against Fairy types. In many cultures, it has been thought that magical creatures had a weakness to iron. Perhaps it's no wonder that the mystical Fairy type seems similarly weak to the cold, hard touch of Steel?

Fairy types take little damage from Fighting, Bug, and Dark types

Fighting-, Bug-, and Dark-type Pokémon will do little good for you in a battle against a pure Fairy-type Pokémon. Note that Dark types will also take supereffective damage from any Fairy-type attacks. You aren't guaranteed to lose with these types in your team, but there may be far better choices out there. However, don't forget about Pokémon with multiple types. A Grass- and Fairy-type Pokémon, for example, will take regular damage from a Bug-type move, due to Grass's weakness to the Bug type. Remember that each additional type will affect overall matchups!

Fairy types are immune to Dragon types

A pure Dragon-type Pokémon has to be one of the worst opponents to pitch against a Fairy-type Pokémon. Not only are Fairy types super effective against Dragon types, but they're also immune to Dragon-type attacks. That means that they have the potential to deal devastating attacks without taking any damage themselves. Keep this in mind when you're up against a Dragon-type user!

Laverre City Gym Battle

Gym Battle Tips

✓ Bring lots of items that recover HP and heal status conditions

✓ Use Fire-, Poison-, and Steel-type Pokémon

The Laverre City Gym has been built inside a massive tree that stands in the city's center. This tree is over 1,500 years old!

The Laverre City Gym is a dollhouse-like environment that can be tricky to navigate. There are nine rooms, and each features a number of warp panels. Step on these warp panels, and you'll be zipped around the various rooms. Some of the rooms contain Trainers, while others are empty.

In this fantastical dollhouse, the yellow warp panels that whisk you off to other rooms go both ways, so if you realize you've arrived someplace you don't wish to be, walk back onto the warp panel and you'll zip back to where you came from. Feeling overwhelmed? Here's a hint: whenever possible, use the warp panel on the right side of the room.

Furisode Girl
Katherine

Gym Leader
Valerie

Furisode Girl
Blossom

Furisode Girl
Kali

Entrance

Furisode Girl
Linnea

Laverre City Gym Leader
Valerie
Fairy-type Pokémon User

Use Fire-, Poison-, and Steel-type moves to deal massive damage

Like all of the Gym's Trainers, Valerie is a Fairy-type Pokémon user. This means that many of her Pokémon's moves are not very effective against Fire-, Poison-, and Steel-type Pokémon. In addition, Poison- and Steel-type moves are often super effective against her Pokémon—but Poison won't even touch her Mawile. Valerie favors a defensive approach, using moves that raise her Pokémon's Defense and Sp. Def stats over several turns. She also carries a couple of Hyper Potions that can quickly patch up her companions.

Valerie's Pokémon

Mawile
♀ Lv. 38 — Steel — Fairy
Weak to: Fire — Ground

Mr. Mime
♀ Lv. 39 — Psychic — Fairy
Weak to: Poison — Ghost — Steel

Sylveon
♂ Lv. 42 — Fairy
Weak to: Poison — Steel

vs Valerie

Fairy Badge
Pokémon up to Lv. 80, including those received in trades, will obey you.

TM99 Dazzling Gleam
The user damages opposing Pokémon by emitting a powerful flash.

The final green warp panel will only be unlocked after you defeat Gym Leader Valerie in battle. It will take you straight back to the entrance—and from there, it's probably back to the Pokémon Center to give your Pokémon some rest after such a hard-fought battle.

NOTE *Your sixth Gym Badge doesn't get you anything new at the Poké Marts, but it does prove to all that you've mastered competing against the new Fairy type!*

TIP *Are you having a tough time taking on those Fairy types? Don't forget that you've recently gotten your hands on a couple of items that can help you in these battles. The Black Sludge you picked up on Route 13 will help your Poison types recover HP, and the Roseli Berry you found on Route 14 will take the sting out of one supereffective Fairy-type move. Consider flying back to your Berry farm, though, to harvest some more before you use this one up. The wild Berry tree will produce another crop, but you'll have to wait a whole week.*

STEP 6 ▶ **With the new Fairy Badge in hand, travel north to the Poké Ball Factory**

Know what? We're going to go tour the Poké Ball Factory!

As you exit the Laverre City Gym, Shauna and Trevor greet you, eager to admire your latest Badge. They also tell you of their plan to tour the nearby Poké Ball Factory. What a great idea! Rest your Pokémon at the Pokémon Center before heading north to join your friends.

243

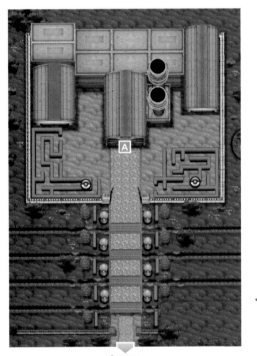

Poké Ball Factory

Have you ever wondered where all of those Poké Balls you've been throwing are made? Well, now you know! Every Poké Ball in the Kalos region is fashioned with painstaking care here at the Poké Ball Factory. Feel free to tour this wondrous place as long as you like—just don't expect to uncover any trade secrets!

Field Moves Needed

A

Laverre
City

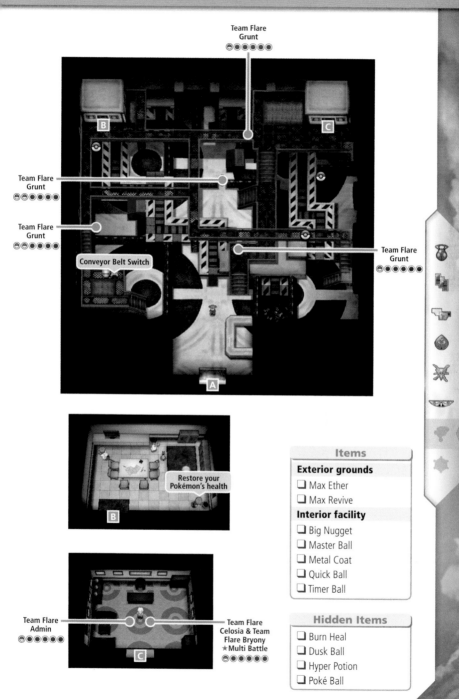

Team Flare Grunt
🅐🅐🅐🅐🅐🅐

Team Flare Grunt
🅐🅐🅐🅐🅐🅐

Team Flare Grunt
🅐🅐🅐🅐🅐🅐

Conveyor Belt Switch

B

C

Team Flare Grunt
🅐🅐🅐🅐🅐🅐

A

Restore your Pokémon's health

B

Team Flare Admin
🅐🅐🅐🅐🅐🅐

C

Team Flare Celosia & Team Flare Bryony
★Multi Battle
🅐🅐🅐🅐🅐🅐

Items
Exterior grounds
❑ Max Ether
❑ Max Revive
Interior facility
❑ Big Nugget
❑ Master Ball
❑ Metal Coat
❑ Quick Ball
❑ Timer Ball

Hidden Items
❑ Burn Heal
❑ Dusk Ball
❑ Hyper Potion
❑ Poké Ball

STEP 1 » Search the outer grounds

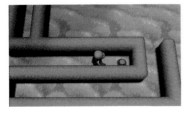

Trouble is brewing at the Poké Ball Factory... Team Flare is running amok! Shauna will create a distraction that lures the lone outdoor guard away from his post, giving you and Serena/Calem a chance to slip inside. Take a moment to search the outer grounds for valuables before entering the facility.

STEP 2 » Enter the Poké Ball Factory and confront Team Flare

I'll take care of this! You go on ahead!

You won't get far in the Poké Ball Factory before a Team Flare hooligan gets in your way. Fortunately Serena/Calem arrives and battles the Team Flare Grunt for you, letting you move on ahead. What a pal!

STEP 3 » Ride the conveyor belts around the factory

You must ride along the Poké Ball Factory's many conveyor belts in order to navigate around it. Run up the rust-colored ramps to reach the belts, and you'll ride along until you reach a stop. Get off at each stop to battle Team Flare Grunts and discover a few items that are stashed around the factory.

STEP 4 » Take a rest on the second floor

Both you and your Pokémon should take a nice rest for a while.

When you finally reach the stairs, go up and make your way to the northwest office. Speak to everyone inside, because a woman there will kindly offer to rest your Pokémon, restoring their HP and PP if they need it.

5 » Hit the switch to reach the northeast office

After resting your Pokémon, exit the northwest office and go south. Sprint downstairs to find a machine that controls the conveyor belts. Activate the machine to reverse the direction in which the belts are moving, and then continue downstairs and ride the belts over to a new staircase. Take the stairs up, and enter the northeast office to confront some of Team Flare's top brass.

STEP
6 » Battle the Team Flare Admin in the northeast office

Several high-ranking Team Flare members are harassing the president of the Poké Ball Factory in his office in the northeast corner of the factory. The Team Flare Admin challenges you first. Time for a fight!

Vs. Team Flare Admin's Pokémon

Scraggy ♀ Lv. 37 — Dark, Fighting
Weak to: Fairy, Fighting, Flying

Houndoom ♀ Lv. 38 — Dark, Fire
Weak to: Water, Fighting, Ground, Rock

STEP
7 » Join forces with Serena/Calem to defeat Celosia and Bryony

The Team Flare Admin's failure forces Team Flare's scientists Celosia and Bryony to get involved. It's two against one—but as luck would have it, Serena/Calem arrives just in time to help you turn the tide in an exciting Multi Battle!

Serena/Calem's Pokémon

If you chose Chespin:

Meowstic
♀/♂ Lv.37 Psychic
Weak to: Bug Ghost Dark

Delphox
♂ Lv.39 Fire Psychic
Weak to: Water Ground Rock Ghost Dark

Absol
♂ Lv.37 Dark
Weak to: Fighting Bug Fairy

If you chose Fennekin:

Meowstic
♀/♂ Lv.37 Psychic
Weak to: Bug Ghost Dark

Greninja
♂ Lv.39 Water Dark
Weak to: Grass Electric Fighting Bug Fairy

Absol
♂ Lv.37 Dark
Weak to: Fighting Bug Fairy

If you chose Froakie:

Meowstic
♀/♂ Lv.37 Psychic
Weak to: Bug Ghost Dark

Chesnaught
♂ Lv.39 Grass Fighting
Weak to: 4×! Flying Fire Ice Poison Psychic Fairy

Absol
♂ Lv.37 Dark
Weak to: Fighting Bug Fairy

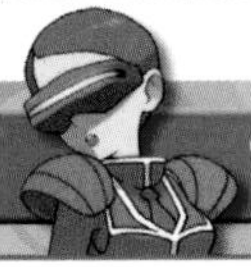

Vs. Team Flare Celosia's Pokémon

Manectric
♀ Lv.41 Electric
Weak to: Ground

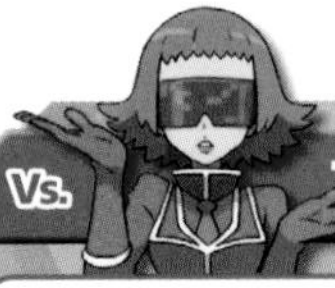

Vs. Team Flare Bryony's Pokémon

Liepard
♀ Lv.41 Dark
Weak to: Fighting Bug Fairy

STEP 8 ⟩⟩ Receive your just rewards

I'll give you a Master Ball or a Big Nugget.
Pick whichever one you'd like.

Master Ball
Big Nugget

Team Flare makes a tactical retreat after losing the Multi Battle, and the Poké Ball Factory's president couldn't be more pleased to be rid of his well-groomed guests. He asks you to choose between a Master Ball and a Big Nugget as your reward. However, it doesn't really matter which one you choose, because he generously decides to give you both items as a special bonus!

TIP *The Big Nugget can be sold for fast cash, while the Master Ball is the ultimate Poké Ball that always succeeds in capturing a wild Pokémon. This is the only Master Ball you are guaranteed to get, so use it wisely! You can try your hand at the Loto-ID Centre in Lumiose City for more Master Balls, but you'll have to be very lucky indeed to win the jackpot prize for one!*

STEP 9 ⟩⟩ Meet up with your friends and plan your next stop

According to the Town Map,
Dendemille Town is next...

Shauna, Trevor, and Tierno arrive as you head for the factory's exit. They've given the Team Flare guard the slip, and now they have their eyes set on visiting Dendemille Town to the east. Step outside and you'll receive a Holo Clip from the famous Holo Caster announcer, Malva. After catching up on your news, return to Laverre City and make a pit stop at the Pokémon Center before proceeding through the east gate to Route 15.

Route 15 (Brun Way)

Route 15 is a leaf-covered trail that runs between Laverre City and Dendemille Town. Route 16 is accessible to the south. You can find many valuables among Route 15's dense fallen leaves and crumbling ruins, though some of these items cannot be obtained until you've learned the Waterfall field move. That's not all that lurks beneath the brilliantly colored leaves, though...

Field Moves Needed

Rock Smash Strength
Surf Waterfall

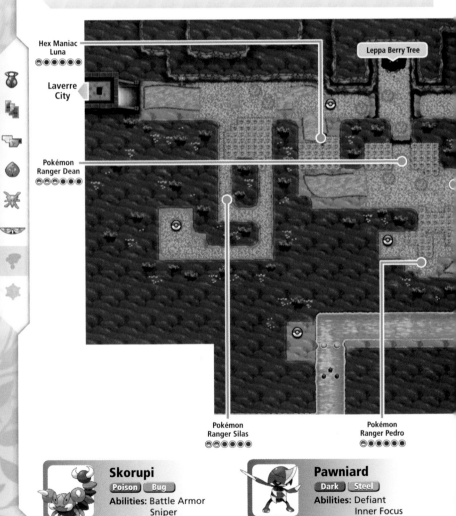

Hex Maniac Luna

Leppa Berry Tree

Laverre City

Pokémon Ranger Dean

Pokémon Ranger Silas

Pokémon Ranger Pedro

Skorupi

Poison Bug

Abilities: Battle Armor
Sniper

Pawniard

Dark Steel

Abilities: Defiant
Inner Focus

Hidden Items

First visit
- ❏ Antidote
- ❏ Pretty Wing
- ❏ Tiny Mushroom
- ❏ X Defense

After learning the Waterfall field move
- ❏ HP Up

Items

First visit
- ❏ Dire Hit
- ❏ Full Heal
- ❏ Leppa Berry
- ❏ Macho Brace
- ❏ Net Ball
- ❏ PP Up
- ❏ Protein
- ❏ Revive

After learning the Waterfall field move
- ❏ Stone Plate
- ❏ TM97 Dark Pulse

Pokémon Ranger Keith

Hex Maniac Carrie

Lost Hotel

Dendemille Town

Mysterious Sisters Rune & Rime
★Double Battle

Fairy Tale Girl Mahalyn

Route 16 (to Lumiose City)

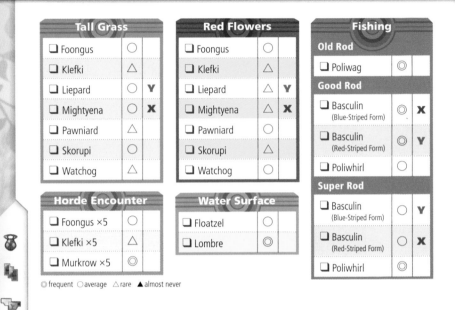

Tall Grass		
❑ Foongus	○	
❑ Klefki	△	
❑ Liepard	○	Y
❑ Mightyena	○	X
❑ Pawniard	△	
❑ Skorupi	○	
❑ Watchog	△	

Red Flowers		
❑ Foongus	○	
❑ Klefki	△	
❑ Liepard	△	Y
❑ Mightyena	△	X
❑ Pawniard	○	
❑ Skorupi	△	
❑ Watchog	○	

Fishing		
Old Rod		
❑ Poliwag	◎	
Good Rod		
❑ Basculin (Blue-Striped Form)	◎	X
❑ Basculin (Red-Striped Form)	◎	Y
❑ Poliwhirl	○	
Super Rod		
❑ Basculin (Blue-Striped Form)	○	Y
❑ Basculin (Red-Striped Form)	○	X
❑ Poliwhirl	◎	

Horde Encounter		
❑ Foongus ×5	○	
❑ Klefki ×5	△	
❑ Murkrow ×5	◎	

Water Surface		
❑ Floatzel	○	
❑ Lombre	◎	

◎ frequent ○ average △ rare ▲ almost never

STEP 1 ▶ Explore Route 15

SURPRISE!
I know you didn't invite me, but here I am! ▼

Route 15's dense fallen leaves hide many secrets. Run all around to scatter the leaf piles and discover lost items that have become buried. Be on your guard, however, for hidden Trainers will emerge from many a leaf pile!

> **TIP** *Use the Surf field move to cross Route 15's rivers and reach even more treats.*

STEP 2 ▶ Use Rock Smash to shatter cracked walls in the ruins

▶ Yes
No

Would you like to use Rock Smash?

As you near Route 15's east end, you'll begin to pass some old ruins. Use the Rock Smash move to shatter the ruins' cracked walls so you may explore them more thoroughly. Don't worry, no wild Pokémon will pop out!

STEP
3 See what Lysandre has to say

Do all people and Pokémon have such potential, or is it hidden within a chosen few?

As you cross the bridge on the east end of Route 15, you will receive a message from Lysandre on your Holo Caster. He has heavy topics weighing on his mind like usual, and this time he wonders whether all Pokémon—and all humans—carry the same potential within them. Are select Pokémon and humans really chosen for greatness? If so, what is their responsibility to the world?

STEP
4 Check out the Lost Hotel and Route 16

Before you go east into Dendemille Town, you may want to check out the Lost Hotel (p. 254) and Route 16 (p. 258). You don't have to visit them to move forward, but you'll find more items, Trainers, and Pokémon if you do. The Lost Hotel is accessible by descending the stairs within Route 15's east ruin, while the Strength field move is needed to shove the large boulder to the south and enter Route 16.

STEP
5 Continue on to Dendemille Town

Whether or not you choose to explore the Lost Hotel or Route 16, your next major destination is Dendemille Town (p. 262). That is where your friends have decided to head next. You might as well join them in checking it out because you'll have to pass through it to reach the next city. That city is where you'll find the next Pokémon Gym and where you can try to earn your seventh Gym Badge!

Lost Hotel

A group of wayward young people has taken over the basement of this once-inviting hotel. Now the place lies in ruins, with bookshelves overturned and trash strewn all about. While exploring the Lost Hotel is optional, you can partake in some worthy battles and discover some long-lost valuables here.

Field Moves Needed

Rock Smash

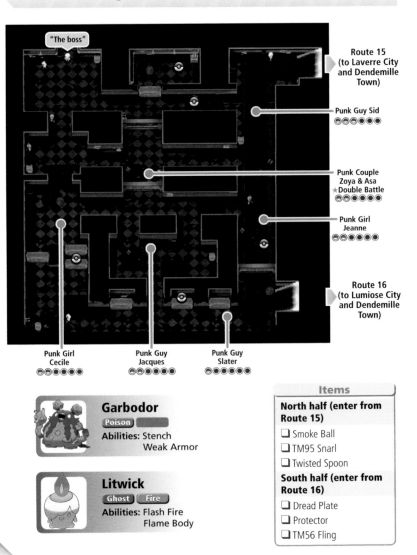

"The boss"

Route 15 (to Laverre City and Dendemille Town)

Punk Guy Sid
◕◕◕◔◔◔

Punk Couple Zoya & Asa
★Double Battle
◕◕◕◔◔◔

Punk Girl Jeanne
◕◕◕◔◔◔

Route 16 (to Lumiose City and Dendemille Town)

Punk Girl Cecile
◕◕◕◔◔◔

Punk Guy Jacques
◕◕◕◔◔◔

Punk Guy Slater
◕◕◔◔◔◔

Garbodor
Poison
Abilities: Stench
Weak Armor

Litwick
Ghost **Fire**
Abilities: Flash Fire
Flame Body

Items

North half (enter from Route 15)
❑ Smoke Ball
❑ TM95 Snarl
❑ Twisted Spoon

South half (enter from Route 16)
❑ Dread Plate
❑ Protector
❑ TM56 Fling

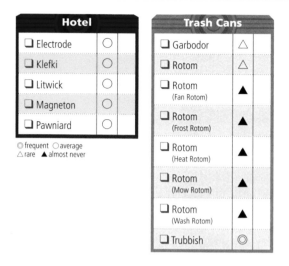

Hotel	
❑ Electrode	◯
❑ Klefki	◯
❑ Litwick	◯
❑ Magneton	◯
❑ Pawniard	◯

◎ frequent ◯ average
△ rare ▲ almost never

Trash Cans	
❑ Garbodor	△
❑ Rotom	△
❑ Rotom (Fan Rotom)	▲
❑ Rotom (Frost Rotom)	▲
❑ Rotom (Heat Rotom)	▲
❑ Rotom (Mow Rotom)	▲
❑ Rotom (Wash Rotom)	▲
❑ Trubbish	◎

STEP 1 » Explore the Lost Hotel

The Lost Hotel's basement is about what you'd expect: dark and dingy. Several Trainers will test your battle skills as you explore this uninviting place, and you'll also be pulled into random encounters with the wild Pokémon that dwell here.

TIP *If you're in a hurry, use Repels to avoid random encounters and hasten your exploration of the Lost Hotel.*

STEP 2 » Inspect shaking trash cans

Many of the Lost Hotel's green trash cans hold little of interest, but look closely and you might notice that some of them occasionally shake. Inspect a shaking trash can to initiate battle against some curious wild Pokémon. The smell might be a bit on the strong side, but try to catch these different Pokémon so you can add their data to your Pokédex.

It seems that the Pokémon that appear might vary by the day of the week. Try checking these shaking trash cans on Tuesdays and you might find a rare form of Rotom!

STEP
3 Show off your roller skating skills

What d'you think you're wearing? You ain't got no sense of style.

Make your way to the Lost Hotel's northwest corner, and a Punk Guy guard will stop you in your tracks. Impress him with your awesome Roller Skate tricks. If you've learned the backflip and the 360, you'll be cool enough to get in—no matter what you're wearing. If your current Roller Skate technique doesn't pass muster, then you won't be allowed to proceed north and meet "the boss." Fly back to Lumiose City and learn all of the Roller Skate tricks if you want to meet this mysterious stranger!

NOTE *Lost on where to learn these awesome tricks? Go to page 398 to find a complete list of all the Roller Skate tricks and where you might find the Roller Skaters who can tell you about them.*

STEP
4 Talk with the boss

If you know the backflip and the 360, the Punk Guy guard will let you pass. Now you can talk to the boss and also discover a few more valuable items around the Lost Hotel's north end, including TM95 Snarl. Speak to the mysterious head honcho to learn that he has been waiting for an individual who was born into this world for the great purpose of beautiful skating. Yes, you're the one! The boss believes that you'll be able to learn an extremely difficult trick called the cosmic flip, and kindly teaches it to you.

STEP
5 Onward to Route 16 or Dendemille Town

Once you've seen everything this half of the Lost Hotel has to offer, emerge out of the dark and get a lungful of fresh air up on Route 15. From here you'll be able to choose to continue onward to Dendemille Town (p. 262) to give your Pokémon a bit of a rest at the Pokémon Center, or continue south onto Route 16 (p. 258) for a bit more adventure. That's where you'll find the other entrance to the Lost Hotel, if you wish to explore its southern half.

AFTER VISITING ROUTE 16:
✿ Explore the Lost Hotel's southern half

The Lost Hotel's basement has two entrances, and you must use its southern entrance to explore its southern half. The southern entry is found in the ruin near Route 16's northeast end, not far from the boulder that requires you to use the Strength field move to shove it aside. Visit Route 16 and reenter the Lost Hotel via its southern entrance to probe its southern rooms and hallways, where more Trainers and items can be found.

Talk to the Roller Skater down south and you won't learn any more tricks, but you will pick up another TM for your collection!

Route 16 (Mélancolie Path)

If you're up for a little fishing, surfing, and romping through some very tall grass, then this is the route for you. Exploring Route 16 is purely optional, but you'll find a wide variety of wild Pokémon here. Just make sure you've got plenty of field moves at the ready!

Field Moves Needed

Cut Strength

Surf Waterfall

Items

- ❑ Dive Ball ×21
- ❑ Fist Plate
- ❑ Lum Berry
- ❑ Max Potion
- ❑ Rare Candy
- ❑ Super Rod

Hidden Items

- ❑ Big Mushroom
- ❑ Max Revive
- ❑ Rare Candy
- ❑ Repel

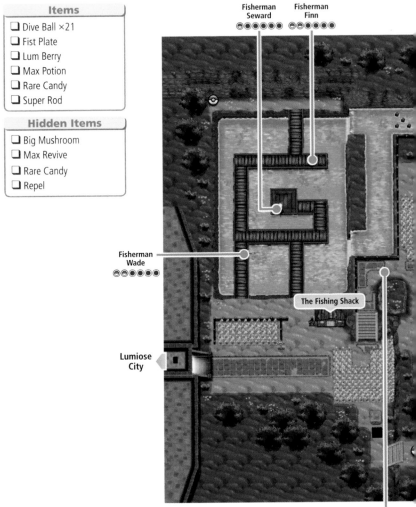

Fisherman Seward

Fisherman Finn

Fisherman Wade

The Fishing Shack

Lumiose City

Fairy Tale Girl Alice

Lombre
Water Grass
Abilities: Swift Swim
Rain Dish

Foongus
Grass Poison
Ability: Effect Spore

Murkrow
Dark Flying
Abilities: Insomnia
Super Luck

Pumpkaboo
Ghost Grass
Abilities: Pickup
Frisk

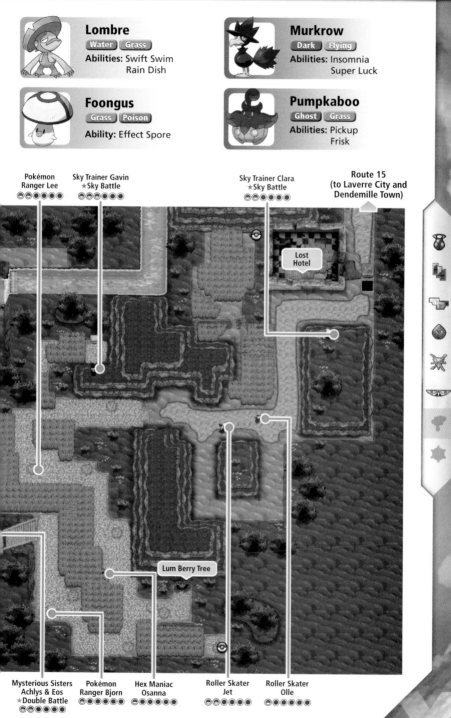

Pokémon
Ranger Lee

Sky Trainer Gavin
★Sky Battle

Sky Trainer Clara
★Sky Battle

Route 15
(to Laverre City and
Dendemille Town)

Lost
Hotel

Lum Berry Tree

Mysterious Sisters
Achlys & Eos
★Double Battle

Pokémon
Ranger Bjorn

Hex Maniac
Osanna

Roller Skater
Jet

Roller Skater
Olle

259

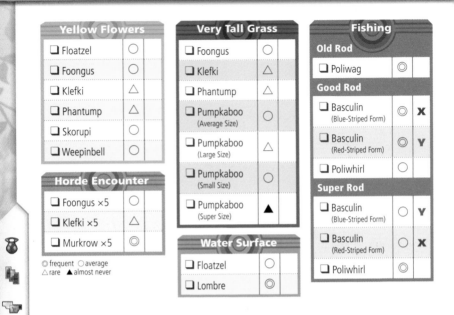

Yellow Flowers

❏ Floatzel	○
❏ Foongus	○
❏ Klefki	△
❏ Phantump	△
❏ Skorupi	○
❏ Weepinbell	○

Horde Encounter

❏ Foongus ×5	○
❏ Klefki ×5	△
❏ Murkrow ×5	◎

◎ frequent ○ average
△ rare ▲ almost never

Very Tall Grass

❏ Foongus	○
❏ Klefki	△
❏ Phantump	△
❏ Pumpkaboo (Average Size)	○
❏ Pumpkaboo (Large Size)	△
❏ Pumpkaboo (Small Size)	○
❏ Pumpkaboo (Super Size)	▲

Water Surface

❏ Floatzel	○
❏ Lombre	◎

Fishing

Old Rod

❏ Poliwag	◎	

Good Rod

❏ Basculin (Blue-Striped Form)	◎	X
❏ Basculin (Red-Striped Form)	◎	Y
❏ Poliwhirl	○	

Super Rod

❏ Basculin (Blue-Striped Form)	○	Y
❏ Basculin (Red-Striped Form)	○	X
❏ Poliwhirl	◎	

STEP
1 » Explore Route 16

Don't you underestimate us!

This large trail is similar in many ways to Route 15. Here you'll find more fallen leaves that hide items and Trainers, along with very tall grass that wild Pokémon just love to frolic in.

TIP *After you've acquired the Waterfall field move, use it to scale Route 16's north waterfall, and then surf the river back to Route 15 to discover a super-secret TM.*

STEP
2 » Revisit the Lost Hotel

Explore Route 16's northern ruin to discover another entrance to the Lost Hotel. Use this entry to visit the Lost Hotel's southern half, where you'll be sure to find more Trainers and more loot.

STEP
③ Take part in some Sky Battles

It's time to get your head out of the grass and look to the sky again! Two Sky Trainers await you on Route 16, one at the north end near the entrance to the Lost Hotel and the other in the middle of the route. If you're up to taking them both on now, the sky's your limit! But if your flying or levitating Pokémon aren't up to the challenge just now, remember to come back after resting your team in either Lumiose City to the west or Dendemille Town to the east.

STEP
④ Obtain the Super Rod

Make your way west toward Lumiose City, and you'll find Route 16's tranquil docks and the fishing shack. Enter the fishing shack to receive a Super Rod from a friendly Fisherman. Another Fisherman in the shack will give you a whopping 20 Dive Balls if you can manage to hook more than seven Pokémon in a row while fishing. It isn't easy, but with the Super Rod, you can make this happen!

NOTE *Your consecutive-fishing combo is broken whenever you cast and fail to catch anything. If you want to reel in those Dive Balls, find a good spot where the Pokémon are really biting!*

STEP
⑤ Return to Route 15 and go east to Dendemille Town

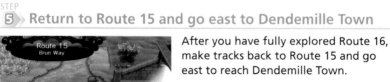

After you have fully explored Route 16, make tracks back to Route 15 and go east to reach Dendemille Town.

Dendemille Town

Soft flakes of gently falling snow fill the brisk air in this quiet mountain town. Here you'll find the warm haven of a Pokémon Center, along with two very handy people to know: Madam Reminder and the Move Deleter.

Field Moves Needed

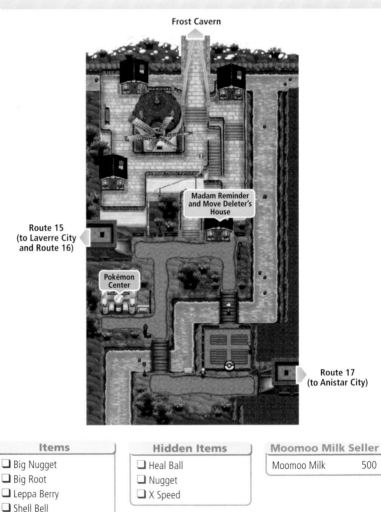

Frost Cavern

Madam Reminder and Move Deleter's House

Route 15 (to Laverre City and Route 16)

Pokémon Center

Route 17 (to Anistar City)

Items
❑ Big Nugget
❑ Big Root
❑ Leppa Berry
❑ Shell Bell
❑ Sitrus Berry
❑ TM42 Facade

Hidden Items
❑ Heal Ball
❑ Nugget
❑ X Speed

Moomoo Milk Seller	
Moomoo Milk	500

1 » Have a chat with Professor Sycamore and Dexio

Professor Sycamore and his faithful assistant, Dexio, catch up to you as you enter Dendemille Town. The good professor imparts information regarding the Kalos region's Legendary Pokémon. Depending on the version of the game you're playing, this will be either Xerneas (*Pokémon X*) or Yveltal (*Pokémon Y*).

2 » Purchase some Moomoo Milk

Go south to reach the Pokémon Center, but before you enter, speak to the Hex Maniac outside, who sells Moomoo Milk at 500 per bottle. This nutritious beverage is a bargain compared to other HP-restoring items that can be purchased at the Poké Mart, so consider stocking up.

3 » Meet Mr. Bonding at the Pokémon Center

Your old pal Mr. Bonding is hanging out at the local Pokémon Center. Talk to him to be awarded the O-Power Accuracy Power. Another generous person inside the Pokémon Center will give you a Sitrus Berry. Rest your Pokémon here and visit the Poké Mart before stepping back outside.

4 » Learn about Madam Reminder's special talent

Enter the house that lies north of Dendemille Town's crop field to chat with a warmhearted old woman known as Madam Reminder. For the price of just one Heart Scale, this kindly woman will help your Pokémon recall a move that it's forgotten over the course of the adventure. This comes in handy at times when you've instructed your Pokémon to forget a move that in retrospect was quite helpful.

5 » Meet the Move Deleter

Conveniently, a forgetful old fellow called the Move Deleter also lives in the same house as Madam Reminder. Though this gentleman's mind isn't what it used to be, he can still recall how to help your Pokémon forget any of the moves that they currently know. This helps to make room for new moves that you wish your Pokémon to remember with the aid of Madam Reminder. Forgetting moves with the help of the Move Deleter is a free service—no Heart Scales needed!

TIP *Do you need more Heart Scales to remember all those moves you've made space for? They can be found in the field by smashing cracked rocks, so Fly back to a city near an area that is full of such rocks, like Route 8, and get ready to Rock Smash!*

STEP
6 » Have your Mountain Kalos Pokédex rated

Continue up the cobbled street that winds around the town's famous windmill. The Monsieur in the next house is interested in seeing how many Pokémon you've recorded in your Mountain Kalos Pokédex. If your Mountain Kalos Pokédex has registered 70 or more Pokémon, the man will reward you with a Shell Bell!

STEP
7 » Show off your gigantic Gourgeist

If you caught a rare Pumpkaboo (Super Size) along Route 16 and evolved it to Gourgeist, the Preschooler in the next house will reward you well. No one believes him when he claims to have seen such a huge specimen of Gourgeist, and he's so glad you've proved him right that he gives you a Big Nugget! Big Nuggets sell for big bucks at the Poké Mart, so make every effort to show the kid what he wants to see.

STEP
⑧ Receive a Leppa Berry and TM42 Facade

In yet another of Dendemille Town's humble homes, an Ace Trainer will give you a Leppa Berry if you show her a certain TM. The TM she asks you to show her changes daily. So get a lot of TMs and visit her every day. Speak to the Youngster in this same house to receive the excellent TM42 Facade.

STEP
⑨ Go north and investigate the Frost Cavern

Route 17 leads to Anistar City, but the route is completely covered in heaps of snow. A friendly Pokémon named Mamoswine is usually happy to help people pass through Route 17, but this Mamoswine is distracted by some sort of disturbance at the nearby Frost Cavern. You'd better head up north and see if you can find out what is going on if you ever hope to continue on to get your next Gym Badge!

AFTER CLEARING THE FROST CAVERN:
⊙ Continue east to Route 17

Return to Dendemille Town after setting things right at the Frost Cavern. It's probably a good idea to stop at the Pokémon Center to heal your team and pick up some items before heading east to Route 17 (p. 273). Anistar City is just ahead!

Frost Cavern

This frigid cavern is crawling with wild Pokémon and a wide variety of hardened Trainers. Something is amiss here, and only a thorough exploration of the Frost Cavern's icy depths will lead to the clues you need.

Field Moves Needed
Surf   Waterfall

Outside

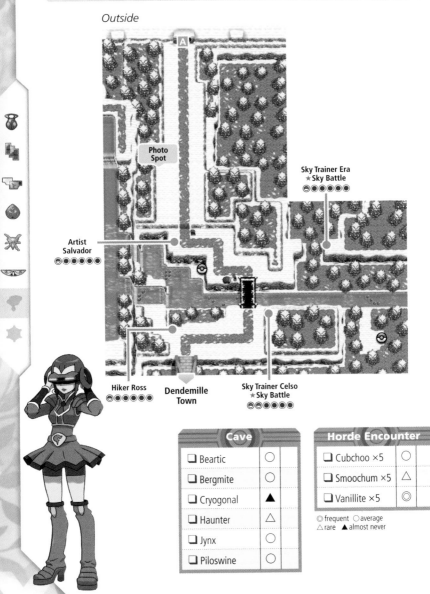

Photo Spot

Sky Trainer Era
★ Sky Battle

Artist Salvador

Hiker Ross   Dendemille Town   Sky Trainer Celso ★ Sky Battle

Cave	
❏ Beartic	○
❏ Bergmite	○
❏ Cryogonal	▲
❏ Haunter	△
❏ Jynx	○
❏ Piloswine	○

Horde Encounter	
❏ Cubchoo ×5	○
❏ Smoochum ×5	△
❏ Vanillite ×5	◎

◎ frequent ○ average
△ rare ▲ almost never

266

1F

Hiker Alain
◎◎◎◎◎◎

Ace Trainer
Cordelia
◎◎◎◎◎◎

Ace Trainer Neil
◎◎◎◎◎◎

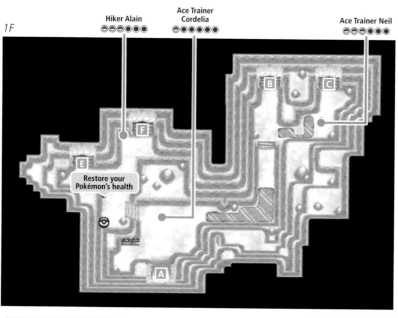

Restore your
Pokémon's health

Fishing

Old Rod

| ❑ Poliwag | ◎ | |

Good Rod

❑ Basculin (Blue-Striped Form)	◎	X
❑ Basculin (Red-Striped Form)	◎	Y
❑ Poliwhirl	○	

Super Rod

❑ Basculin (Blue-Striped Form)	○	Y
❑ Basculin (Red-Striped Form)	○	X
❑ Poliwhirl	◎	

Water Surface

| ❑ Floatzel | ○ | |
| ❑ Lombre | ◎ | |

Items

Outside
After learning the Waterfall field move
- ❑ Heart Scale
- ❑ TM71 Stone Edge

First floor
- ❑ Hyper Potion
- ❑ Icy Rock

Second floor
- ❑ Ice Heal
- ❑ Max Repel
- ❑ Never-Melt Ice
- ❑ TM79 Frost Breath

Third floor
- ❑ Abomasite
- ❑ Ether
- ❑ Zinc

Hidden Items

Outside
- ❑ Escape Rope
- ❑ X Sp. Def

First floor
- ❑ Dusk Ball
- ❑ Ice Heal

Second floor
- ❑ Dire Hit
- ❑ Ice Heal
- ❑ Pearl
- ❑ Super Potion

Third floor
- ❑ Elixir
- ❑ PP Up

Beartic
`Ice`

Ability: Snow Cloak

Jynx
`Ice` `Psychic`

Abilities: Oblivious
Forewarn

Cryogonal
`Ice`

Ability: Levitate

Piloswine
`Ice` `Ground`

Abilities: Oblivious
Snow Cloak

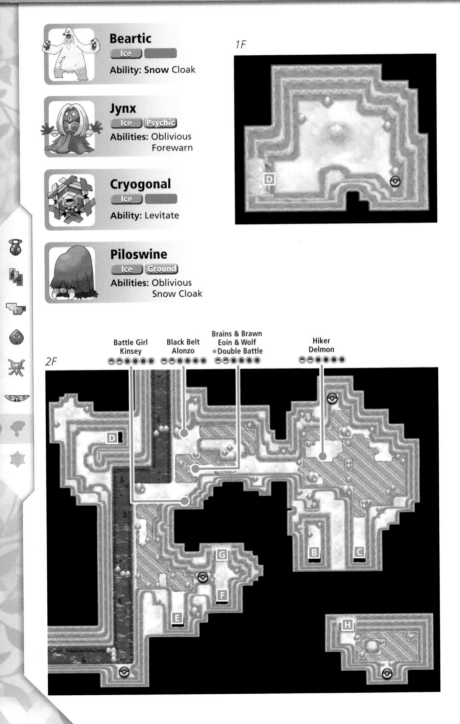

1F

2F

Battle Girl
Kinsey

Black Belt
Alonzo

Brains & Brawn
Eoin & Wolf
★Double Battle

Hiker
Delmon

3F

Team Flare
Mable
⊖⊖⊕⊕⊕⊕

Team Flare
Grunt
⊖⊖⊕⊕⊕⊕

Hiker
Brent
⊖⊖⊕⊕⊕⊕

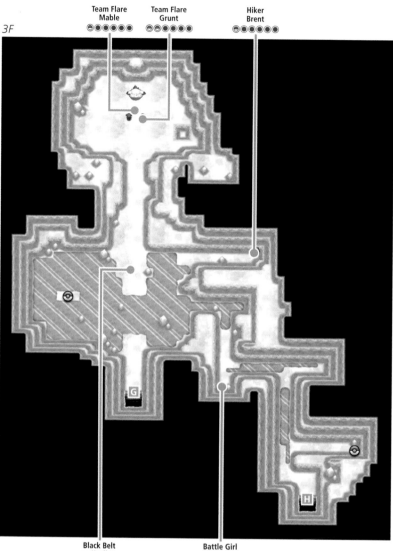

Black Belt
Kenji
⊖⊕⊕⊕⊕⊕

Battle Girl
Gabrielle
⊖⊖⊕⊕⊕⊕

Vanillite

Ice

Ability: Ice Body

Smoochum

Ice   Psychic

Abilities: Oblivious
Forewarn

1 Find a couple of Sky Trainers

Two Sky Trainers are braving the cold winds that roar around Frost Cavern, eyeing your arrival from their lofty perches. You will spot one as soon as you head east to cross the bridge. The other is beyond the bridge and around the narrow ledge that curls around the eastern edge of the cliffs.

2 Meet Mamoswine on your way to the cavern's first floor

The Frost Cavern's outer grounds are blanketed in snow. Once you have the Waterfall field move, you'll be able to ride down the waterfalls and discover a couple of useful items. For now, proceed north to encounter Mamoswine and its Trainer. Mamoswine is indeed upset over something in the Frost Cavern, and it won't budge from its spot. Proceed north to enter the cavern and investigate.

3 Cross the Frost Cavern's icy floors

The Frost Cavern is a puzzling maze of slippery, frozen floors. In order to progress, you need to figure out how to slide along the ice. For example, when you reach the second floor, you need to slide northward, walk east across the snow, and then slide back down to the south. When you stop, slide east again, and then slide south into a nook. Slide west, and then slide north again to reach another patch of snow. Walk south a bit on the snow—don't slip out onto the ice—and you'll be able to slide west and reach a Trainer.

NOTE *There may be more than one way to get across the ice. Find the ways that work best for you to navigate this frosty expanse.*

TIPS *Use the maps to navigate the Frost Cavern. Look for patches of snow that provide traction, as well as icy stalagmites that will halt your slides. When looking at the maps, it helps to start at the place where you want to end up and work backward in your mind to determine how you'll get there.*

Note that you can also slide diagonally across the ice. It may be the easiest way to reach some locations—or perhaps the only way!

STEP
④ Surf across the water to reach some chilling discoveries

Use Surf to cross the glacier-blue river and reach another path to the west. Follow it around and down the stairs, and you will discover a small chamber deeper underground. Within it is a huge stone covered completely in a thick sheet of ice. It doesn't seem to do anything right now, but perhaps it will prove to have some greater purpose in the future. For now, you'll find an Icy Rock, which might be of more immediate use!

NOTE *If you try to go farther south down the river, a row of frosted rocks will stand in your way. Clamber back onto dry land (or at least solid ice) and slide your way south around them, before surfing out on the water again to reach a Never-Melt Ice!*

STEP
⑤ Explore the third floor

To reach the third floor, make your way south along the river on the second floor and go down the stairs at the end. You'll find another set of stairs on the east. Climb them to reach the third floor. Before you rush north to find out what is wrong with Frost Cavern, though, take time to explore this new area. You'll find numerous items to the west and east, including TM79 Frost Breath in another subterranean chamber! There will be some Trainers along the way, though, so heal your Pokémon before you finally head into the heart of the Frost Cavern.

STEP
⑥ Battle against Team Flare to free Abomasnow

At last you've discovered the source of Mamoswine's misgivings: Team Flare! The stylish thugs are harassing a monstrous Pokémon, and its rage is somehow causing the blizzard outside. You can't let Team Flare get away with this! Defeat the Team Flare Grunts with the help of Trevor, who arrives on the scene soon after you, and then defeat Mable to rescue the poor, embattled Pokémon. Once you have, it's time to head back to Dendemille Town and then on at last to Route 17!

NOTE *Even after you chase off Team Flare, the Abomasnow that they were hassling remains to show you its gratitude. Approach it after the battle, and it will reward you with an Abomasite!*

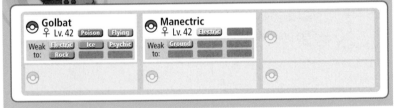

Vs. **Team Flare Grunt's Pokémon**

Golbat
♀ Lv. 42 Poison Flying
Weak to: Electric Ice Psychic Rock

Manectric
♀ Lv. 42 Electric
Weak to: Ground

Vs. **Team Flare Mable's Pokémon**

Houndoom
♀ Lv. 48 Dark Fire
Weak to: Water Fighting Ground Rock

Due to constant snowstorms and heavy snowfall, humans have no hope of traversing this road on foot.

Route 17 (Mamoswine Road)

This inhospitable route lies between Dendemille Town and Anistar City, but it cannot be traversed until you've resolved the issue at the Frost Cavern. After that, you'll be able to ride on Mamoswine's back and make your way through Route 17's heaps of snow.

Field Moves Needed

Sky Trainer Anila
★Sky Battle
◎◎◎◎◎◎

Dendemille Town

Anistar City

Items

- ❑ Calcium
- ❑ Icicle Plate
- ❑ Rare Candy

Hidden Items

- ❑ Paralyze Heal
- ❑ Timer Ball

Abomasnow

Grass Ice

Ability: Snow Warning

Delibird

Ice Flying

Abilities: Vital Spirit
Hustle

Sneasel

Dark Ice

Abilities: Inner Focus
Keen Eye

Deep Snow

❑ Abomasnow	▲
❑ Delibird	◎
❑ Sneasel	○
❑ Snover	○

◎ frequent ○ average
△ rare ▲ almost never

STEP 1 » Hitch a ride on Mamoswine

Trainer, you should ride on Mamoswine's back to the other side!

Now that the crisis at the Frost Cavern has been resolved, Mamoswine is happy to help you navigate Route 17. Speak to Mamoswine's Trainer to learn more about why the gentle Pokémon was so upset, and then climb onto Mamoswine's back and steer the massive Pokémon into the deep snow ahead.

NOTES *You cannot ride Mamoswine while using an item, such as the Dowsing Machine.*

Wild Pokémon live in Route 17's deep snow, and they will periodically attack when Mamoswine accidentally steps on them.

STEP 2 » Smash rocks with Mamoswine's tusks

It's not long before large rocks get in your way. Not to worry, for Mamoswine's massive tusks can make short work of these obstacles. Simply press Ⓐ to smash these rocks to bits whenever you encounter them.

STEP 3 » Seek out items and battle a Sky Trainer

It's takeoff time!

Each time you emerge from the deep snow, dismount Mamoswine and do a little exploring on foot. Side paths await you and lead you further northeast and southwest, far beyond where Mamoswine can take you. Use the Dowsing Machine to locate a hidden item in the driving snow, collect a couple other items, and test your skills against the Sky Trainer who waits in the route's far northeast corner.

STEP
4 After exploring Route 17, proceed east to Anistar City

This time, I challenge you to a battle in front of Anistar City's Gym!

Anistar City is your next stop, and it lies to the east. You'll receive a Holo Clip from your friend Serena/Calem as you near the Anistar City gate. Serena/Calem wants another rematch against you and challenges you to a battle in front of the Anistar City Gym. At least you have a little forewarning this time!

Some say the enigmatic device used as a sundial came from outer space.

Anistar City

This modern city is famous throughout the Kalos region for its massive and mysterious sundial. Rumor has it that a man who knows much about the fable of the Kalos region's Legendary Pokémon resides here.

Field Moves
Needed

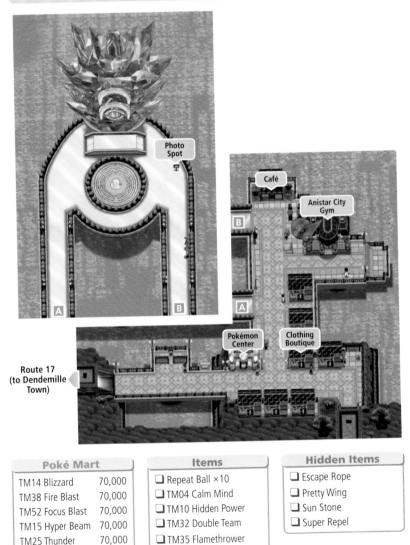

Photo Spot

Café

Anistar City Gym

B

A

B

A

Pokémon Center

Clothing Boutique

Route 17
(to Dendemille Town)

Poké Mart		Items	Hidden Items
TM14 Blizzard	70,000	❏ Repeat Ball ×10	❏ Escape Rope
TM38 Fire Blast	70,000	❏ TM04 Calm Mind	❏ Pretty Wing
TM52 Focus Blast	70,000	❏ TM10 Hidden Power	❏ Sun Stone
TM15 Hyper Beam	70,000	❏ TM32 Double Team	❏ Super Repel
TM25 Thunder	70,000	❏ TM35 Flamethrower	
		❏ TM77 Psych Up	
		❏ TM90 Substitute	

276

STEP
1 » Have a chat with Sina and receive some Repeat Balls

Oh, I almost forgot! I brought you some gifts!
Put them to good use!

Professor Sycamore's assistant, Sina, greets you as you enter Anistar City. She informs you that someone in this city knows about the Kalos region's Legendary Pokémon. She gives you 10 Repeat Balls to help you in your journey. What a friendly gesture!

STEP
2 » Marvel at the Memory Girl's skills

Do you want to know the memory of your Pokémon?

Yes
No

A mysterious maiden known as the Memory Girl stands right outside the local Pokémon Center. The Memory Girl's unique insight allows her to recount the memories of your Pokémon. Simply show her any Pokémon that you've obtained, and she'll tell you its most prevailing memories.

STEP
3 » Meet Mr. Bonding in the Pokémon Center

Let's get started, shall we?
It's bonding time!

Step inside the Pokémon Center to rest your Pokémon. You guessed it: Mr. Bonding is present and accounted for, and he grants you a new O-Power: Exp. Point Power. Now you can increase the number of Experience Points that your Pokémon receive after battles!

STEP
4 » Receive TMs from the friendly Hex Maniac

I may not be able to share my love with you, but I can certainly share some TMs!

A Hex Maniac in the Pokémon Center will give you not one, but four TMs just for speaking to her. There is a catch, though. She'll only give you one per day and at different times. Keep coming back at different hours on different days to collect all four.

STEP
5 >> Check out the Anistar Sundial

Speaking of time, detour north of the Pokémon Center and take a moment to marvel at Anistar City's famous sundial. Have Phil the Photo Guy snap your picture here if you like, and fire up the Dowsing Machine to discover a hidden item. Wondering why people call it a sundial? Show up when the sun is setting and you will see the fantastic sculpture come to life—the golden rings spinning in harmony as a stream of sunlight falls on them through the crystal sculpture that was perhaps created by some ancient civilization.

STEP
6 >> Obtain TM10 Hidden Power

You there! Use this and awaken your Pokémon's hidden powers!

Enter the house that's right next to the boutique and speak with the Psychic inside to receive a unique TM. Most Pokémon can use this TM to unlock their hidden power! The move's type will change depending on the Pokémon that learns the move. Talk to the Psychic again, and he'll tell you which type of move your Pokémon will use when it unleashes TM10 Hidden Power in battle.

STEP
7 >> Learn the stories of the Legendary Pokémon

It's my guess that you've come to ask about the Legendary Pokémon of the Kalos region, Xerneas.

Enter the house north of the boutique to speak with a knowledgeable Monsieur who recounts the story of the Kalos region's Legendary Pokémon. Depending on the version of the game you're playing, this will be either Xerneas (Pokémon X) or Yveltal (Pokémon Y), each with its own unique tale.

The Legends of Xerneas   X

About 800 years ago, the Pokémon known as Xerneas used its shining horns to illuminate the lands of Kalos. At that very moment, people and Pokémon throughout the land felt great energy and vitality surge through their bodies. At the same time, a vast forest sprang up, with Xerneas at its center. Legend has it that, when it nears the end of its thousand-year life span, Xerneas releases all of its remaining energy, sharing it with all living things nearby.

Another tale suggests that 3,000 years ago, the Kalos region was engulfed in a terrible war. The story goes that one Pokémon came to the rescue of all of the wounded Pokémon that had been caught up in the conflict. Some people suspect the Pokémon that appeared was Xerneas, but there's no way to know. Supposedly, after Xerneas released its remaining energy, it transformed into a dried-up tree. It remains in hiding deep within the forest.

The Legends of Yveltal

About 800 years ago, the Pokémon known as Yveltal spread its ominous wings, engulfing the lands of Kalos in darkness. At that moment, people and Pokémon throughout the land began to fall one by one. Yveltal let out a piercing cry and took to the sky, vanishing to an unknown location. Stories say that when it nears the end of its thousand-year life span, Yveltal absorbs the life force of the living things around it in order to charge its own energy.

Another tale suggests that 3,000 years ago, the Kalos region was engulfed in a terrible war. The story goes that one Pokémon appeared and stole the life force of countless living beings. Some people suspect the Pokémon that appeared was Yveltal, but there's no way to know. Supposedly, after Yveltal finished storing the energy it had absorbed, it transformed into a kind of cocoon, remaining in hiding deep in the mountains.

STEP 8 ▸ Lend a Pokémon to a lonely old man

Would you be so kind as to lend me one of your Pokémon? You know--to keep me company.

Continue going north and enter the next house, where you'll visit a lonely old man who could use some cheering up. Give the man a Pokémon that's Lv. 5 or under, and you'll fill his heart with joy. Everyone needs a little company, after all!

Do you have any Pokémon left in your PC Boxes that are still untrained and Lv. 5 or below? If not, return to the early areas of the game, like Santalune Forest, to catch one such partner for this old man.

STEP
⑨ Have a battle against Serena/Calem

Let me show you how much stronger I am!

The Anistar City Gym lies to the north, and Serena/Calem will catch you there, still eager for battle. This is your most challenging battle against your friend so far, so give it all you've got! Once you've proved your might, it's time to move on to the Gym battle.

Vs. Serena/Calem's Pokémon

If you chose Chespin:

Meowstic
♀/♂ Lv. 44 Psychic
Weak to: Bug Ghost Dark

Jolteon
♂ Lv. 44 Electric
Weak to: Ground

Delphox
♂ Lv. 46 Fire Psychic
Weak to: Water Ground Rock Ghost Dark

Absol
♂ Lv. 44 Dark
Weak to: Fighting Bug Fairy

If you chose Fennekin:

Meowstic
♀/♂ Lv. 44 Psychic
Weak to: Bug Ghost Dark

Flareon
♂ Lv. 44 Fire
Weak to: Water Ground Rock

Greninja
♂ Lv. 46 Water Dark
Weak to: Grass Electric Fighting Bug Fairy

Absol
♂ Lv. 44 Dark
Weak to: Fighting Bug Fairy

If you chose Froakie:

Meowstic
♀/♂ Lv. 44 Psychic
Weak to: Bug Ghost Dark

Vaporeon
♂ Lv. 44 Water
Weak to: Grass Electric

Chesnaught
♂ Lv. 46 Grass Fighting
Weak to: Flying Fire Ice Poison Psychic Fairy

Absol
♂ Lv. 44 Dark
Weak to: Fighting Bug Fairy

Anistar City Gym Battle

Gym Battle Tips

✓ Bring lots of Super Potions and items that heal status conditions

✓ Use Bug-, Ghost-, and Dark-type Pokémon

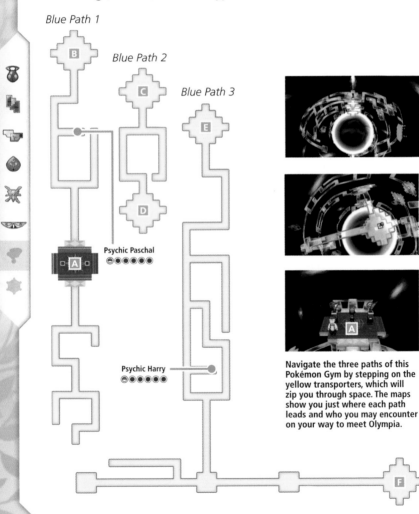

Blue Path 1

Blue Path 2

Blue Path 3

B

C

E

D

A

Psychic Paschal

Psychic Harry

F

Navigate the three paths of this Pokémon Gym by stepping on the yellow transporters, which will zip you through space. The maps show you just where each path leads and who you may encounter on your way to meet Olympia.

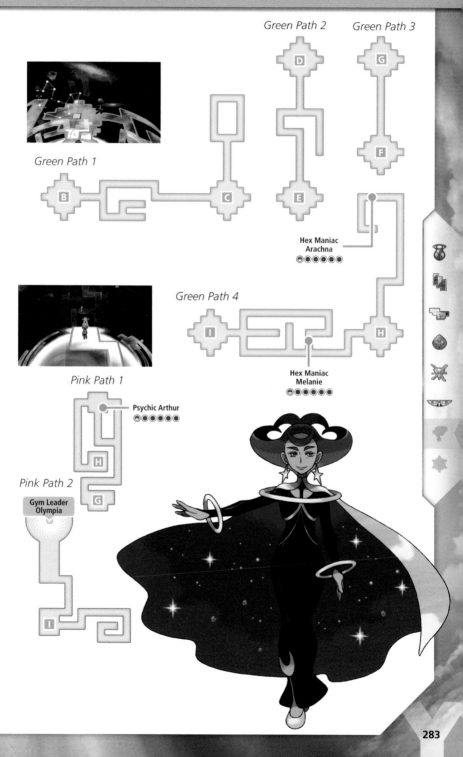

Green Path 2

Green Path 3

D

G

F

Green Path 1

B

C

E

Hex Maniac
Arachna
◉◉◉◉◉◉

Green Path 4

I

H

Hex Maniac
Melanie
◉◉◉◉◉◉

Pink Path 1

Psychic Arthur
◉◉◉◉◉◉

H

Pink Path 2

G

Gym Leader
Olympia

I

Anistar City Gym Leader

Olympia
Psychic-type Pokémon User

Use Bug-, Ghost-, and Dark-type moves to deal massive damage

The Anistar City Gym is a colorful, spherical maze filled with dead ends and powerful Psychic Trainers. As you navigate the maze, look for yellow warp panels that will zap you to new areas when you step on them. Use them to progress through the maze, advancing from blue to green to pink areas until you finally reach Gym Leader Olympia.

Olympia's first Pokémon, Sigilyph, uses Reflect to raise her party's Defense stat. This makes her Pokémon tough to defeat before she can heal them up with her Hyper Potions. She only has two Hyper Potions at her disposal, fortunately, so just hang tight and keep your Pokémon in good shape, and you'll wear down her party before long.

Olympia's Pokémon

Sigilyph
♀ Lv. 44 `Psychic` `Flying`
Weak to: `Electric` `Ice` `Rock` `Ghost` `Dark`

Slowking
♀ Lv. 45 `Water` `Psychic`
Weak to: `Grass` `Electric` `Bug` `Ghost` `Dark`

Meowstic
♀ Lv. 48 `Psychic`
Weak to: `Bug` `Ghost` `Dark`

+ vs Olympia +

Psychic Badge
Pokémon up to Lv. 90, including those received in trades, will obey you.

TM04 Calm Mind
The user quietly focuses its mind and calms its spirit to raise its Sp. Atk and Sp. Def stats.

TIP *Is your party thin on Bug-, Ghost-, or Dark-type Pokémon? Luckily you're in the right part of the region for them. There are good Bug- and Dark-type Pokémon to be found on Route 15. And a number of Ghost types can be found in the Lost Hotel and on Route 16. Take advantage of those side treks—they are worth it!*

STEP 10 With the Psychic Badge in hand, receive a Holo Clip from Team Flare

After you clear the Anistar City Gym and obtain the Psychic Badge, you'll receive a disturbing Holo Clip from Team Flare's leader. In a sickening revelation, you find that someone very familiar to you is actually behind the threatening group. What's worse, they plan on using something they call the "ultimate weapon" to wipe out everyone in the Kalos region who isn't with them. Not good!

STEP 11 Return to Lumiose City and search for Team Flare's hideout

Team Flare must be stopped! Serena/ Calem advises you to search for Team Flare's hideout in Lumiose City. There's no time to lose, so ignore Route 18 for the moment and hightail it back to Lumiose City via Routes 17 and 16 (or use the field move Fly) and begin your search for Team Flare!

Lumiose City (North)

This is your third time under the bright lights of Lumiose City, but this is no time for a relaxing day of shopping and fine dining. The members of Team Flare have revealed their cruel plan to wipe out everyone in the Kalos region except for themselves, and they must be stopped!

Field Moves Needed

Trainers you may find in alleys:

Black Belt Killian ⬡●●●●●	Waitress Paget ⬡●●●●●
Beauty Anais ⬡●●●●●	Garçon Jacopo ⬡●●●●●
Owner Toro ⬡●●●●●	Punk Girl Lillian ⬡●●●●●
Beauty Aimee ⬡●●●●●	Punk Guy Faust ⬡●●●●●
Beauty Cassandra ⬡●●●●●	Chef Kamaboko ⬡●●●●●

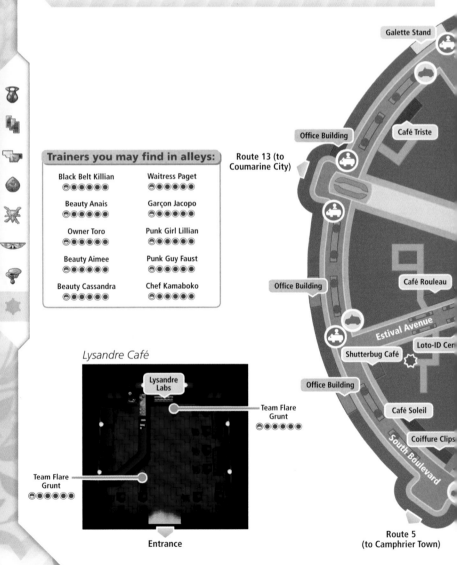

Lysandre Café

Lysandre Labs

Team Flare Grunt ⬡●●●●●

Team Flare Grunt ⬡●●●●●

Entrance

Galette Stand

Café Triste

Office Building

Route 13 (to Coumarine City)

Café Rouleau

Office Building

Estival Avenue

Loto-ID Cen

Shutterbug Café

Office Building

Café Soleil

Coiffure Clips

South Boulevard

Route 5 (to Camphrier Town)

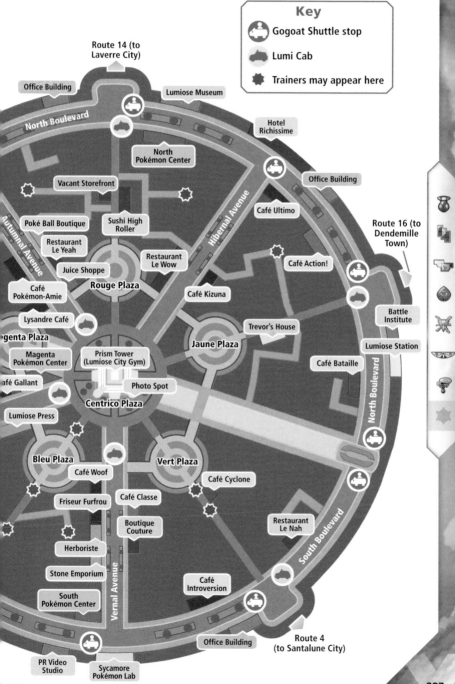

Key
Gogoat Shuttle stop
Lumi Cab
Trainers may appear here

Route 14 (to Laverre City)

Office Building
Lumiose Museum
North Boulevard
Hotel Richissime
North Pokémon Center
Office Building
Vacant Storefront
Café Ultimo
Autumnal Avenue
Poké Ball Boutique
Sushi High Roller
Restaurant Le Yeah
Restaurant Le Wow
Café Action!
Route 16 (to Dendemille Town)
Juice Shoppe
Rouge Plaza
Café Kizuna
Café Pokémon-Amie
Hibernal Avenue
Trevor's House
Battle Institute
Lysandre Café
Magenta Plaza
Jaune Plaza
Lumiose Station
Magenta Pokémon Center
Prism Tower (Lumiose City Gym)
Café Bataille
Café Gallant
Photo Spot
North Boulevard
Centrico Plaza
Lumiose Press
Bleu Plaza
Vert Plaza
Café Woof
Café Cyclone
Friseur Furfrou
Café Classe
Restaurant Le Nah
Boutique Couture
South Boulevard
Herboriste
Vernal Avenue
Stone Emporium
Café Introversion
South Pokémon Center
Office Building
Route 4 (to Santalune City)
PR Video Studio
Sycamore Pokémon Lab

287

1 Locate Lysandre Café

This flaming-red café is perfect for hot young stars like us.

Lysandre Café is a well-known Team Flare hangout, which makes it a good place to begin your search for their secret base. Time is short, but you might want to stock up on items at Lumiose City's various shops and Pokémon Centers before you head in. You're sure to face stiff opposition from Team Flare going forward!

TIP *You've been to Lysandre Café before—Professor Sycamore summoned you there during your last trip to the city. It's the red building that's close to the central Pokémon Center in Magenta Plaza, with the Team Flare member standing nearby. If you're having trouble locating the Lysandre Café, hop into any Lumi Cab and pay a small fee to get there.*

STEP
2 Defeat the Team Flare Grunts inside Lysandre Café

Today, our special is... get out of here or else!

Take on two Team Flare Grunts inside Lysandre Café to learn that there's a secret door here that leads to Lysandre Labs. After defeating both Team Flare Grunts, you'll learn the door's password is "open sesame." No style points for that one, Lysandre!

STEP
3 Find the secret door and enter Lysandre Labs

"Open sesame"!

After defeating both Team Flare Grunts inside the café, examine the cabinet on the far wall. Yes, it's a secret door! After reciting Lysandre's woefully obvious password, the cabinet slides away, granting you access to Lysandre Labs.

A top-secret laboratory hidden beneath the surface of Lumiose City.

Lysandre Labs

Lysandre's laboratory houses many secrets and a host of Team Flare fanatics with familiar faces. Be ready to face a number of battles as you explore its confounding depths.

Field Moves Needed

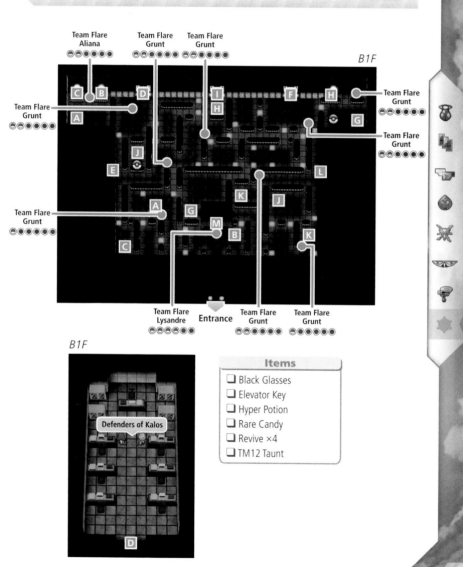

B1F

B1F

Defenders of Kalos

Items

- ☐ Black Glasses
- ☐ Elevator Key
- ☐ Hyper Potion
- ☐ Rare Candy
- ☐ Revive ×4
- ☐ TM12 Taunt

289

B1F

Team Flare
Celosia

Team Flare
Bryony

B1F

Team Flare
Mable

B1F

Restore your
Pokémon's health

E

B1F

B2F

B3F

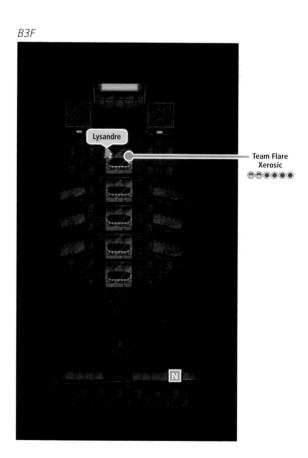

Team Flare
Xerosic

1 » Test your skills against the head of Team Flare

Only the chosen ones will obtain a ticket to tomorrow.

Follow the dark corridor to the north to find Lysandre, the boss of Team Flare, awaiting you in an eerily lit underground chamber. What is this high-tech place doing under the streets of old and beautiful Lumiose City? Lysandre is yearning to test your power. Show him what you're made of, Trainer!

Vs. Team Flare Lysandre's Pokémon

Mienfoo
♂ Lv. 45 Fighting
Weak to: Flying Psychic Fairy

Murkrow
♂ Lv. 45 Dark Flying
Weak to: Electric Ice Rock Fairy

Gyarados
♂ Lv. 49 Water Flying
Weak to: 4x Electric Rock

Pyroar
♂ Lv. 47 Fire Normal
Weak to: Water Fighting Ground Rock

2 » Explore Lysandre Labs

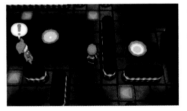

After Lysandre storms off, take a look around his eerie laboratory. Note the two special types of floor panels: spin panels and warp panels. Spin panels push and spin you forward in the direction the panel's arrow is pointing, and you'll just keep spinning until you hit a wall. Warp panels send you warping around the premises, just like the panels you used in the Laverre City Gym.

STEP
3 » Defeat Team Flare Aliana

Why, if it isn't that fascinating little Trainer from the Kalos Power Plant.

Heading west is your only option at the moment. The first warp panel you step on zips you over to the lab's northwest corner, where the scientist Aliana has been watching for you. You beat this mad scientist back at the Kalos Power Plant, but she has grown even stronger since then. Defeat Aliana once again to access another pair of warp panels.

Vs. Team Flare Aliana's Pokémon

Mightyena ♀ Lv. 46 Dark	Druddigon ♀ Lv. 48 Dragon	
Weak to: Fighting Bug Fairy	Weak to: Ice Dragon Fairy	

TIP *Picking the yellow warp panel will only have you going in circles, depositing you back at the elevator. You've been through two battles now against the higher-ups in Team Flare and there are far more waiting. If you're running low on the restorative items you're sure to need ahead, pick the yellow warp panel and exit Lysandre Labs for a time to better prepare yourself. Otherwise, pick the green one and move ahead.*

STEP
4 » Receive some Revives from the defenders of Kalos

We're looking for a really tall guy...

Follow along the path, punctuated by spin panels and Team Flare Grunts. If you pass through the lab's northwest door, you will find the defenders of Kalos in a small office. The masked heroes are searching for a very tall person, but they can't be more specific than that. They do give you a few Revives to help you out, however. Isn't it nice having friends?

STEP
5 Take a break in the barracks

You! Do you think you can really use this TM?

After encountering the defenders of Kalos, exit the office and use the spin panels to twirl around the lab, heading south. You'll end up near a door in the lab's west wall. Go inside to visit a barracks, where a Team Flare member mistakes you for a comrade and gives you TM12 Taunt. You can also find another Revive here, and you can rest in any of the beds to recover your Pokémon's HP and PP.

STEP
6 Battle Celosia and Bryony in the northeast office

Let's get him, yeah?

Next, head back out and make your way to the lab's northeast office to battle a pair of powerful Team Flare scientists. You'll fight Celosia and Bryony one at a time, so there's no Double Battle to worry about. After you best them both, they'll reveal more of Team Flare's sinister plot. It seems that they are using the power of the mysterious stones to siphon power from Pokémon back at Geosenge Town. These stones are the graves of unfortunate Pokémon that perished when the ultimate weapon was unleashed 3,000 years ago—and Team Flare is planning to strap Pokémon to them once again to steal their energy!

Vs. **Team Flare Celosia's Pokémon**

Manectric ♀ Lv. 46 Electric	Drapion ♀ Lv. 48 Poison Dark	
Weak to: Ground	Weak to: Ground	

Vs. Team Flare Bryony's Pokémon

Liepard
♀ Lv. 46 [Dark]
Weak to: [Fighting] [Bug] [Fairy]

Bisharp
♀ Lv. 48 [Dark] [Steel]
Weak⁴ˣ¹ to: [Fighting] [Fire] [Ground]

STEP
7 » Navigate the lab to reach the east office

Oh, oh, oh, oh? You're that kid from the Frost Cavern...

Continue exploring the lab after you defeat Celosia and Bryony, using spin panels and warp panels to reach a few more valuable items around the main floor, including a Rare Candy in the middle-north office. Work your way to the east office, where you'll encounter Team Flare's scientist Mable. Win this battle to acquire the Elevator Key at last!

TIP *Take the time to read the records that fill the bookshelves and cover the desk in the room where you found a Rare Candy. They will help illuminate the dark past of the Kalos region and Lysandre's own history. Remember: those who do not know the mistakes of the past are bound to repeat them.*

Vs. Team Flare Mable's Pokémon

Houndoom
♀ Lv. 46 [Dark] [Fire]
Weak to: [Water] [Fighting] [Ground] [Rock]

Weavile
♀ Lv. 48 [Dark] [Ice]
Weak⁴ˣ¹ to: [Fighting] [Fire] [Bug] [Rock] [Steel] [Fairy]

STEP 8 » Use the Elevator Key to ride to the second basement floor

Now that you have the Elevator Key, make your way back to the elevator that Lysandre used to escape after you beat him. Use the Elevator Key to activate the elevator and ride down to B2F.

STEP 9 » Learn the story of Kalos's troubled past

The elevator delivers you to a long corridor. Go west until you find Lysandre. You'll also see an extremely tall man who's being held behind bars. It's the same mysterious stranger that you encountered briefly in the Lumiose Badlands! He recounts a tale of sorrow and loss that sheds new light on the destructive events that rocked Kalos 3,000 years ago.

STEP 10 » Battle Xerosic on the third basement floor

I need to do a little research on you! Come, let us begin!

After the mysterious stranger concludes his sad tale, Lysandre walks away from the old man, telling you to follow him to B3F. Return to the elevator, and this time, you can ride down to the third basement floor. Do so, and you'll find Lysandre once again, together with a Team Flare scientist named Xerosic in a high-tech chamber. After Lysandre departs, Xerosic tests your skill and heroism in a Pokémon battle.

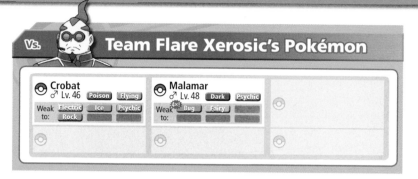

Team Flare Xerosic's Pokémon

Crobat ♂ Lv. 46 — Poison, Flying
Weak to: Electric, Ice, Psychic, Rock

Malamar ♂ Lv. 48 — Dark, Psychic
Weak to: Bug (4x), Fairy

STEP 11 — Beware the ultimate weapon!

Behind me you'll find a red button and a blue button.

Xerosic is impressed by your talent and instructs you to press one of the two colored buttons behind him. He says one button will summon the ultimate weapon, while the other one won't. Lysandre said that if you choose correctly, Team Flare will leave the ultimate weapon be and abandon their plans for domination. Unfortunately, Xerosic has other plans. Your only option is to pick a button and see what happens...

STEP 12 — Hurry to Geosenge Town

The ultimate weapon emerges from Geosenge Town's circle of standing stones, wreaking havoc on the humble settlement. You've got to do something! Leave Lysandre Labs in a hurry, and use Fly to zoom to Geosenge Town.

NOTE *Even if you wish to take the scenic route, you'll find it hard to reach Geosenge Town on foot. You'll find Route 10 blocked by Team Flare Grunts if you try to approach the town via Menhir Trail.*

Geosenge Town (Second Visit)

This once-quiet town has been completely transformed by the emergence of the ultimate weapon. Many of its buildings have been ruined, and only the Pokémon Center, Hotel Marine Snow, and a couple of houses remain intact.

Field Moves Needed

To Team Flare Secret HQ

Team Flare Grunt

Pokémon Center   **Hotel Marine Snow**

Route 11 (to Azure Bay and Shalour City)

STEP
1 Defeat the Team Flare guard

You'd better have come here prepared! Both you and your Pokémon!

The ultimate weapon has toppled nearly all of Geosenge Town's structures, but miraculously, its Pokémon Center still stands. Rest here before going northwest toward Team Flare's secret hideout. You'll need to defeat a Team Flare Grunt along the way.

NOTE *The path to Route 10 is blocked by Team Flare. The ultimate weapon is harnessing the power of the many Pokémon that Team Flare has captured, using the ancient gravestones there.*

STEP
2 Enter the Team Flare Secret HQ

C'mon! Let's stop Team Flare... No... We have to stop Lysandre himself!

Serena/Calem catches up to you as you near the entrance to Team Flare's hideout and insists on coming with you. This is the kind of friend who would never dream of letting you go alone on such an important mission. It's good to have such a loyal and brave companion!

Team Flare Secret HQ

At last, you've reached Team Flare's secret headquarters. Now you can stop Lysandre and his legion of snazzily dressed zealots from activating the ultimate weapon! Make haste, Trainer, for the ultimate weapon will soon have all the power it needs to be unleashed. The fate of the Kalos region rests in your hands!

Field Moves Needed

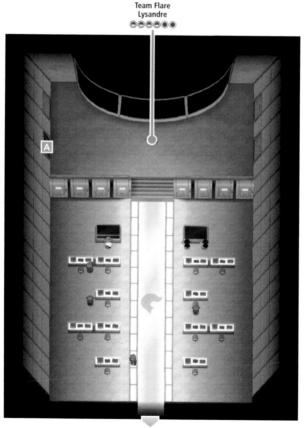

Team Flare
Lysandre

A

Entrance

Team Flare Admin &
Team Flare Grunt
★Multi Battle

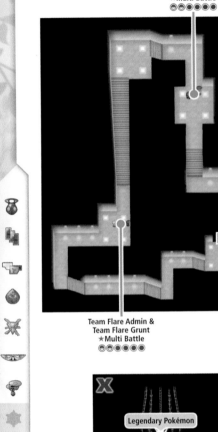

A

Team Flare Admin &
Team Flare Grunt
★Multi Battle

B

Team Flare Admin &
Team Flare Grunt
★Multi Battle

Team Flare Admin &
Team Flare Grunt
★Multi Battle

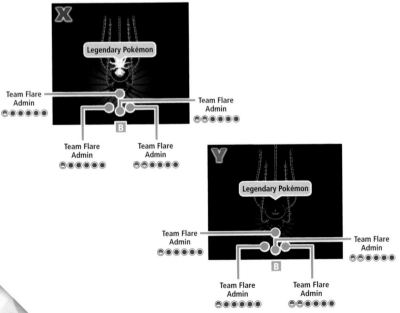

X

Legendary Pokémon

Team Flare
Admin

Team Flare
Admin

B

Team Flare
Admin

Team Flare
Admin

Y

Legendary Pokémon

Team Flare
Admin

Team Flare
Admin

B

Team Flare
Admin

Team Flare
Admin

STEP
1 » Battle Lysandre inside the secret headquarters

You want to stop the ultimate weapon, and I refuse to do so.

Lysandre lurks inside the Team Flare headquarters, anticipating your arrival. He has no plans to stop the ultimate weapon now that it's been deployed. Instead, he battles you to buy time for the weapon to amass the vast power it needs to be unleashed.

Vs. Team Flare Lysandre's Pokémon

Mienshao
♂ Lv. 47 Fighting
Weak to: Flying Psychic Fairy

Gyarados
♂ Lv. 51 Water Flying
Weak to: 4× Electric Rock

Pyroar
♂ Lv. 49 Fire Normal
Weak to: Water Fighting Ground
Rock

Honchkrow
♂ Lv. 47 Dark Flying
Weak to: Electric Ice Rock
Fairy

STEP
2 » Race to reach the Legendary Pokémon

You've beaten Lysandre for a second time, but you're far from finished here. Serena/Calem suggests that you seek out the Legendary Pokémon, whose powerful life force is being used to charge the ultimate weapon. Hurry to the northwest door to begin your exploration of the Team Flare Secret HQ.

Approach the background glass behind Lysandre for a peek at the Legendary Pokémon far below.

STEP
③ Take on Team Flare Admins and Grunts in Multi Battles

I'm afraid we're going to have to ask you to turn back.

As you might expect, Team Flare's secret headquarters is filled with Team Flare Grunts and high-ranking Team Flare Admins. As you race to the basement where the Legendary Pokémon is being held, you must defeat several pairs of Team Flare fanatics in Multi Battles. You're not alone, for your friend Serena/Calem battles by your side.

Serena/Calem's Pokémon

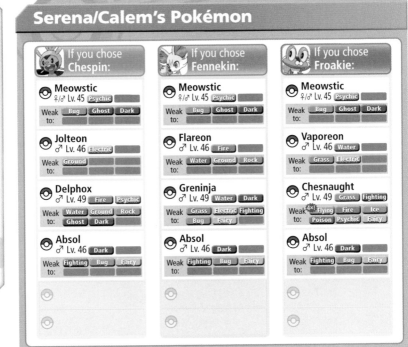

If you chose Chespin:

Meowstic
♀/♂ Lv. 45 Psychic
Weak to: Bug Ghost Dark

Jolteon
♂ Lv. 46 Electric
Weak to: Ground

Delphox
♂ Lv. 49 Fire Psychic
Weak to: Water Ground Rock Ghost Dark

Absol
♂ Lv. 46 Dark
Weak to: Fighting Bug Fairy

If you chose Fennekin:

Meowstic
♀/♂ Lv. 45 Psychic
Weak to: Bug Ghost Dark

Flareon
♂ Lv. 46 Fire
Weak to: Water Ground Rock

Greninja
♂ Lv. 49 Water Dark
Weak to: Grass Electric Fighting Bug Fairy

Absol
♂ Lv. 46 Dark
Weak to: Fighting Bug Fairy

If you chose Froakie:

Meowstic
♀/♂ Lv. 45 Psychic
Weak to: Bug Ghost Dark

Vaporeon
♂ Lv. 46 Water
Weak to: Grass Electric

Chesnaught
♂ Lv. 49 Grass Fighting
Weak to: 4x Flying Fire Ice Poison Psychic Fairy

Absol
♂ Lv. 46 Dark
Weak to: Fighting Bug Fairy

First Multi Battle

Vs. Male Admin's Pokémon

Toxicroak
♂ Lv. 50 Poison Fighting
Weak to: Psychic Ground Flying

Vs. Female Grunt's Pokémon

Liepard
♀ Lv. 48 Dark
Weak to: Fighting Bug Fairy

Second Multi Battle

Vs. Female Admin's Pokémon

Manectric
♀ Lv. 50 Electric
Weak to: Ground

Vs. Male Grunt's Pokémon

Mightyena
♂ Lv. 48 Dark
Weak to: Fighting Bug Fairy

STEP
④ **Have a chat with a surprise visitor**

About halfway down into the depths of Team Flare's headquarters, a friendly voice calls out to you. It's Shauna! She's managed to follow you and wants to help out. Be a pal and invite Shauna to join you—after all, you can always use the company of another friend!

Third Multi Battle

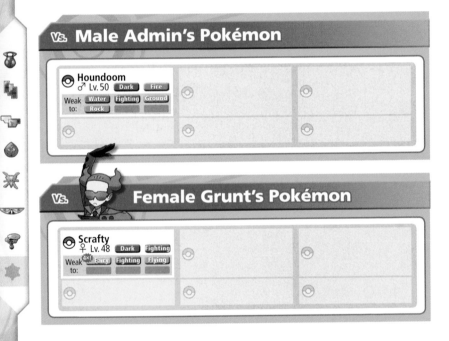

Vs. Male Admin's Pokémon

Houndoom
♂ Lv. 50 Dark Fire
Weak to: Water Fighting Ground Rock

Vs. Female Grunt's Pokémon

Scrafty
♀ Lv. 48 Dark Fighting
Weak to: 4x Fairy Fighting Flying

STEP
⑤ **Open the sealed door**

When you reach the basement door, you'll find it sealed with a high-tech electronic lock. This isn't a problem for Shauna, though, because she has a special device that Clemont gave her for figuring out puzzles! Shauna uses the device to unlock the door in a jiffy. Hurry inside—the Legendary Pokémon needs you!

STEP
⑥ Defeat the last of Team Flare

But just to make double sure nothing goes wrong, let's take these runts out!

Team Flare makes its final stand in the eerie chamber where the Legendary Pokémon is being held. Shauna and Serena/Calem lure several Team Flare members away, leaving you to take out the rest. Beat the four remaining Team Flare Admins, one by one, using items to restore your Pokémon's HP between each battle.

STEP
⑦ Catch the Legendary Pokémon

Xsaaaaaah!

Yvaaaaaar!

You've fought hard to reach this point, and now the Kalos region's Legendary Pokémon is within your grasp! By defeating Team Flare, you've rescued this mighty Pokémon from the brink of oblivion—but it must still be caught before it will join you. Fight hard to wear down the Legendary Pokémon, then use your best Poké Ball to catch it.

TIPS

Remember: inflicting status conditions such as Poison and Paralysis makes Pokémon easier to catch.

If you've saved the Master Ball from the Poké Ball Factory, consider using it to simplify matters here.

Catch Xerneas!

⊙ Xerneas Lv. 50 [Fairy]

Weak to: [Poison] [Steel]

Ability: Fairy Aura

Moves: Gravity, Geomancy, Moonblast, Megahorn

Xerneas is unlike anything you've ever seen before—the first Legendary Fairy-type Pokémon. This Pokémon is said to be a benevolent force in nature, and when it reaches the end of its 1,000 year life, it releases all of the energy it has gathered and shares its vitality with all living things. After exhausting itself, it takes the form of a withered tree, tucked away in some forgotten forest of the world. This is the condition it was in when Team Flare found it and brought it here in order to use its stored energy for their own purposes. It has been awakened from its dormant state due to Lysandre's meddling, and now it seems interested in fighting alongside you to help end Team Flare's twisted ambitions.

Xerneas has a brand-new Ability, Fairy Aura, which will power up any Fairy-type attack moves that are used in battle. This includes its Fairy-type move—Moonblast. Moonblast will deal heavy damage to your team, with its power of 95, and it may even lower your Pokémon's Sp. Atk. Geomancy is a two-turn move, which allows Xerneas to sharply increase its own Sp. Atk, Sp. Def, and Speed on the second turn. Megahorn can deal massive damage, with its power of 120 and Xerneas's high Attack. You should have learned your lesson by now, but don't make the mistake of thinking that the Fairy type is weak or helpless!

Catch Yveltal!   **Y**

⊙ **Yveltal** Lv. 50   **Dark** **Flying**

Weak to: **Electric** **Ice** **Rock** **Fairy**

Ability: Dark Aura

Moves: Snarl, Oblivion Wing, Disable, Dark Pulse

Yveltal is a Dark- and Flying-type Legendary Pokémon, a combination never before seen among Legendary Pokémon. This Pokémon of destruction is said to absorb the life force of all living things when it reaches the end of its 1,000 year life. After this destructive act, it takes the form of a hardened husk, hiding away somewhere in the world. This is the condition it was in when Team Flare found it and brought it here in order to use its stored energy for their own purposes. It has been awakened from its dormant state due to Lysandre's meddling, and now it seems interested in fighting alongside you to help end Team Flare's twisted ambitions.

Yveltal has a brand new Ability, Dark Aura, which will power up any Dark-type attack moves that are used in battle. This includes its Dark Pulse move. Oblivion Wing is a new move, which only Yveltal can learn. It not only damages your Pokémon, but also allows Yveltal to absorb most of that damage to restore its own health! With a power of 80 and an accuracy of 100, this move is one to watch out for, and it can quickly turn your imminent victory into disaster. In addition to this, its Disable move can seal your moves, making your Pokémon unable to use their best attacks against this beastly Pokémon. Choose each action with care, because if you assume that you can keep unleashing supereffective attack after supereffective attack, you may be in for an unpleasant surprise when your moves get disabled!

Team Flare Lysandre

Lysandre's Pokémon

Mienshao
♂ Lv. 49 `Fighting`
Weak to: `Flying` `Psychic` `Fairy`

Honchkrow
♂ Lv. 49 `Dark` `Flying`
Weak to: `Electric` `Ice` `Rock` `Fairy`

Gyarados
♂ Lv. 53 `Water` `Flying`
Weak to: `4x Electric` `Rock`

Pyroar
♂ Lv. 51 `Fire` `Normal`
Weak to: `Water` `Fighting` `Ground` `Rock`

The time has come for your final confrontation against Lysandre. He has extremely strong bonds with his Pokémon, but perhaps it is not so surprising when you consider his origins. Once, long ago, Lysandre hoped more than anything to help the people of the world—but he grew bitter when he saw how fruitless all his efforts seemed to be. As terrible as his current goal may be, his frustration is something we all may grapple with at times. Even your friendly rival seemed lost on how to respond when Lysandre claimed that not everything in this world can be shared. Can you prove to him that your way of thinking is right, and convince him that destruction is not the only way to build his beautiful new future?

STEP
⑧ Defeat the Team Flare Boss

I'll be taking the Legendary Pokémon back now!

You've rescued and caught the Kalos region's Legendary Pokémon, thus preventing the ultimate weapon from being powered. But the battle isn't over yet. Lysandre returns to challenge you one last time. Beware: he will use every trick possible in a last-ditch effort to secure victory. Put all of your training and talent to use in this final clash against the head of Team Flare!

Luckily, your Pokémon have recovered from their battle against the Legendary Pokémon in time for this last challenge against Team Flare's boss. If you caught Xerneas and had it join your party, its Fairy-type moves will be super effective against many of Lysandre's Pokémon. If you caught Yveltal and had it join your party, its moves may not be super effective, but it is resistant to a couple of Lysandre's Pokémon. Either Legendary Pokémon will be a great partner in this battle. The greatest hurdle is likely to be Lysandre's Gyarados. With its Dragon Dance move, it can increase its Attack, as well as boost its Speed. By using Rain Dance, it can summon a rain that will increase the power of its Water-type move Hydro Pump by 50%. This is one opponent that you do not want to give the time to build itself up in battle, or victory will quickly become impossible. And don't think for a second you've seen everything yet. Lysandre could have a few tricks up his sleeve, so it might be a good idea to bring along some Pokémon with Fighting-, Bug-, or Fairy-type moves. When defeating Lysandre's other Pokémon, be sure that you keep at least one Pokémon ready to stand up against Gyarados—one that is healthy and ready to switch in the moment it is needed.

STEP
9
Stand back as the ultimate weapon is unleashed

You've beaten Lysandre and saved the Legendary Pokémon, but the ultimate weapon has siphoned just enough power for one use. Lysandre foolishly fires the ultimate weapon, unleashing a massive blast of energy that soars into outer space before crashing down upon Geosenge Town. As luck would have it, that blast falls directly back down on the ultimate weapon, obliterating the dangerous device. The Kalos region is safe again.

Geosenge Town (Third Visit)

The deployment and subsequent destruction of the ultimate weapon has left a gaping hole in the center of this town, home of the standing stones. Many buildings lie in ruin, but a few remain intact.

Field Moves Needed

To Team Flare
Secret HQ

Route 11
(to Azure
Bay and
Shalour
City)

Pokémon
Center

Hotel Marine
Snow

Route 10
(to Cyllage City)

STEP 1 » Regroup with your friends

So, we won't have to deal with Team Flare anymore. ▾

With Team Flare's scheme undone, you and your friends take a moment to regroup in Geosenge Town. The defenders of Kalos are also present, and you discover that they are actually Sina and Dexio in disguise. (As if you hadn't noticed!)

STEP 2 » Meet the mysterious man again

A long, long time ago.
A very long time ago. ▾

Your friends are excited to get back to their own goals, and everyone hurries on ahead of you. Before you can follow them and Fly back to Anistar City, though, the mysterious stranger appears again, surveying the wreckage. Finding no trace of his beloved Pokémon, he departs with a heavy heart. Maybe you'll see him again someday, but now it's time to resume your own journey.

This path is best known for its trolley, once used for the coal mine, and the curious Inverse Battle house.

Route 18 (Vallée Étroite Way)

This lush mountain trail links Anistar City and Couriway Town. The mysterious Terminus Cave can be accessed by delving into the mining tunnels. Visiting this cave is optional, but if you're in the mood for adventure, go ahead and explore it. You'll find a lot of goodies and encounter new Pokémon. Also, the Inverse Battle house is definitely worth a look.

Field Moves Needed

Cut · Rock Smash

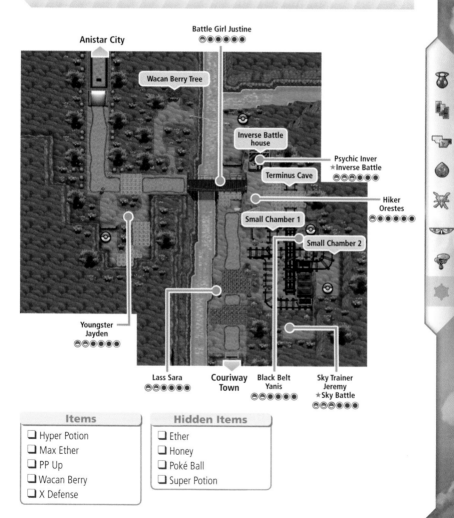

Anistar City

Battle Girl Justine

Wacan Berry Tree

Inverse Battle house

Psychic Inver ★Inverse Battle

Terminus Cave

Hiker Orestes

Small Chamber 1

Small Chamber 2

Youngster Jayden

Lass Sara

Couriway Town

Black Belt Yanis

Sky Trainer Jeremy ★Sky Battle

Items	Hidden Items
❑ Hyper Potion	❑ Ether
❑ Max Ether	❑ Honey
❑ PP Up	❑ Poké Ball
❑ Wacan Berry	❑ Super Potion
❑ X Defense	

Lairon
Rock **Steel**
Abilities: Sturdy
Rock Head

Pupitar
Rock **Ground**
Ability: Shed Skin

Tall Grass		
❏ Durant	△	
❏ Graveler	△	
❏ Gurdurr	◎	
❏ Heatmor	▲	
❏ Lairon	△	✗
❏ Pupitar	△	Y
❏ Sandslash	△	
❏ Torkoal	◎	

Red Flowers		
❏ Durant	△	
❏ Graveler	△	
❏ Gurdurr	△	
❏ Heatmor	▲	
❏ Lairon	◎	✗
❏ Pupitar	◎	Y
❏ Sandslash	◎	
❏ Torkoal	△	

Horde Encounter	
❏ Durant ×5	◎
❏ Durant ×4 Heatmor ×1	△
❏ Geodude ×5	◎

Cracked Rock	
❏ Graveler	◎
❏ Shuckle	▲

Shaking Bush	
❏ Durant	◎
❏ Heatmor	△

◎ frequent ◎ average △ rare ▲ almost never

STEP
1 ▶ Swing by the Inverse Battle house

Would you care to try an Inverse Battle?

Enter the small house on the hill beyond Route 18's lone bridge, and you'll encounter an unusual Psychic who has invented a new type of Pokémon battle—the Inverse Battle! In these unusual battles, the type matchup chart is completely reversed. So, for example, Fire-type moves would be super effective against Water-type Pokémon—when normally they are not very effective at all! You can have an Inverse Battle against Psychic Inver once each day. If you win, he'll reward you with a Rare Candy, Berry, or Evolution stone. If none of your Pokémon faint during the battle, he'll give you three prizes instead of one. What a generous guy!

TIP *Here's the list of what you can get from Inver: Oran Berry, Sitrus Berry, Occa Berry, Passho Berry, Wacan Berry, Rindo Berry, Yache Berry, Chople Berry, Kebia Berry, Shuca Berry, Coba Berry, Payapa Berry, Tanga Berry, Charti Berry, Kasib Berry, Haban Berry, Colbur Berry, Fire Stone, Water Stone, Leaf Stone, Thunder Stone, Moon Stone, Sun Stone, Shiny Stone, Dusk Stone, Dawn Stone, Everstone, and Rare Candy.*

STEP
2 Check out Terminus Cave

The abandoned coal mine near the Inverse Battle house is known as Terminus Cave. You could explore the cave now if you want to. Three entrances are accessible, and there are many items, Pokémon, and Trainers within! But Professor Sycamore is waiting for you in Couriway Town, so you may want to hurry to Couriway Town first. Perhaps someday you'll come back to investigate the rumors of a monster lurking in its dark tunnels...

STEP
3 Take on a Sky Battle

When you are exploring the many levels of Terminus Cave, head out onto the rickety trestle that holds up the mining cart rails, which have fallen into disuse above Route 18. At the southern end of one such railway, approach the edge and you'll spot a Sky Trainer. He is ready to challenge you to a Sky Battle, so if you're up to yet another challenge after your Inverse Battle, step right up!

STEP
4 Proceed south to Couriway Town

Professor Sycamore is waiting for you in Couriway Town (p. 317), so you'd better get a move on. There's surely some catching up to do after the tumultuous events you survived in Geosenge Town. Simply follow the path southward to get to the town and find the professor.

Terminus Cave

A chill wind blows through this forbidding cave, which lies along Route 18. Many wild Pokémon live here, and there's plenty of treasure for bold adventurers to discover. According to rumor, a powerful monster may dwell in the cave's deepest reaches...

Field Moves Needed

Rock Smash

1F

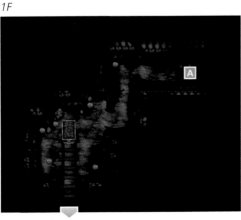

Entrance

B1F

Worker Narek

Worker Dimitri

Worker Yusif

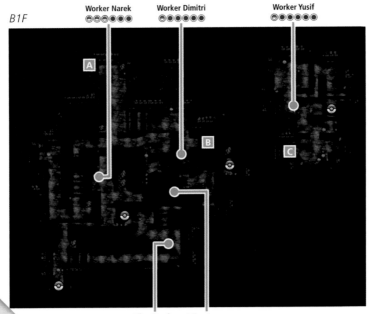

Hiker Bergin   Hiker Aaron

B2F

Black Belt
Gunnar

Battle Girl Hailey

Black Belt
Ricardo

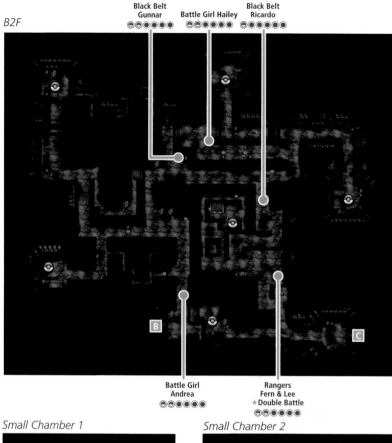

B

C

Battle Girl
Andrea

Rangers
Fern & Lee
★Double Battle

Small Chamber 1

Entrance

Small Chamber 2

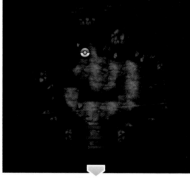

Entrance

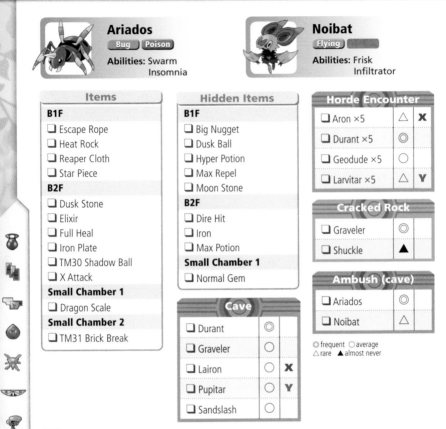

Ariados

Bug | Poison

Abilities: Swarm
Insomnia

Noibat

Flying |

Abilities: Frisk
Infiltrator

Items

B1F
- ❏ Escape Rope
- ❏ Heat Rock
- ❏ Reaper Cloth
- ❏ Star Piece

B2F
- ❏ Dusk Stone
- ❏ Elixir
- ❏ Full Heal
- ❏ Iron Plate
- ❏ TM30 Shadow Ball
- ❏ X Attack

Small Chamber 1
- ❏ Dragon Scale

Small Chamber 2
- ❏ TM31 Brick Break

Hidden Items

B1F
- ❏ Big Nugget
- ❏ Dusk Ball
- ❏ Hyper Potion
- ❏ Max Repel
- ❏ Moon Stone

B2F
- ❏ Dire Hit
- ❏ Iron
- ❏ Max Potion

Small Chamber 1
- ❏ Normal Gem

Cave

❏ Durant	◎	
❏ Graveler	○	
❏ Lairon	○	X
❏ Pupitar	○	Y
❏ Sandslash	○	

Horde Encounter

❏ Aron ×5	△	X
❏ Durant ×5	◎	
❏ Geodude ×5	○	
❏ Larvitar ×5	△	Y

Cracked Rock

❏ Graveler	◎
❏ Shuckle	▲

Ambush (cave)

❏ Ariados	◎
❏ Noibat	△

◎ frequent　○ average
△ rare　▲ almost never

STEP

1 ▶ Find the correct entrance and enter at your peril

Xavier found an Escape Rope!

Terminus Cave features three entrances, but only one of them leads to its main floors. Use the entrance near the Inverse Battle house to start your exploration of Terminus Cave. Once inside, you will find it is a long, dark, and dizzying path. You may want to have an Escape Rope with you if you have any doubts about facing the many wild Pokémon and lurking Trainers in your quest to collect all the many items within. Luckily, you can find one on the first basement floor!

NOTE *Be sure to check the cave's two other entrances as well. Each leads to a small chamber containing additional items.*

Couriway Town

The rushing roar of this mountain town's giant waterfall is surprisingly soothing. You're just passing through here, but don't let that stop you from taking a moment to sit at the lookout and enjoy the awesome spectacle of nature.

Field Moves Needed

Surf   Waterfall

Route 18
(to Anistar City)

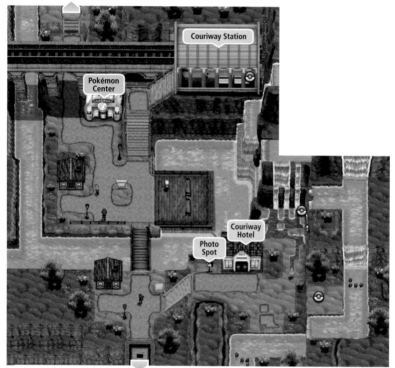

Couriway Station

Pokémon Center

Couriway Hotel

Photo Spot

Route 19
(to Snowbelle City)

Basculin (Blue-Striped Form) **Y**

`Water`

Abilities: Reckless
Adaptability

Basculin (Red-Striped Form) **X**

`Water`

Abilities: Reckless
Adaptability

Items

First visit
- ❑ Charcoal (if you chose Fennekin)
- ❑ Max Potion
- ❑ Miracle Seed (if you chose Chespin)
- ❑ Mystic Water (if you chose Froakie)
- ❑ Oran Berry
- ❑ Rare Candy
- ❑ Relax Ribbon (in the hotel on Friday)
- ❑ Revive
- ❑ TM55 Scald
- ❑ TM89 U-turn

After learning the Waterfall field move
- ❑ TM80 Rock Slide

Hidden Items
- ❑ Burn Heal
- ❑ Ether
- ❑ Poké Ball
- ❑ Pretty Wing
- ❑ Prism Scale

Fishing

Old Rod

❑ Poliwag	◎

Good Rod

❑ Basculin (Blue-Striped Form)	◎	X
❑ Basculin (Red-Striped Form)	◎	Y
❑ Poliwhirl	○	

Super Rod

❑ Basculin (Blue-Striped Form)	○	Y
❑ Basculin (Red-Striped Form)	○	X
❑ Poliwhirl	◎	

Water Surface

❑ Floatzel	○
❑ Lombre	◎

◎ frequent ○ average
△ rare ▲ almost never

Fresh Water Seller

Fresh Water	300*

*A free Oran Berry is included with your first purchase.

STEP
1 Have a friendly battle with Professor Sycamore

everything you learned from your journey and hit me with your very best shot!

As you near Couriway Town's central bridge, Professor Sycamore approaches you. The professor apologizes for being slow in catching the error of Lysandre's ways, and then challenges you to a friendly Pokémon battle. Professor Sycamore has been brushing up on his skills, so expect a tougher battle this time around!

Professor Sycamore's Pokémon

Venusaur	Blastoise	Charizard
♂ Lv. 50 Grass Poison	♂ Lv. 50 Water	♂ Lv. 50 Fire Flying
Weak to: Fire Ice Flying Psychic	Weak to: Grass Electric	Weak to: Rock Water Electric

STEP 2 ▶▶ Talk to the townsfolk and receive lots of goodies

Oh! Your Pikachu!
It knows Nuzzle!

Chatting with Couriway Town's residents is both informative and profitable. Start with the Madame at the Couriway Station who will give you TM89 U-turn. Next, drop in at the house on the north bank, where a Schoolgirl wants to see a Pokémon with the move Nuzzle. If you have a Pokémon that knows this move—like Pikachu, Minun, Pachirisu, Emolga, or Dedenne—show it off in return for a Revive.

STEP 3 ▶▶ Get a special item for your first partner

Xavier obtained a Charcoal!

Cross the bridge to visit the house on the town's south bank. Inside is a Beauty who wants to see how well you know your first Pokémon partner. She will ask you about Chespin, Fennekin, or Froakie, depending on which you chose at the beginning of the game. If you answer correctly, you will get a Miracle Seed, a Charcoal, or a Mystic Water.

Each of these three items can strengthen moves of the same type as your first partner: Miracle Seeds boost the power of Grass-type moves, Charcoal does the same for Fire-type moves, and Mystic Water will aid Water-type moves.

STEP
④ Visit the Couriway Hotel for more rewards

Answering another quizzical question in the hotel lobby will get you TM55 Scald, if you are correct. This is a rare Water-type move that can leave a Burn on the target.

You can also find Mr. Bonding upstairs, waiting to grant you the O-Power Stealth Power.

And if you happen to be visiting on a Friday, a woman upstairs will give you a Relax Ribbon for your lead Pokémon.

STEP
⑤ Proceed south to Route 19

There are still many items to be found around the town, so be sure that you've explored every nook, cranny, and waterway. Why not take a minute to enjoy the falls as well? You can always take a photo to remember them by. After you've fully explored Couriway Town, it's time to move along. Route 19 lies to the south and leads toward your next destination, Snowbelle City.

This great valley can now be crossed thanks to its long bridge, built with the help of many Pokémon.

Route 19 (Grande Vallée Way)

Route 19 is very large, and it runs between Couriway Town and Snowbelle City. It features lots of flowers in which to frolic, along with a less-inviting swampy basin. Numerous Trainers and Pokémon will delay you as you try to make your way across this expansive area, and they will prove quite tough as you advance toward Victory Road. Explore the upper and lower regions of this route, before coming to the long bridge that spans the swampy gorge—this route's most impressive landmark.

Field Moves Needed

Strength   Surf

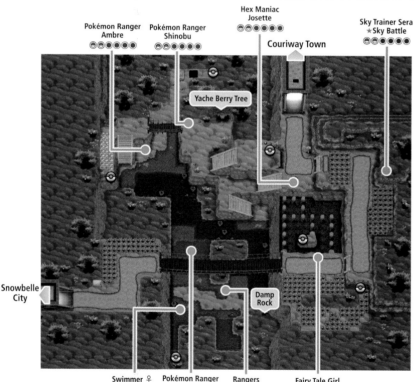

Hex Maniac Josette
◉◉◉◉◉◉

Pokémon Ranger Ambre
◉◉◉◉◉◉

Pokémon Ranger Shinobu
◉◉◉◉◉◉

Couriway Town

Sky Trainer Sera ★Sky Battle
◉◉◉◉◉◉

Yache Berry Tree

Snowbelle City

Damp Rock

Swimmer ♀ Coral
◉◉◉◉◉◉

Pokémon Ranger Clementine
◉◉◉◉◉◉

Rangers Ivy & Orrick ★Double Battle
◉◉◉◉◉◉

Fairy Tale Girl Lovelyn
◉◉◉◉◉◉

Drapion

Poison Dark

Abilities: Battle Armor
Sniper

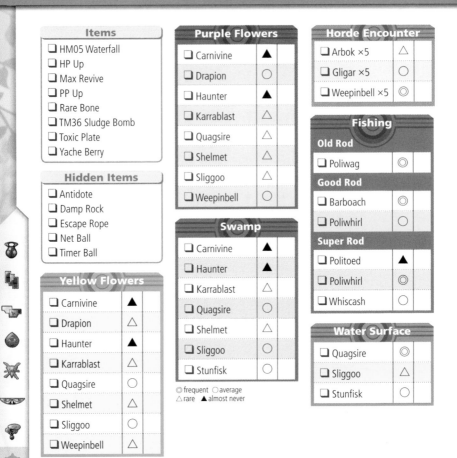

Items

- ❑ HM05 Waterfall
- ❑ HP Up
- ❑ Max Revive
- ❑ PP Up
- ❑ Rare Bone
- ❑ TM36 Sludge Bomb
- ❑ Toxic Plate
- ❑ Yache Berry

Hidden Items

- ❑ Antidote
- ❑ Damp Rock
- ❑ Escape Rope
- ❑ Net Ball
- ❑ Timer Ball

Yellow Flowers

❑ Carnivine	▲	
❑ Drapion	△	
❑ Haunter	▲	
❑ Karrablast	△	
❑ Quagsire	○	
❑ Shelmet	△	
❑ Sliggoo	○	
❑ Weepinbell	△	

Purple Flowers

❑ Carnivine	▲	
❑ Drapion	○	
❑ Haunter	▲	
❑ Karrablast	△	
❑ Quagsire	△	
❑ Shelmet	△	
❑ Sliggoo	△	
❑ Weepinbell	○	

Swamp

❑ Carnivine	▲	
❑ Haunter	▲	
❑ Karrablast	△	
❑ Quagsire	○	
❑ Shelmet	△	
❑ Sliggoo	○	
❑ Stunfisk	○	

◎ frequent ○ average
△ rare ▲ almost never

Horde Encounter

❑ Arbok ×5	△	
❑ Gligar ×5	○	
❑ Weepinbell ×5	◎	

Fishing

Old Rod

❑ Poliwag	◎	

Good Rod

❑ Barboach	◎	
❑ Poliwhirl	○	

Super Rod

❑ Politoed	▲	
❑ Poliwhirl	◎	
❑ Whiscash	○	

Water Surface

❑ Quagsire	◎	
❑ Sliggoo	△	
❑ Stunfisk	○	

STEP

1 Challenge the last Sky Trainer

Flying high in the sky can show you a whole new world!

This is it! Head up the small flight of stairs you find soon after entering Route 19, and cut through the purple flowers to the east. You should find the last of the 14 Sky Trainers that can be challenged in the Kalos region. By now, you have probably become quite an expert on Sky Battles. Use everything that you've learned to blow this Sky Trainer and her two Pokémon away in your greatest Sky Battle yet!

STEP
2 Collect items and experience

Hop to it! The skipping stones that lie to the west will lead you to a handy Max Revive. Some large hurdles loom before you on your way to Victory Road, so you're definitely going to want this item. There is also an HP Up lurking in the lovely lilac flowers, and don't forget to whip out your Dowsing Machine from time to time to find more hidden items. But don't venture across the long rope bridge yet. There is still a lot to explore in the bottom of valley, far below you.

STEP
3 Step into the soggy bottoms

Head back to the entrance to Route 19, and this time head west and down the stairs. Lots of items have dropped down into the swamps over the years, and they're just waiting for you to find them. And the many Trainers will help your Pokémon grow before you take on your friends in some friendly battles. You've all come a long way together, but that doesn't mean they'll just let you win. You may want to swing back by Couriway Town once more to heal your Pokémon. As you head back to the gate, don't miss your chance to pick up a Yache Berry and a nice TM!

4 Come full circle with Shauna

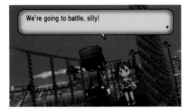

We're going to battle, silly!

It's been a long time since you first met Shauna on your first day in your new hometown. You two have shared many memories from around the Kalos region, and now it is time to make one more. As you cross the long bridge that spans the grand valley, turn to face her in Pokémon battle again. Her team consists of much more now than a single partner she'd just met, and she's learned a lot on her journey as well. Be ready for this battle!

Vs. Pokémon Trainer Shauna's Pokémon

If you chose **Chespin:**	If you chose **Fennekin:**	If you chose **Froakie:**
Greninja ♀ Lv. 51 [Water] [Dark]	**Chesnaught** ♀ Lv. 51 [Grass] [Fighting]	**Delphox** ♀ Lv. 51 [Fire] [Psychic]
Weak to: [Grass] [Electric] [Fighting] [Bug] [Fairy]	Weak to: [Flying] (4x!) [Fire] [Ice] [Poison] [Psychic] [Fairy]	Weak to: [Water] [Ground] [Rock] [Ghost] [Dark]
Delcatty ♀ Lv. 49 [Normal]	**Delcatty** ♀ Lv. 49 [Normal]	**Delcatty** ♀ Lv. 49 [Normal]
Weak to: [Fighting]	Weak to: [Fighting]	Weak to: [Fighting]
Goodra ♂ Lv. 49 [Dragon]	**Goodra** ♂ Lv. 49 [Dragon]	**Goodra** ♂ Lv. 49 [Dragon]
Weak to: [Ice] [Dragon] [Fairy]	Weak to: [Ice] [Dragon] [Fairy]	Weak to: [Ice] [Dragon] [Fairy]

STEP
5 Have a rematch with Tierno

The moment you finish your battle with Shauna, your pals Trevor and Tierno arrive. Tierno wastes little time challenging you to a Pokémon battle. There's no rest for the weary, it seems! It's been ages since you last battled him. Why don't you see how his Pokémon dance team measures up? Tierno may claim that he's not much for battling, but he won't be a pushover in this fight.

Vs. **Pokémon Trainer Tierno's Pokémon**

Talonflame ♂ Lv. 48 [Fire] [Flying]	Crawdaunt ♂ Lv. 52 [Water] [Dark]	Roserade ♀ Lv. 49 [Grass] [Poison]
Weak to: [x4][x1] [Rock] [Water] [Electric]	Weak to: [Grass] [Electric] [Fighting] [Bug] [Fairy]	Weak to: [Fire] [Ice] [Flying] [Psychic]

STEP
6 Help Trevor experience a new kind of battle

Trevor has been a relentless rival every step of your journey, always wanting to compete with you for completion of the Pokédexes of the Kalos region. But he usually shies away from actual Pokémon battles. There are some things that can only be understood by experiencing them, and your bookish friend is ready at last to challenge you to a real Pokémon battle. He likes a fair fight, though, so he heals your Pokémon before the battle. Let nothing stop you from achieving victory!

Pokémon Trainer Trevor's Pokémon

Raichu
♂ Lv. 49 Electric

Weak to: Ground

Aerodactyl
♂ Lv. 49 Rock Flying

Weak to: Water Electric Ice
Rock Steel

Florges
♀ Lv. 51 Fairy

Weak to: Poison Steel

STEP
7 Receive HM05 Waterfall

I've gotta get going!
See you!

That sure was a lot of battling, but don't worry, Serena/Calem is off training with the Mega Evolution guru, so you don't have to face another battle just yet. Instead, Trevor, Tierno, and Shauna depart to catch more Pokémon, but not before Shauna gives you HM05 Waterfall as a special gift!

NOTE *Your Pokémon can use the HM05 Waterfall move in battle, but you won't be able to use it as a field move until you've obtained the eighth Gym Badge.*

STEP
8 Proceed west to Snowbelle City

When you've finished your thorough exploration of Route 19, proceed west across the long bridge. Keep going west to reach Snowbelle City. You could probably use a little break by now, but don't rest too long. Your eighth and final Gym battle is waiting for you—and after that, Victory Road!

Snowbelle City

You've traveled far to reach this snowcapped city, where the eighth Gym Badge can be obtained. Unfortunately, however, the Snowbelle City Gym Leader, Wulfric, isn't around when you first arrive. What a shame! You'll just have to track him down. Whether you do so before or after exploring the town is up to you, but you'll probably want to at least rest your team at the Pokémon Center before setting out into the worrisomely named Winding Wood.

Field Moves Needed

Bisharp

Dark **Steel**

Abilities: Defiant
Inner Focus

Items	Hidden Items	Poké Mart	
❑ Full Restore	❑ Full Heal	Dusk Ball	1,000
❑ Revive	❑ Icy Rock	Heal Ball	300
❑ TM08 Bulk Up	❑ X Sp. Atk	Nest Ball	1,000
❑ TM13 Ice Beam		Net Ball	1,000
❑ Gracidea Flower	**Trade**	Quick Ball	1,000
	❑ Bisharp (trade for Jigglypuff)	Repeat Ball	1,000
		Timer Ball	1,000

STEP
1 ▶ Meet Mr. Bonding at the Pokémon Center

Hey, how's it going, friend?

Your old pal Mr. Bonding is warming up inside Snowbelle City's Pokémon Center. Speak with him to receive a new O-Power, PP Restoring Power. This excellent O-Power lets you restore your lead Pokémon's PP and is a huge help when you are trekking through the long, long path of Victory Road. And that's where you will soon be headed, young Trainer!

STEP
2 ▶ Learn ultimate moves from the Move Tutor

Let me reward your passion with some absolutely astounding moves.

A sage old man known as the Move Tutor resides here in Snowbelle City. Enter his house and speak with him, and he'll offer to teach ultimate moves to your Pokémon. These mighty moves are incredibly powerful, but your Pokémon won't be able to act on its next turn after it uses an ultimate move.

TIP *Speak to the Move Tutor's wife to learn which Pokémon are capable of learning ultimate moves.*

STEP
3 ▶ Receive a TM and other gifts from the locals

Let's trade my Bisharp for a Jigglypuff?

Yes
No

When you stop by the Snowbelle City Gym, you're informed that Leader Wulfric has left to explore the nearby Winding Woods. You won't be able to challenge him anytime soon, so talk to everyone else in town for information. One Battle Girl will give you TM08 Bulk Up, and another woman will offer to trade Pokémon with you. One man will give you a Revive if any of the Pokémon in your team has the Mat Block move.

> TIP
>
> *In the house north of the Pokémon Center, stop in to talk to the Ace Trainer. She'd love to share with you one of her early compositions. This jazzy tune somehow sounds very...jubilant. Don't you think?*

STEP
④ Search for Wulfric in the Winding Woods

You haven't traveled all this way for nothing! If Wulfric has gone to the Winding Woods, then you'll just have to track him down. Prepare your Pokémon, and then follow the southwest path out of Snowbelle City and into the Winding Woods.

AFTER FINDING WULFRIC:
⊗ Prepare to challenge Gym Leader Wulfric

After you've finished looking around the Pokémon Village (p. 334), use Fly to return to Snowbelle City. It sure beats traveling back through the Winding Woods! When you arrive, prepare your Pokémon for the challenges to come in the Snowbelle City Gym.

Route 20 (Winding Woods)

The Winding Woods certainly lives up to its name. This confounding forest has multiple paths, some of which seem to bend the very laws of nature by leading you back to previous areas. Take it nice and slow through this shady route, and do your best to keep your bearings as you search for the Gym Leader, Wulfric.

Field Moves Needed

Cut

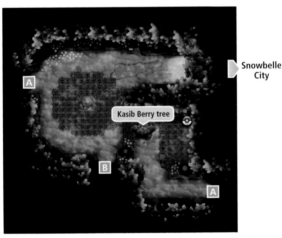

Snowbelle City

Kasib Berry tree

Twins Nana & Nina
★Double Battle

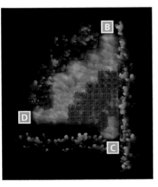

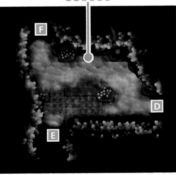

Gothorita

Psychic

Abilities: Frisk
Competitive

Noctowl

Normal Flying

Abilities: Insomnia
Keen Eye

Fairy Tale Girl
Wynne
◉◉◉◉◉◉

Hex Maniac
Desdemona
◉◉◉◉◉◉

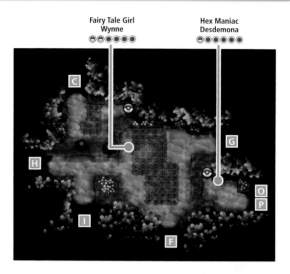

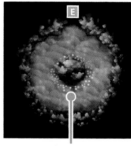

Poké Fan Roisin
◉◉◉◉◉◉

Poké Fan Corey
◉◉◉◉◉◉

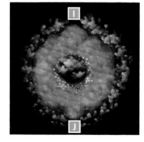

NOTE *Wondering why some entrances are marked with more than one letter? These woods are very tricky, and even going through the same exit does not guarantee that you'll end up in the same place as you did the time before. Try not to get too lost!*

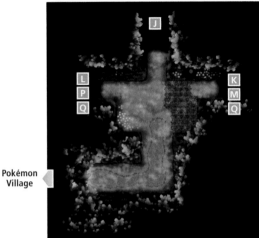

Pokémon
Village

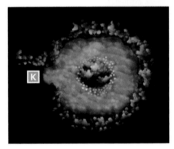

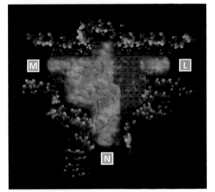

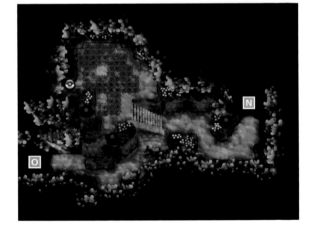

Items

- ❏ Kasib Berry
- ❏ Meadow Plate
- ❏ Paralyze Heal
- ❏ Protein
- ❏ TM53 Energy Ball
- ❏ X Accuracy

Hidden Items

- ❏ Antidote
- ❏ Balm Mushroom
- ❏ Mental Herb
- ❏ Repeat Ball
- ❏ Tiny Mushroom

Tall Grass		
❏ Amoonguss	◯	
❏ Gothorita	△	
❏ Jigglypuff	◯	
❏ Noctowl	◯	
❏ Trevenant	△	
❏ Zoroark	▲	

◎ frequent ◯ average
△ rare ▲ almost never

Red Flowers		
❏ Amoonguss	◯	
❏ Gothorita	◯	
❏ Jigglypuff	△	
❏ Noctowl	△	
❏ Trevenant	◯	
❏ Zoroark	▲	

Horde Encounter		
❏ Foongus ×5	◎	
❏ Trevenant ×5	◯	
❏ Trevenant ×4 Sudowoodo ×1	△	

STEP
① Navigate the Winding Woods

The Winding Woods contains many valuable items, so it's worth giving the route a thorough search. The paths become trickier to navigate as you near the route's end, for certain paths will lead back to previous areas in a baffling manner. Use the maps in this guidebook to stay on course as you explore. Visit each twisting turn to collect all the items and snag a new Berry, and don't stop until you reach daylight!

NOTE *In the first stretch of woods that you enter, you will find an impressive boulder covered in moss. It seems almost as though it was put there for some reason...*

The Pokémon Village

This secret village is home to runaway Pokémon who have been mistreated by cruel Trainers. The Pokémon here are timid as a result, and they will flee at the sight of most humans unless they sense a strong bond of friendship between the visitor and her or his Pokémon.

Field Moves Needed

Cut Surf

Waterfall

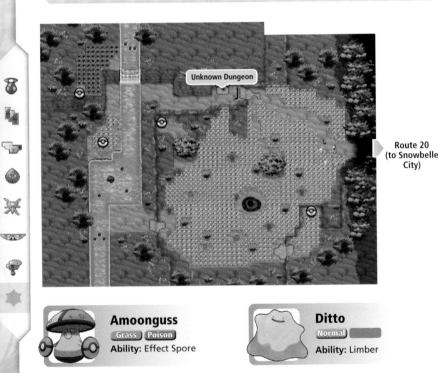

Unknown Dungeon

Route 20 (to Snowbelle City)

Amoonguss

Grass Poison

Ability: Effect Spore

Ditto

Normal

Ability: Limber

Items	Hidden Items
First visit	❑ Honey ×2
❑ Chople Berry	❑ Pretty Wing
❑ Full Restore	
❑ Max Ether	
❑ Pixie Plate	
❑ Pretty Wing	
After learning the Waterfall field move	
❑ TM29 Psychic	

Yellow Flowers	
❏ Amoonguss	◎
❏ Ditto	○
❏ Gothorita	○
❏ Jigglypuff	△
❏ Noctowl	○
❏ Zoroark	△

Purple Flowers	
❏ Amoonguss	○
❏ Ditto	△
❏ Gothorita	△
❏ Jigglypuff	○
❏ Noctowl	○
❏ Zoroark	△

Horde Encounter	
❏ Foongus ×5	◎
❏ Lombre ×5	△
❏ Poliwag ×5	○

Fishing		
Old Rod		
❏ Poliwag	◎	
Good Rod		
❏ Basculin (Blue-Striped Form)	◎	X
❏ Basculin (Red-Striped Form)	◎	Y
❏ Poliwhirl	○	
Super Rod		
❏ Basculin (Blue-Striped Form)	○	Y
❏ Basculin (Red-Striped Form)	○	X
❏ Poliwhirl	◎	

Water Surface	
❏ Lombre	◎
❏ Poliwhirl	○

Trash Can	
❏ Garbodor	◎
❏ Banette	△

◎ frequent ○ average
△ rare ▲ almost never

STEP
1 Have a chat with Gym Leader Wulfric

Oh--excuse my manners. We haven't even had a proper introduction yet. The name's Wulfric.

The Winding Woods lead to this secret village, where at last you discover Leader Wulfric. The powerful Pokémon Trainer knows that you've come to challenge him and apologizes for making you travel all this way. After he assures the local Pokémon that you're a friend, Wulfric departs. He'll return to Snowbelle City, where he'll gladly accept your challenge at the Gym.

Speak to the Pokémon that surrounded Leader Wulfric. They don't have much to say, but one will give you a Pretty Wing, while another will give you a Chople Berry.

STEP
② Explore the Pokémon Village

A strange, black shadow leaped out in a panic!

Take a moment to explore the Pokémon Village before flying back to Snowbelle City. There are wild Pokémon to catch here and several items to find. Additional Pokémon can be caught by inspecting the shaking trash cans, just as you did back at the Lost Hotel. (However, sometimes the Pokémon manage to flee, and all you might find in their wake is an item they dropped in their haste.) And just as was true in the Lost Hotel, it seems that the Pokémon inhabiting these trash cans can vary by day. Check back on different days to try to get rare Pokémon!

 NOTE You can surf the river to the west to reach a cave known as the Unknown Dungeon, but the man who stands outside the cave only lets Champions inside. You'll just have to come back later!

AFTER OBTAINING THE ICEBERG BADGE:
⚙ Swim up mighty waterfalls with ease

After you obtain your eighth and final badge, you will be able to fully use the HM05 Waterfall that Shauna and your friends gave you. Now you can climb up and down waterfalls freely, opening up some new areas for you to explore. They contain useful items, so consider a quick trip around Kalos to retrieve them all before taking on Victory Road.

NOTE There are waterfalls waiting to be climbed on Routes 15, 16, and 22, as well as outside the Frost Cavern and in Couriway Town. Keep an eye out for waterfalls you can climb on Victory Road as well.

Snowbelle City Gym Battle

Gym Battle Tips

✓ Bring lots of Hyper Potions and items that heal status conditions
✓ Use Fire-, Fighting-, Rock-, and Steel-type Pokémon

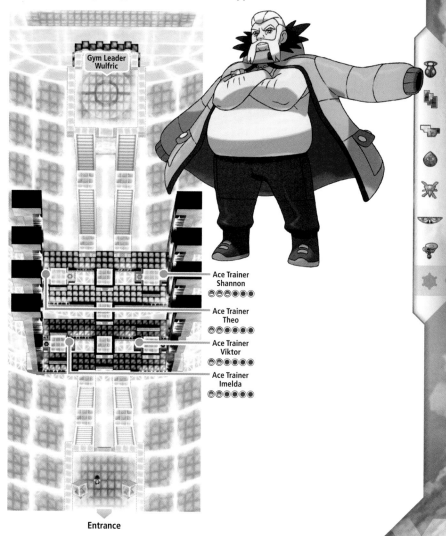

Gym Leader Wulfric

Ace Trainer Shannon
◉◉◉◉◉◉

Ace Trainer Theo
◉◉◉◉◉◉

Ace Trainer Viktor
◉◉◉◉◉◉

Ace Trainer Imelda
◉◉◉◉◉◉

Entrance

Wulfric

Ice-type Pokémon User

Deal massive damage with Fire-, Fighting-, Rock-, and Steel-type moves

At first glance, the Snowbelle City Gym seems very straightforward, but there's actually some complexity involved. Each of the Gym's four Trainers stands near a colored button. Defeat each Trainer, and you'll be able to step on the buttons that they guard. Each time you step on a colored button, the matching section of the Gym rotates, altering the arrangement of the connecting paths. You'll sometimes need to backtrack and activate previous buttons in order to reach Leader Wulfric at the Gym's north end.

As is obvious by now, Leader Wulfric favors powerful Ice-type Pokémon. Defeat his Pokémon quickly with Fire-, Fighting-, Rock-, and Steel-type moves. Fire- and Steel-type Pokémon will be especially helpful, since their type moves are not only super effective against Ice types, but they also take only half the damage from Ice-type attacks! Try not to give Wulfric a chance to mount much offense, for his Pokémon's moves can inflict the Frozen status condition. This can really put your offense on ice by preventing your Pokémon from taking any action. Use Ice Heals or items that remove all status conditions to thaw your frozen friends. Moves that prevent status conditions, such as Safeguard, are also helpful.

Wulfric's Pokémon

Abomasnow
♂ Lv. 56 Grass Ice
Weak to: Fire Fighting Poison Flying Bug Rock Steel

Avalugg
♂ Lv. 59 Ice
Weak to: Fire Fighting Rock Steel

Cryogonal
Lv. 55 Ice
Weak to: Fire Fighting Rock Steel

Iceberg Badge

All Pokémon, including those received in trades, will obey you.

TM13 Ice Beam

The target is struck with an icy-cold beam of energy. This may also leave the target frozen.

STEP 3 › After clearing the Snowbelle City Gym, proceed west to Route 21

Congratulations, you've won the eighth and final Gym Badge! This means that you're finally able to brave Victory Road and battle to become the Kalos region's Champion. Warm up at the Pokémon Center before traveling west to Route 21, which leads to Victory Road.

Route 21 (Dernière Way)

This final route before Victory Road runs between Victory Road and Snowbelle City. While its main trail is short and easy to navigate, several worthy items lie off the beaten path, so it pays to explore.

Field Moves Needed

Cut Strength

Surf

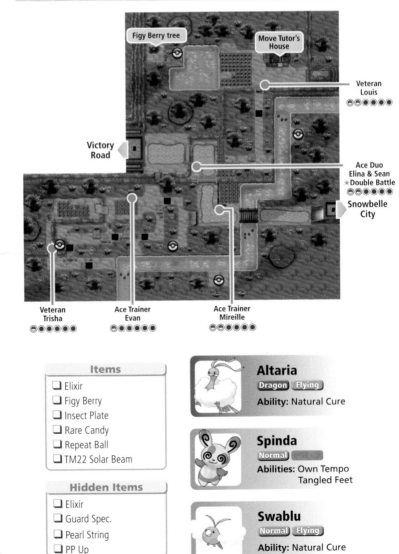

Figy Berry tree

Move Tutor's House

Veteran Louis
⊙⊙⊙⊙⊙⊙

Victory Road

Ace Duo Elina & Sean
★ Double Battle
⊙⊙⊙⊙⊙⊙

Snowbelle City

Veteran Trisha
⊙⊙⊙⊙⊙⊙

Ace Trainer Evan
⊙⊙⊙⊙⊙⊙

Ace Trainer Mireille
⊙⊙⊙⊙⊙⊙

Items

- ❑ Elixir
- ❑ Figy Berry
- ❑ Insect Plate
- ❑ Rare Candy
- ❑ Repeat Ball
- ❑ TM22 Solar Beam

Hidden Items

- ❑ Elixir
- ❑ Guard Spec.
- ❑ Pearl String
- ❑ PP Up

Altaria
Dragon Flying
Ability: Natural Cure

Spinda
Normal
Abilities: Own Tempo
Tangled Feet

Swablu
Normal Flying
Ability: Natural Cure

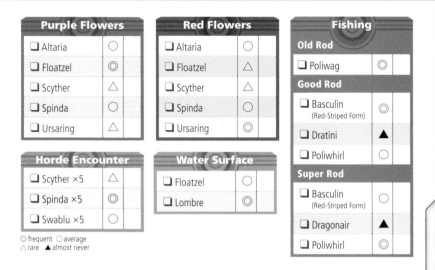

Purple Flowers		
❏ Altaria	◎	
❏ Floatzel	◉	
❏ Scyther	△	
❏ Spinda	◎	
❏ Ursaring	△	

Red Flowers		
❏ Altaria	◎	
❏ Floatzel	△	
❏ Scyther	△	
❏ Spinda	◎	
❏ Ursaring	◉	

Fishing		
Old Rod		
❏ Poliwag	◉	
Good Rod		
❏ Basculin (Red-Striped Form)	◉	
❏ Dratini	▲	
❏ Poliwhirl	◎	
Super Rod		
❏ Basculin (Red-Striped Form)	◎	
❏ Dragonair	▲	
❏ Poliwhirl	◉	

Horde Encounter		
❏ Scyther ×5	△	
❏ Spinda ×5	◉	
❏ Swablu ×5	◎	

Water Surface		
❏ Floatzel	◎	
❏ Lombre	◉	

◉ frequent ◎ average
△ rare ▲ almost never

STEP
1 ⟩ **Explore Route 21 in preparation for entering Victory Road**

If you wish, I can teach your Pokémon the strongest Dragon-type move. ▼

Victory Road beckons, and its entrance lies to the west. But take a few moments to explore Route 21 before you go there. Raid the route for valuables, and stop by the Move Tutor's house up north to have your Dragon-type Pokémon learn a powerful new move. Surf across the pond beside his house to get a new Berry, a Repeat Ball, and an Elixir. And don't miss that Pearl String somewhere in the purple flowers!

STEP
2 ⟩ **Overcome the obstacles in your path**

You used Strength once already to reach the Move Tutor's house, but you're not done with the boulders yet...Turn the page for a full guide if you're having trouble with the maze of boulders in the southwest corner of this route.

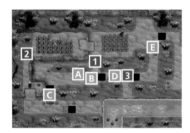

1. Walk down the dirt slope just before the gate to reach another area beside the river.

2. Head west around a patch of red flowers to cut down thorn bush 1 in the middle of the area.

3. Push boulder A as far west as you can.

4. Run back and push boulder B west as well.

5. Move to the north side of boulder B and push it south, filling the hole.

6. Circle back around to the north side of boulder A so that you can push it east until it fills the hole near its original location.

7. Walk over the hole that boulder B filled and push boulder C south.

STEP
3 » Keep pushing on

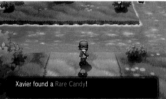

1. Run back up north then west through red flowers and cut thorn bush 2.

2. Head south, defeat the Trainer, then push boulder C east until it fills the hole between you and the river.

3. Surf east and alight at the first path you find to your north then cut down thorn bush 3.

5. Return to the river and surf farther east to collect a Rare Candy.

6. Return to the southwest path and run back up past boulder C, before turning east to finally reach boulder D. Push it through the recently cleared path and into its hole.

7. Approach boulder E from the south and push it north then east to fill the hole and find TM22 Solar Beam at the end of the path.

When you're finished exploring the route, go west to Victory Road.

Victory Road

This long, difficult road is the ultimate proving ground for Trainers. Only those who have collected all eight Gym Badges from around the Kalos region are allowed entry. Survive the many challenges that await you here, and you'll find yourself at the foot of the Pokémon League, mere battles away from being crowned the Kalos region's new Champion!

Field Moves Needed

Rock Smash · Strength · Surf · Waterfall

Items

Inside 1
- ❑ Dusk Ball
- ❑ TM03 Psyshock

Outside 2
- ❑ Rare Candy

Inside 2
- ❑ Carbos

Outside 3
- ❑ Max Elixir
- ❑ Max Revive ×2
- ❑ PP Up
- ❑ Quick Ball
- ❑ Zinc

Inside 3
- ❑ Dragon Fang
- ❑ Full Restore

Outside 4
- ❑ TM02 Dragon Claw

Entrance

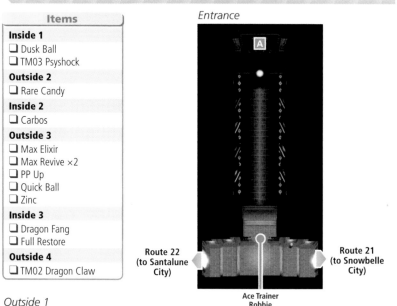

Route 22
(to Santalune City)

Route 21
(to Snowbelle City)

Ace Trainer
Robbie
◉◉◉◉◉◉

Outside 1

Hidden Items

Inside 1	Inside 3
❑ X Attack	❑ Escape Rope
Outside 2	❑ Max Repel
❑ Full Heal	**Outside 4**
❑ Hyper Potion	❑ Max Ether
Inside 2	❑ X Defense
❑ Smooth Rock	**Inside 4**
❑ Ultra Ball	❑ Star Piece
Outside 3	
❑ Pretty Wing	
❑ Revive	

Inside 1

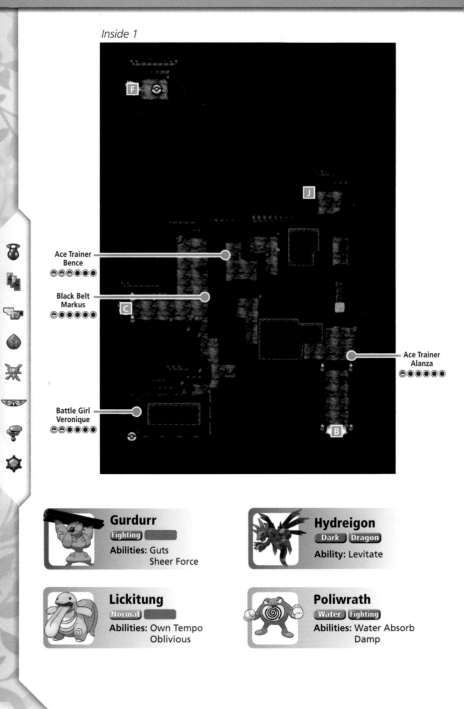

Ace Trainer Bence

Black Belt Markus

Ace Trainer Alanza

Battle Girl Veronique

Gurdurr
Fighting
Abilities: Guts
Sheer Force

Lickitung
Normal
Abilities: Own Tempo
Oblivious

Hydreigon
Dark Dragon
Ability: Levitate

Poliwrath
Water Fighting
Abilities: Water Absorb
Damp

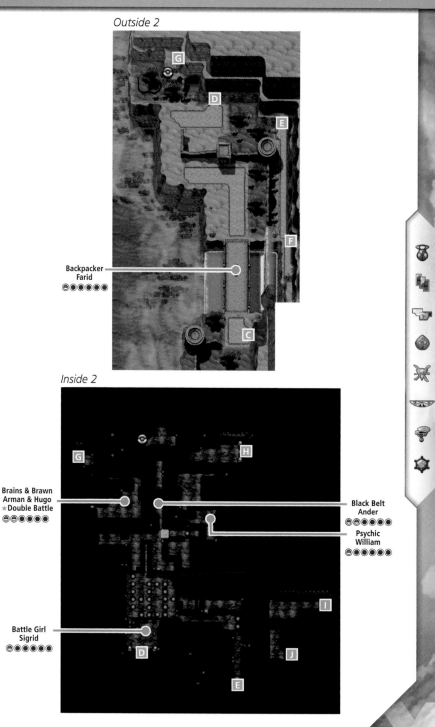

Outside 2

Backpacker
Farid

Inside 2

G

H

Brains & Brawn
Arman & Hugo
★Double Battle

Black Belt
Ander

Psychic
William

Battle Girl
Sigrid

D

E

I

J

Outside 3

Hex Maniac
Raziah
◉●●●●●

Restore your
Pokémon's
health

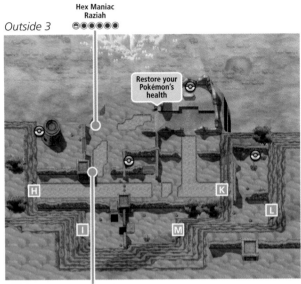

H

I

K

L

M

Fairy Tale Girl
Corinne
◉●●●●●

Inside 3

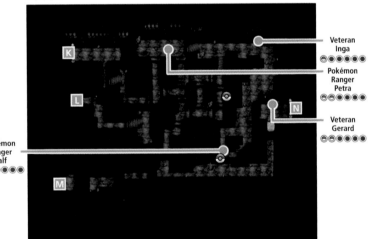

K

L

M

N

Veteran
Inga
◉●●●●●

Pokémon
Ranger
Petra
◉●●●●●

Veteran
Gerard
◉●●●●●

Pokémon
Ranger
Ralf
◉●●●●●

Outside 4

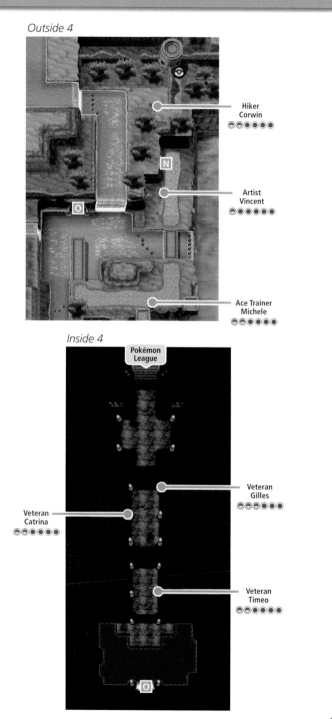

Hiker
Corwin

Artist
Vincent

Ace Trainer
Michele

Inside 4

Pokémon
League

Veteran
Gilles

Veteran
Catrina

Veteran
Timeo

Cave		
❑ Druddigon	○	
❑ Graveler	○	
❑ Gurdurr	○	
❑ Haunter	△	
❑ Lickitung	△	
❑ Zweilous	▲	

Ambush (cave)		
❑ Ariados	◎	
❑ Graveler	◎	
❑ Noibat	○	

Ambush (aerial)		
❑ Fearow	◎	
❑ Hydreigon	▲	
❑ Skarmory	△	

◎ frequent ○ average
△ rare ▲ almost never

Cracked Rock		
❑ Graveler	◎	
❑ Shuckle	▲	

Horde Encounter		
❑ Floatzel* ×5	○	
❑ Geodude ×5	◎	
❑ Graveler** ×5	○	
❑ Lickitung ×5	△	

*Only appears in caves 1 & 4
**Only appears in caves 2 & 3

Water Surface		
❑ Floatzel	○	
❑ Lombre*	◎	
❑ Poliwhirl**	◎	

*Only appears outdoors.
**Only appears in caves.

Fishing		
Old Rod		
❑ Poliwag	◎	
Good Rod		
❑ Basculin (Blue-Striped Form)	◎	X
❑ Basculin (Red-Striped Form)	◎	Y
❑ Poliwhirl	○	
Super Rod		
❑ Basculin (Blue-Striped Form)	○	Y
❑ Basculin (Red-Striped Form)	○	X
❑ Poliwhirl	◎	
❑ Poliwrath*	▲	

*Only appears in cave 4.

STEP
1 ❯ Pass through the Badge checkpoint

Wow! You have all eight.
Well then, allow me to test your abilities. ▼

Ace Trainer Robbie stands watch over Victory Road, and he only lets those who have collected all eight Gym Badges pass. Show Robbie your epic Badge collection, and he'll test your skills in battle. Win the battle, and you'll be allowed to enter Victory Road.

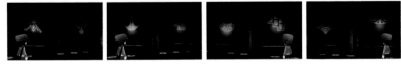

STEP
2 **Begin the long trek to the top**

Watch the path open before you and climb up to the dizzying heights of Victory Road. You will be making your way in and out of caves, which are swarming with Trainers, items, and surprising paths. Even when you break free from the dark depths of the caves, you will find yourself high on perilous cliffs above Kalos—and still facing expert Trainers at every bend. Use everything that you have learned to wind your way back and forth, overcome obstacles, and collect every item that is there for the taking.

STEP
3 **Create a shortcut**

When you come out of the second level of caves into a place filled with crumbling ruins, you may want to take the time to make yourself a handy shortcut back to the entrance to Victory Road. Run out of the cave exit and east along the stone wall until you come to a large boulder. Use Strength to drop it into the convenient hole in front of it, and then reenter the caves from the small side entrance you can now reach. Take the stairs down to the next floor, and eventually you'll find a boulder that you may have noticed on your first pass through. Drop it into the hole with Strength and you are back at the beginning of Victory Road.

TIP

You've already been through a lot of tough battles, and Serena/ Calem is waiting just ahead in the ruins. You can get your Pokémon's health restored by a Pokémon Ranger in the ruins, but if you're feeling low on items, you might want to take this chance to visit a Pokémon Center. With your new shortcut, you'll be able to run straight up the back stairs and be back where you were in a flash, even if you leave Victory Road for a time.

Battle against Serena/Calem as you navigate Victory Road

As you explore some old ruins about halfway up Victory Road, your old rival Serena/Calem arrives to challenge one last time before you face the Champion. Hopefully, you took advantage of the nearby Pokémon Ranger who can restore your Pokémon's health! Whether or not you did, be sure to do so after the battle—you've still got ground to cover before you reach the Pokémon League.

ⓥ Serena/Calem's Pokémon

If you chose Chespin:

Absol ♂ Lv. 59 `Dark`
Weak to: `Fighting` `Bug` `Fairy`

Altaria ♀ Lv. 58 `Dragon` `Flying`
Weak to: `4x!` `Ice` `Rock` `Dragon` `Fairy`

Meowstic ♀/♂ Lv. 57 `Psychic`
Weak to: `Bug` `Ghost` `Dark`

Delphox ♂ Lv. 61 `Fire` `Psychic`
Weak to: `Water` `Ground` `Rock` `Ghost` `Dark`

Jolteon ♂ Lv. 57 `Electric`
Weak to: `Ground`

If you chose Fennekin:

Absol ♂ Lv. 59 `Dark`
Weak to: `Fighting` `Bug` `Fairy`

Altaria ♀ Lv. 58 `Dragon` `Flying`
Weak to: `4x!` `Ice` `Rock` `Dragon` `Fairy`

Meowstic ♀/♂ Lv. 57 `Psychic`
Weak to: `Bug` `Ghost` `Dark`

Greninja ♂ Lv. 61 `Water` `Dark`
Weak to: `Grass` `Electric` `Fighting` `Bug` `Fairy`

Flareon ♂ Lv. 57 `Fire`
Weak to: `Water` `Ground` `Rock`

If you chose Froakie:

Absol ♂ Lv. 59 `Dark`
Weak to: `Fighting` `Bug` `Fairy`

Altaria ♀ Lv. 58 `Dragon` `Flying`
Weak to: `4x!` `Ice` `Rock` `Dragon` `Fairy`

Meowstic ♀/♂ Lv. 57 `Psychic`
Weak to: `Bug` `Ghost` `Dark`

Chesnaught ♂ Lv. 61 `Grass` `Fighting`
Weak to: `4x!` `Flying` `Fire` `Ice` `Poison` `Psychic` `Fairy`

Vaporeon ♂ Lv. 57 `Water`
Weak to: `Grass` `Electric`

STEP
5 Climb the final heights

Head back into the dark of the caves, and don't be in too much of a hurry. There are still many items to be found, and you'll have to go through the caves ahead at least a couple of times to get them all. You can keep visiting the Pokémon Ranger to have your team healed, so there's no reason not to get all these handy items for free when you've got the chance! When you finally come out into the light again, you'll find that the path ends—except for a savvy Trainer who can use Surf. Climb the waterfall to the east before sailing into the final cave, and from there it is on to the Pokémon League.

Pokémon League

This is it—the Pokémon League! Here you'll find some of the most powerful Trainers in the Kalos region, known as the Elite Four. Beat each of them in battle, and you'll earn the right to face the Champion. Just be sure you're ready to battle, for once you begin, there's no turning back!

Field Moves
Needed

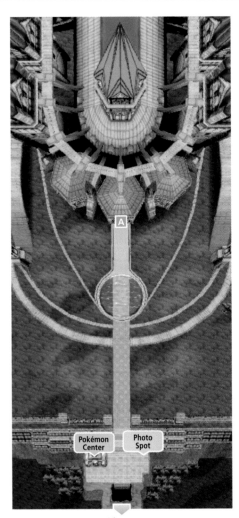

A

Pokémon
Center

Photo
Spot

Victory
Road

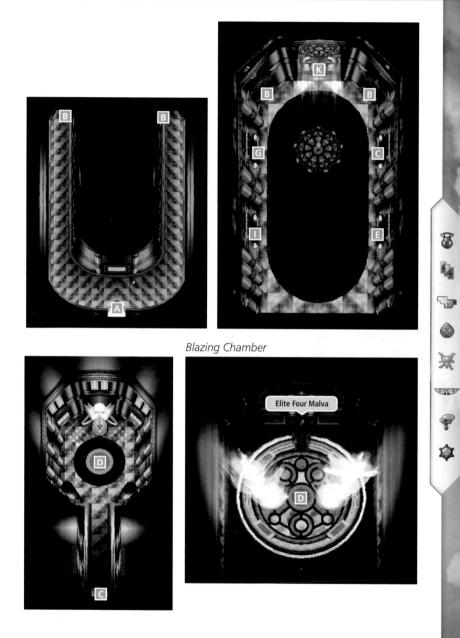

Blazing Chamber

Flood Chamber

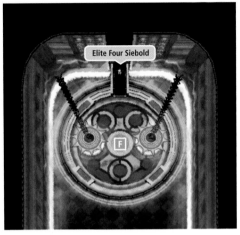

Elite Four Siebold

Ironworks Chamber

Elite Four Wikstrom

Dragonmark Chamber

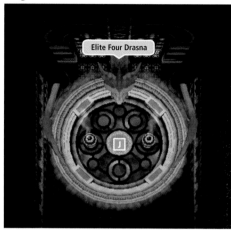

Radiant Chamber

1 Catch your breath at the Pokémon Center

Hello, and welcome to the Pokémon Center. Would you like to rest your Pokémon?

Yes
No

A Pokémon Center comes as a welcome sight when you arrive at the Pokémon League. Rest your faithful companions here and use the following techniques to prepare for the upcoming battles against the Elite Four and the Champion.

Defeat the Elite Four

TECHNIQUE 1
Examine your party with an expert eye

Take a look at the moves that the Pokémon in your party know. It's important that they know moves that will be effective against the Pokémon used by the Elite Four and the Champion. In addition to using TMs, enlist the aid of the Move Tutors in Snowbelle

City and Route 21, who can teach your Pokémon moves that will exploit the weaknesses of your opponent's Pokémon.

TECHNIQUE 2
Give Pokémon items to hold in battle

Give your Pokémon items that are useful in battle if they aren't already holding some. For example, if one of your Pokémon has a low Speed stat, give it a Quick Claw to hold. If it has moves with low accuracy ratings, give it a Wide Lens.

TECHNIQUE 3
Stock up on medicine

Healing is important during battles, but you'll also want to have plenty of healing items on hand to restore your Pokémon's HP and help them recover from any status conditions after each battle. Ensure that you have lots of Full Restores and Revives before you begin.

NOTE   *Once you enter the Pokémon League, you won't be able to leave until you either win against the Elite Four and the Champion, or you are defeated. It is therefore vital that you prepare with care before entering the Pokémon League.*

with these techniques!

TECHNIQUE 4
Save the most challenging opponent for last

Each of the Elite Four specializes in one of the following types: Fire, Water, Steel, or Dragon. The order in which you challenge them is up to you. Examine your party and decide which opponents will be easiest, then make them your first battles. By defeating the easiest opponents first, your Pokémon will become just a little bit stronger before you face your most difficult opponent.

TECHNIQUE 5
Use Rare Candies to level up your Pokémon

If you are having trouble against even the first member of the Elite Four you choose to challenge, try using Rare Candies to raise the levels of the Pokémon in your party. The higher a Pokémon's level, the stronger it becomes. You can obtain more Rare Candies even after you enter the Hall of Fame, so don't worry about using up all the ones you have at this point.

NOTE   *Each of the Elite Four has two Full Restores to use in battle, and the Champion has three. This heightens the importance of landing powerful moves that wipe out Pokémon without giving their Trainer the chance to heal them.*

Elite Four
Malva

Water-, Ground-, and Rock-type moves are the keys to victory

The sizzling moves used by Malva's Pokémon can burn your Pokémon if you aren't quick to take her Pokémon out. Fortunately, all of Malva's Pokémon are vulnerable to Water- and Rock-type moves, and most are also vulnerable to Ground-type moves. This gives you plenty of options when it comes to selecting and switching out your Pokémon during battle.

Malva's Pokémon

Chandelure
♀ Lv. 63 Ghost Fire
Weak to: Water Ground Rock Ghost Dark

Pyroar
♀ Lv. 63 Fire Normal
Weak to: Water Fighting Ground Rock

Talonflame
♀ Lv. 65 Fire Flying
Weak to: Rock 4×! Water Electric

Torkoal
♀ Lv. 63 Fire
Weak to: Water Ground Rock

Elite Four
Siebold

**Water-type
Pokémon User**

Use Grass- and Electric-type moves to gain the advantage

Siebold's Pokémon will unleash a torrent of mighty moves against you. Keep your head above water and sink Siebold's Pokémon with Electric-type moves, which are super effective against all of his Pokémon. Grass-type moves are also super effective against all of Siebold's Pokémon with the exception of Gyarados.

Siebold's Pokémon

Barbaracle
♂ Lv. 65   Rock   Water
Weak to: 4×1 Grass   Electric   Fighting   Ground

Clawitzer
♂ Lv. 63   Water
Weak to: Grass   Electric

Gyarados
♂ Lv. 63   Water   Flying
Weak to: 4×1 Electric   Rock

Starmie
Lv. 63   Water   Psychic
Weak to: Grass   Electric   Bug   Ghost   Dark

Elite Four

Wikstrom

Steel-type
Pokémon User

Fire- and Ground-type moves give you an edge

Wikstrom's Pokémon have been tempered through countless battles. They're sturdy and resilient, so it's vital that you capitalize on their weaknesses. Almost all of Wikstrom's Pokémon are weak to Fire-type moves. In addition, almost all of his Pokémon are weak to Ground-type moves, which are also super effective against many of Malva's Pokémon. So be sure to include at least one Ground-type Pokémon in your party!

Wikstrom's Pokémon

Aegislash ♂ Lv. 65	Steel	Ghost	
Weak to:	Fire	Ground	Ghost
	Dark		

Klefki ♂ Lv. 63	Steel	Fairy
Weak to:	Fire	Ground

Probopass ♂ Lv. 63	Rock	Steel
Weak to:	4×! Fighting 4×! Ground	Water

Scizor ♂ Lv. 63	Bug	Steel
Weak to:	4×! Fire

Elite Four
Drasna

**Dragon-type
Pokémon User**

Use Ice-, Dragon-, and Fairy-type moves to deal massive damage

Drasna's Dragon-type Pokémon are strong and ferocious, but every one of them is vulnerable to Ice-type moves. Her Pokémon are also vulnerable to Dragon-type moves, but avoid using Dragon-type Pokémon against her, for many of her Pokémon's moves are super effective against Dragon-type Pokémon. Instead, put Drasna's dangerous Dragon-type Pokémon on ice by making good use of the TM13 Ice Beam that you recently received from Wulfric in Snowbelle City. It wouldn't hurt to prepare a good Fairy type either—it will be helpful in taking on the Champion as well.

Drasna's Pokémon

Altaria ♀ Lv. 63 `Dragon` `Flying`	Weak to: `Ice` 4x! `Rock` `Dragon` `Fairy`	
Dragalge ♀ Lv. 63 `Poison` `Dragon`	Weak to: `Ice` `Ground` `Psychic` `Dragon`	
Druddigon ♀ Lv. 63 `Dragon`	Weak to: `Ice` `Dragon` `Fairy`	
Noivern ♀ Lv. 65 `Flying` `Dragon`	Weak to: `Ice` 4x! `Rock` `Dragon` `Fairy`	

Champion

Diantha

Multi-type
Pokémon User

Switch out your Pokémon as needed to best exploit your opponent's weakness

Unlike the Elite Four, Champion Diantha's Pokémon don't all belong to any one type. You'll need to switch out your Pokémon more often during this epic battle than you did with the Elite Four. Many of Diantha's Pokémon do share a weakness to Ice-, Steel-, and Fairy-type moves, so look to take advantage of that. Fight smart, fight hard, and let nothing stop you from securing your legacy as the new Champion! You'll find that defeating Diantha's Gardevoir may be your greatest hurdle. It's Lv. 68 and it can display great Attack, Speed, and Sp. Def stats, but its Sp. Atk stat is where it really shines. When you face it, make sure to have a Pokémon with a very good Sp. Def stat of its own. A Gardevoir of this level typically knows Captivate, Imprison, Hypnosis, and Future Sight. Captivate can be countered by using a Pokémon of the opposite gender or one whose gender is unknown. You could also take advantage of the Oblivious Ability, if any of your Pokémon happen to have it. Imprison can prevent your team from using any of the same moves that Gardevoir happens to know. Hypnosis has a good chance of putting your Pokémon to sleep, unless they have an Ability that prevents sleep, and that is not a good state to be in when it comes to Gardevoir's last move: Future Sight. This Future Sight move can be brutal, as its power is enhanced by the unusually high Sp. Atk of Diantha's Gardevoir. You will have two moves before it hits your team, so act quickly or switch your Pokémon out for one who can take the damage if you don't want to lose your best battlers for this final challenge!

Diantha's Pokémon

Aurorus ♂ Lv. 65	Rock	Ice
Weak to:	4x! Fighting 4x! Steel	Water
	Grass Ground	Rock

Hawlucha ♀ Lv. 64	Fighting	Flying
Weak to:	Electric Ice	Flying
	Psychic Fairy	

Goodra ♀ Lv. 66	Dragon	
Weak to:	Ice Dragon	Fairy

Gardevoir ♀ Lv. 68	Psychic	Fairy
Weak to:	Poison Ghost	Steel

Gourgeist ♀ Lv. 65	Ghost	Grass
Weak to:	Fire Ice	Flying
	Ghost Dark	

Tyrantrum ♂ Lv. 65	Rock	Dragon
Weak to:	Ice Fighting	Ground
	Dragon Steel	Fairy

Congratulations, Trainer!

You've won your rightful place in the Hall of Fame and proven to all what it means to be a Pokémon Trainer! You and your team have grown together and shown that you can overcome any challenge. Watch as your loyal partners get the recognition they deserve and have their names—and yours—inscribed for perpetuity in the Kalos region's Hall of Fame!

This marks the completion of a major goal in your journey—but your adventure isn't over yet. See what awaits you beyond the Pokémon League, and after you watch the credits, you'll once again set out from Vaniville Town on a new journey. But that's a tale for another time!

Pokémon-Amie

Battling with Pokémon is great fun, but have you ever wanted to just relax and play with your Pokémon? Maybe pet them and feed them tasty treats to show them how much you care? Well, you're in luck, because Pokémon-Amie lets you do just that!

Pokémon-Amie is a unique Touch Screen mode that becomes available early in the adventure. Using this mode will make your Pokémon more affectionate toward you through a variety of fun activities, including petting your Pokémon, playing minigames with them, and feeding them delicious snacks called Poké Puffs.

NOTE *Playing with your Pokémon makes them more affectionate toward you. This can have numerous benefits in battle, from Pokémon spontaneously curing themselves of status conditions to avoiding attacks or landing more critical hits. Battles will go better than ever if you play with your Pokémon a lot!*

Getting started

Use ⓛ and ⓡ to bring up the Pokémon-Amie menu on the Touch Screen. Then simply tap "PLAY" to begin your Pokémon-Amie experience.

When you first begin playing Pokémon-Amie, your party's lead Pokémon will be automatically selected. Tap this Pokémon to bring up three options: "DECORATE," "PLAY," and "SWITCH."

Switching Pokémon and checking stats

Switch Pokémon!

Pikachu

Affection

Fullness

Enjoyment

Switch Pokémon!

Select the Pokémon you'd like to play with!

To switch out your Pokémon for another one in your party, first tap your Pokémon to select it, and then tap "SWITCH." While examining your party Pokémon in this menu, pay attention to their three Pokémon-Amie stats: Affection, Fullness, and Enjoyment. If you want to keep your Pokémon happy, make sure these stats are in good standing. See below for how to increase each stat.

Affection: This stat increases when you pet your Pokémon, play the Making Faces game, or feed it Poké Puffs.

Fullness: This stat increases when you feed Poké Puffs to your Pokémon.

Enjoyment: This stat increases when you pet your Pokémon, play Pokémon-Amie minigames, or the Making Faces game with your Pokémon.

NOTE *Some actions can also lower certain stats. Playing Pokémon-Amie minigames or the Making Faces game lowers your Pokémon's Fullness stat, and petting your Pokémon can sometimes lower its Enjoyment stat instead of increasing it.*

Playing with your Pokémon

Playing with your Pokémon is what Pokémon-Amie is all about. Just tap your Pokémon to select it, and then tap "PLAY." The scene then changes to a close-up of your Pokémon.

First, you may need to get your Pokémon's attention. If your Pokémon is faced away from you, just tap it a few times until it turns around.

Once your Pokémon is facing you, you're able to play with it in a variety of ways. Pet and scratch your Pokémon by rubbing it with the stylus until it shakes with glee. Each Pokémon has a preference for where it likes to be touched, so try petting your Pokémon in different spots. You can also talk or sing into your Nintendo 3DS microphone to entertain your Pokémon through verbal communication.

This icon shows that you can trigger the Making Faces game!

Notice the little smiley icon that appears in the lower-left corner of the Touch Screen. This icon appears when the Nintendo 3DS Camera is picking you up. If you take an action while this icon appears, like smiling, tilting your head to the side, blinking, opening your mouth wide, and so on, your Pokémon will imitate it. Do this three times to trigger the Making Faces game! Your Pokémon will tell you to make certain faces or perform certain actions. Try to keep the game going as long as you can! Making Faces won't score you any Poké Puffs, but it will make your Pokémon very happy, and thus more affectionate toward you.

Feeding your Pokémon

To increase your Pokémon's Affection and Fullness stats, you need to feed it. Pokémon just love delicious snacks called Poké Puffs, and as luck would have it, these treats are easy to earn by playing Pokémon-Amie minigames!

While playing with your Pokémon, tap the upper-left button on the Touch Screen to bring up your current supply of Poké Puffs. Tap and drag a Poké Puff down to your Pokémon's mouth, and then hold the Poké Puff there while the Pokémon gobbles it up. Don't release the stylus or the Poké Puff will plummet! Just keep feeding your Pokémon until it shakes its head, indicating that the Pokémon is totally stuffed and its Fullness stat is maxed out.

NOTE *If your Pokémon turns away from eating, drag your Poké Puff back to the pink icon in the upper-left of the screen to save it for later. Don't just drop it on the ground, or you will lose it!*

All about Poké Puffs

Poké Puffs come in five flavors (Sweet, Mint, Citrus, Mocha, and Spice) and four levels (Basic, Frosted, Fancy, and Deluxe). The fancier the Poké Puff, the more Affection your Pokémon will gain from it. There are also special Poké Puffs to collect.

Supreme Wish Poké Puff	Received on your birthday.
Supreme Honor Poké Puff	Received when you enter the Hall of Fame.
Supreme Spring Poké Puff	Received when you beat a Pokémon-Amie minigame in unlimited mode with 5 stars.
Supreme Summer Poké Puff	Received when you beat Head It in unlimited mode with 5 stars.
Supreme Autumn Poké Puff	Received when you beat Berry Picker in unlimited mode with 5 stars.
Supreme Winter Poké Puff	Received when you beat Tile Puzzle in unlimited mode with 5 stars.

Pokémon-Amie minigames

Pokémon-Amie also lets you play fun minigames with your Pokémon, including Berry Picker, Head It, and Tile Puzzle. These simple minigames are easy to grasp, yet challenging to master. Play together with your Pokémon to increase their Enjoyment stats and earn more Poké Puffs to feed them as snacks!

You must have at least three healthy Pokémon on your team to play minigames. You'll unlock more advanced minigame levels as your performance improves on each game, and the more advanced levels will reward you with fancier Poké Puffs as prizes.

Berry Picker

In Berry Picker, your goal is to feed Berries to your Pokémon as quickly as possible. Three different Berries hang from the trees in easy mode, and your Pokémon periodically pop up from the bottom of the screen with a Berry inside a thought bubble. Tap and drag the correct Berry down to the Pokémon to feed it. Take too long or give the wrong Berry, and your Pokémon will leave annoyed. See how many Pokémon you can feed before time runs out. But know that the more successful you are, the faster the demands will come flying at you! Easy mode will have you picking from three different Berries, five in normal mode, and seven in hard mode. Once you unlock unlimited mode, you can see how long you can keep your Pokémon happy. It's three strikes and you're out in this mode, where three wrong or missed Berries will end the game.

Head It

In Head It, you must help your Pokémon headbutt falling balls of yarn back up into the sky. Simply tap your Pokémon just as a ball of yarn is about to reach it or fall past it. Be careful not to tap your Pokémon too soon! Keep hitting the balls of yarn without missing, and you'll soon rack up a combo. Try to keep that combo going for as long as possible to earn big points. The more successful hits in a row that you manage, the faster the balls will come flying at you—meaning that you can get a far higher combo! The main difference between easy, normal, and hard mode in this game is simply the speed at which the balls of yarn fall toward your Pokémon. Unlimited mode once again gives you three chances: miss three balls of yarn and it is game over!

 Hit the big ball of yarn that falls at the end of the game to score some serious bonus points.

Tile Puzzle

Tile Puzzle is perhaps the most challenging minigame. In Tile Puzzle, you must reassemble a scrambled image as quickly as you can by tapping the pieces to swap them around. Study the picture at the start and try to memorize the order of the three Pokémon. After the picture is scrambled, hurry to swap those tiles around and put it back together. When you place a tile correctly, it will sparkle as it snaps into place. You can't move that tile again, so don't worry about it anymore! In easy mode, the puzzle is made up of 20 pieces, in normal mode it's 30 pieces, and in hard mode it's 48 pieces. In unlimited mode, you solve as many increasingly complicated puzzles as you can before time runs out, and each successful puzzle completed will put some time back on the clock.

> **TIP** *When you're stuck, look for edge and corner pieces. These are usually easy to identify and can be quickly swapped into their proper spot.*

Decorating

The "DECORATE" option lets you change your Pokémon-Amie wallpaper and put out fancy Décor items such as cushions for Pokémon to enjoy. You can also put out Poké Puffs in the hope of attracting nearby players' Pokémon to visit. Visiting Pokémon may give you gifts of Décor items or Poké Puffs, so they're always welcome. There are over 200 Décor items to collect. Enjoy decorating with Décor items and customizing your Pokémon-Amie experience!

Super Training

Once you've caught some Pokémon, what do you need to know to raise them to be strong? Their stats (HP, Attack, Defense, Sp. Atk, Sp. Def, and Speed) increase every time they level up, but things aren't as simple as that. How much each stat can increase is affected by a Pokémon's base stats. One Lv. 20 Pikachu might have a Sp. Atk of 30 and another Lv. 20 Pikachu may have a Sp. Atk of 40, and that is in part due to the difference in their base stats. In the past, you could raise base stats using items or services, or by battling particular Pokémon. In Kalos, you can quickly raise your Pokémon's base stats with Super Training!

Why use Super Training?

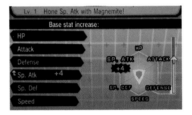

For the first time in the Pokémon series, Super Training lets players raise their Pokémon's base stats from the start, which helps competitive players, since base stats can only be increased to a certain point. The total limit is 510 points for all combined base stats, which means that you can only max out two base stats. The limit for each base stat is 252 points, leaving you with six points to spend on the other three base stats.

A special training bag, the Reset Bag, allows you to reset all of a Pokémon's base stats to their initial states. So if you didn't take advantage of Super Training early in the game, you can start again with a fresh slate and work at maxing out those all-important base stats.

Hoping to train your ideal Pokémon? Each Pokémon has its inherent strengths and weaknesses, with some Pokémon naturally having a higher Speed stat and others having a higher Attack stat than others of their species. Somewhere you'll find the Judge, who can tell whether your Pokémon excels in a certain stat relative to others of its kind. Catch many of the same kind of Pokémon and train the one with the strengths you are most interested in.

Base stats and stat growth

Super Training affects your Pokémon's base stats. To understand base stats, you need to understand the stats that they affect and how stats grow.

Your Pokémon all have six **stats**: HP, Attack, Defense, Special Attack (Sp. Atk), Special Defense (Sp. Def), and Speed. These affect how much damage they can dish out in battle and how much damage they receive from attacks, as well as which Pokémon get to strike first. These six stats grow at different rates as your Pokémon take part in battles, train, and level up. The rate at which each stat grows is affected by a number of factors, one being the Pokémon's **base stats**.

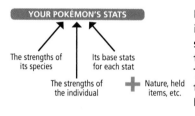

YOUR POKÉMON'S STATS

The strengths of its species

Its base stats for each stat

The strengths of the individual

Nature, held items, etc.

STAT GROWTH RATES
HP
Attack
Defense
Sp. Atk
Sp. Def
Speed

Pokémon Species A

STAT GROWTH RATES
HP
Attack
Defense
Sp. Atk
Sp. Def
Speed

Pokémon Species B

If gaining a level triggers an increase in a Pokémon's stats, you'll see it on screen. You can see increases gained through other means, such as Super Training, items, or battles, by checking the Summary page about your Pokémon (main menu).

The strengths of the Pokémon's species:

Each species of Pokémon has relative strengths in stat growth compared to other Pokémon species. For example, any Pikachu's Speed will increase at a decent rate, but the average Crobat will greatly outpace it. These strengths can be seen in any version of the Regional or National Pokédexes, expressed as boxes or dots of various colors. You'll be able to see whether a species is strong in a particular area compared to the average of all other Pokémon species. More boxes means that the average specimen of that species will see greater stat growth each time it trains compared with a Pokémon of a different species. These species strengths greatly influence a Pokémon's final stats, so it's wise to pay attention to them if you hope to create a real powerhouse Pokémon. *You cannot affect these strengths.*

The individual strengths of the Pokémon:

Additionally, each Pokémon has its own strengths. If you catch two Pikachu, the first Pikachu might have a much higher Sp. Atk stat than an average Pikachu, but the second Pikachu might only have a slightly better Sp. Atk stat—but a greater Speed stat than an average Pikachu. Since all Pikachu already have a pretty good Speed as a species, this Pikachu will probably be able to move first in many battles, if you train it right. *You can catch Pokémon with different individual strengths, but you can't alter the strength that your Pokémon naturally has.*

The way you train your Pokémon:

There are three main ways to raise your Pokémon's base stats, which are special values that affect a Pokémon's overall stats. The first way is to battle other Pokémon, the second way is to use items on your Pokémon, and the third way is to use Super Training. Every Pokémon you battle will give some base-point yield to your Pokémon. Which of the stats get a boost depends on what kind of Pokémon they are. All Pokémon who participate in the battle will get this boost to their base stats. If you have the Exp. Share turned on, then all of the Pokémon in your party will share the base-stat earnings, regardless of whether they appear in battle or not. However, Super Training enables you to train exactly the base stats that interest you. Work to increase your base stats in a certain stat area, and once you reach a certain point, that stat will increase. There is a limit to how far base stats can be increased, and you can get a good visual at the main Super Training screen. *This is the primary way that you can affect how well your Pokémon stands up to others in battle.*

Plan ahead when training base stats

There is a limit to how much you can raise your base stats, so be careful about how many base points your Pokémon gain from battles. If you accidentally raise base stats that you're not interested in, you may later be unable to max out the base stats that you *are* interested in. There are two ways to reset all of your Pokémon's base stats: use a Reset Bag in Super Training or give your Pokémon a Perilous Soup from the Juice Shoppe in Lumiose City. Note that these methods will undo all of the work you've done for *all* of its base stats.

> **TIP** To decrease a single base stat, feed the Pokémon certain Berries that decrease base stats: Pomeg Berry (lowers HP base stat); Kelpsy Berry (lowers Attack base stat); Qualot Berry (lowers Defense base stat); Hondew Berry (lowers Sp. Atk base stat); Grepa Berry (lowers Sp. Def base stat); and Tamato Berry (lowers Speed base stat). They can be tricky to find in the Kalos region.

Use items to help train base stats

Certain items, like Muscle Wings and Proteins, will also raise your Pokémon's base stats. The Wing-type items slightly increase one base stat, while nutritious drinks give a more significant boost. You can also have juices made for your Pokémon at the Berry Shoppe in Lumiose City to increase a base stat. Finally, certain held items will also make it easier to increase your base stats through battling: Macho Brace, Power Weight, Power Bracer, Power Belt, Power Lens, Power Band, and Power Anklet. Note that they also slow your Pokémon down.

Nature versus nurture in the world of Pokémon

Another trait that will affect your Pokémon's stats over time is its Nature. Different Natures tend to make one stat grow more quickly than average, while making another grow more slowly than average. You'll need to discover a Pokémon with the right Nature to achieve your absolutely ideal Pokémon.

> **TIP** On your Pokémon's Summary page, you may see that one stat appears in light pink and another in light blue. The light pink stat will grow more quickly, thanks to your Pokémon's Nature, while the blue grows more slowly.

Super Training modes

There are two ways to increase a Pokémon's base stats in Super Training: Core Training and Super-Training Regimens.

Core Training

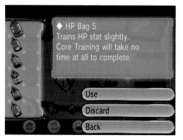

Core Training is all about training bags. Training bags are mostly received as rewards for completing Super-Training Regimens. While pounding away at the plain bag that initially appears on the Core Training screen, training bags may drop down from above. Some training bags will increase the Pokémon's base stats, while other training bags will temporarily boost its skills for its Super-Training Regimens. Finally, special training bags can reset all base stats or make your Pokémon friendlier toward you.

The S/M/L designation reflects the size of the training bag's effect on your Pokémon's stats—a larger size means a greater effect, but the more times a Pokémon will have to hit it.

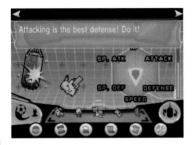

If you leave your Pokémon on its own, it will slowly work on the training bag, hitting it once per minute. If you want to pick up the pace, just keep tapping the screen. Your Pokémon will hit the bag every time you tap, speeding up its Core Training big time!

Training Bags
HP Bag S / HP Bag M / HP Bag L
Attack Bag S / Attack Bag M / Attack Bag L
Defense Bag S / Defense Bag M / Defense Bag L
Sp. Atk Bag S / Sp. Atk Bag M / Sp. Atk Bag L
Sp. Def Bag S / Sp. Def Bag M / Sp. Def Bag L
Speed Bag S / Speed Bag M / Speed Bag L
Strength Bag / Toughen-Up Bag / Swiftness Bag / Big-Shot Bag / Double-Up Bag
Team Flare Bag / Reset Bag / Soothing Bag

NOTE The Strength Bag, Toughen-Up Bag, Swiftness Bag, Big-Shot Bag, and Double-Up Bag all affect your Pokémon's performance in its next Super-Training Regimen. A Pokémon can only reap benefits from one such training bag at a time, though. Only the effects of the last training bag used will remain, so don't use multiple of these training bags in between Super-Training Regimens or you will have lost a possible advantage.

Super-Training Regimens

Super-Training Regimens have three basic levels, each containing six stages—one for each of the six major Pokémon stats. The higher the Regimen's level, the greater the challenge. You unlock new levels by clearing all six stages of a level. Once you've maxed out one Pokémon's stats, making it a Fully Trained Pokémon, you will unlock the 12 stages of the Secret Super-Training Regimens. Unlock each of these stages in turn by beating the stage before it. Unlock all 12 and take on the final challenge in the 12th Secret Super-Training Regimen stage: the battle for the best!

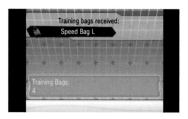

The further you make it through the Super-Training Regimens, the better the rewards. You'll earn more powerful training bags as you progress, and you may also receive rare items! As your Pokémon's stats go up, they'll perform better in their Regimens. For example, they'll be able to score more points with their shots or maintain their barriers for longer periods.

Have a strong Pokémon collect lots of valuable training bags by beating the higher-level Super-Training Regimens repeatedly, then use these higher-level training bags to quickly raise your weaker Pokémon!

Super Training 101

Super Training's main mode plays like a virtual sports game in which your chosen Pokémon faces off against Balloon Bots. Use the Circle Pad to dodge the balls that are launched by the Balloon Bots while simultaneously tapping the Touch Screen to shoot your own balls into the goals. You'll score points for goals, but being hit by a ball will subtract points from your total. To clear the challenge, reach the required score before time runs out!

You can also press ⬆ and ⬇ on the +Control Pad to move toward and away from the Balloon Bot as well. Moving closer to the Balloon Bot makes goals easier to score, but gives you less time to react and avoid inbound balls.

Tapping a Pokémon in Core Training selects it for both Core Training and Super-Training Regimens.

Goal types

Normal white goals

Red bonus goal

There are two basic types of goal: normal white goals and red bonus goals. White goals are the most common. They vanish after you hit them, giving you a certain number of points. They'll also disappear after a certain amount of time, turning orange to warn you before they disappear. Red bonus goals are more rare, and they do not vanish when hit. Instead, these special goals remain in play for a brief amount of time, letting you rack up lots of points as you hit them repeatedly. Often a bonus goal will appear after you have made all of the normal white goals disappear by successfully hitting them with your shots. Take full advantage of those rare bonus goals!

Shot types

Energy Shot

Charged Shot

See the circle in the bottom of the screen, beside the score? That is your Pokémon's energy meter. When it is empty, your Pokémon will only be able to shoot regular gray balls, but when it has stored some energy up, it can let loose with Energy Shots. Tap the Touch Screen to fire an individual shot, or keep tapping to fire off a volley—but watch that you don't run out of energy or your shots will become far less effective!

Your Pokémon can also use Charged Shots. If you hold the stylus to the Touch Screen, you'll begin to store up energy. Your Pokémon will begin to glow and when the light flares up around its body, it is time for you to let go! These shots will score you far more points than regular shots or even Energy Shots, but don't charge them for too long. If you do, the Charged Shot will fail in a plume of smoke. Charged Shots are the key to getting great records in your Super-Training Regimens, and timing is vital!

Energy Shot varieties

There are five kinds of Energy Shots that different Pokémon can use as long as there is some energy in their energy meters. Each Pokémon's Energy Shot is determined by its species.

Black Balls: Have an average power, speed, size, and energy consumption. These can be fired off quickly in succession.

Yellow Balls: Have a low power, average speed, and small size, but with low energy consumption. These can be fired off quickly in succession.

Orange Balls: Have an average speed, energy consumption, and time between shots. Their power is a bit weak, but the shots are large and less likely to miss.

Green Balls: Have a high power, but high energy consumption. These shots are slow, but a bit bigger than average.

Blue Balls: Have an average power, but they are fast. These balls are small and consume quite a lot of energy.

Barriers

Graveler Balloon

In the later stages of Super Training, the use of barriers becomes an important tactic. Simply press ⓛ to put up a barrier that temporarily shields you from the Balloon Bot's inbound balls. When Balloon Bots bring up barriers of their own, blast the roaming target to bring the barrier down quickly.

Barriers can't be held forever, so be sure you time their usage well or you might be left exposed at an inopportune moment. Don't make the mistake of thinking that you can keep ⓛ held down forever—instead you should throw your barriers up when you need them and let them drop between incoming shots.

Bitbots

Bitbots are small bits of errant data that Balloon Bots can summon around them. They may look like innocent balloons, but they can fire shots at you just like their parent Balloon Bot. They can also get in the way of your shots, making it harder to hit the Balloon Bot's goals. You can knock them out of the park with a well-aimed shot, but that won't provide relief for long, because these tricky Bitbots regenerate over time.

Awards and rewards

Your Pokémon can earn awards for completing Super-Training Regimens within the target time. Get rewards on every single Regimen and your Fully Trained Pokémon will become a Supremely Trained Pokémon! And you already knew that you could get new training bags for completing Super Training Regimens, but don't forget that you can also get items in the more advanced Regimens. Unlock the Secret Super-Training Regimens by fully training your Pokémon and you can get great rewards, like Leaf Stones, Stardust, Pretty Wings, and PP Maxes! These are just a few of the rare and valuable items you can get, so be sure to try Secret Super-Training Regimens for yourself!

Base stats and performance

As your base stats grow, they will not only help your Pokémon grow stronger for real battles, but they will also improve how they can perform in Super Training. This table gives an easy breakdown of the gains you can expect to see in your Super-Training Regimens.

Increased base stat	Effects
HP	Increases the size of the Pokémon's shots, making it easier to hit targets.
Attack	Increases the power of the Pokémon's shots, making them earn more points.
Defense	Increases how quickly you gain energy for Energy Shots and how long you can hold a barrier.
Sp. Atk	Increases the power of the Pokémon's shots, making them earn more points.
Sp. Def	Increases how quickly you gain energy for Energy Shots and how long you can hold a barrier.
Speed	Allows Pokémon to fire shots more quickly and move around the field more swiftly.
Any	Reduces the number of points you lose when an enemy shot enters your goal.

Berry Farming

Berries are valuable items that can boost your Pokémon's battle prowess in a variety of ways. Some Berries heal status conditions, while others have even more useful benefits. Although most Berries are hard to come by, you can grow as many as you like in the Berry fields on Route 7.

> **NOTE** *The best part about Berries is that your Pokémon will automatically use them as needed in battle if they have appropriate Berries. For example, if your Pokémon is holding a Persim Berry and becomes afflicted with the Confused status condition, that Pokémon will automatically eat the Persim Berry and heal its confusion. You won't need to spend a turn using a recovery item from your Bag!*

The friendly farmer

The first time you visit the Berry fields, the friendly old Berry farmer will hand you five Oran Berries, five Pecha Berries, and a watering tool called a Sprinklotad. After that, he will set himself up in his cozy home in the northeast corner of the Berry fields, where he will always be happy to answer any questions you have about farming. His granddaughter also stands at the ready to tell you all you could ever want to know about Mulch!

Planting Berries

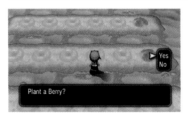

The Berry fields offer plenty of spots to plant your Berries. Approach any vacant plot of soft soil and press Ⓐ to inspect it. If no other Berry has been planted yet, you'll be able to plop any Berry you possess into the soft soil.

After you plant a Berry, the next step is to water it. Inspect the soft soil to see if it needs watering. If it does, go ahead and water it with the Sprinklotad. Berry trees won't sprout in parched plots!

Making Mulch

Do you want to compost some Berries to make Mulch?

You can simply plant all of your Berries and water them if you like, or you can use one of the composters around the Berry fields to make Mulch out of some of your Berries first. Although this will use up some of your Berries, Mulch can provide some special benefits.

Mulch-making guide

Rich Mulch: Use three different-colored Berries.

Surprise Mulch: Use three same-colored Berries.

Boost Mulch: Use two same-colored Berries and one different-colored Berry.

Amaze Mulch: There are two Berries that can make Amaze Mulch if you add either one of them to a Mulch mix. Try adding lots of different Berries and see if you can discover which ones are the necessary ingredients!

> **TIP** *The two Berries needed to make Amaze Mulch are both Berries that have never been found in another region. But where can you get Berries that have not been discovered before? Perhaps they arise from some sort of mutation...*

Mulch effects

Rich Mulch: Increases your Berry harvest without any extra care. Useful for those without the time to care for their Berry trees.

Surprise Mulch: Makes mutations more likely. Useful for those who want to discover new Berry types.

Boost Mulch: Dries out the soil, forcing you to water more often. But the more you water your trees, the more Berries will grow. Useful for dedicated farmers.

Amaze Mulch: Has the effects of the other three Mulches in one. It increases your Berry harvest, dries out the soil, and makes mutations more likely.

Mutations

Mutations can sometimes occur when two different trees are planted next to each other. For example, an Aspear Berry and a Leppa Berry planted next to each other will sometimes give rise to a mutation. Thirteen Berries are only available through mutations. They cannot be obtained within the game itself by any other means. Try planting as many different trees next to each other as you can, and see what develops!

I'm researching sudden mutations of Berries!

After your first mutation occurs, a Scientist will appear and stop you as you try to leave the Berry fields. She sets herself up in the old farmer's house and collects data for you. By talking to the Scientist, you can check how Berry mutations were created in the past and what combinations created them. This is helpful if you forget a recipe or if you weren't paying attention to how a mutation developed.

 NOTE *In addition to the thirteen Berries that can only be cultivated through mutation, another fourteen Berries do not appear in Pokémon X and Pokémon Y, and can be obtained only by trading them from other regions.*

Checking on your Berry trees

The Oran Berry tree has 7 Berries!

Berry trees don't just spring out of the ground right away. It takes time for your trees to grow large enough to yield Berries. To ensure a healthy crop, keep them watered and pull up any weeds. Once your trees mature, you'll be able to harvest numerous Berries, which you may then use to make Mulch or plant even more Berry trees. Of course, you can also hoard your Berries for use in battles, or sell excess Berries to stores for some quick cash.

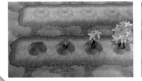

Berry tree bugs

Pokémon adore Berries, and it's not uncommon to discover Bug-type Pokémon while checking on your trees. To keep your trees healthy, be sure to defeat any Bug-type Pokémon that show up. The type of Pokémon that appear differ by the type of tree.

Burmy: Rawst Berry, Lum Berry, Aguav Berry, Wepear Berry, Hondew Berry, Rabuta Berry, Durin Berry, Rindo Berry, Kebia Berry, Tanga Berry, Babiri Berry, Salac Berry, Starf Berry, Micle Berry

Combee: Aspear Berry, Sitrus Berry, Iapapa Berry, Pinap Berry, Qualot Berry, Grepa Berry, Nomel Berry, Wacan Berry, Shuca Berry, Charti Berry, Chilan Berry, Jaboca Berry, Kee Berry

Illumise: Chesto Berry, Wiki Berry, Bluk Berry, Cornn Berry, Pamtre Berry, Belue Berry, Payapa Berry, Kasib Berry, Colbur Berry, Ganlon Berry

Ledyba: Cheri Berry, Leppa Berry, Figy Berry, Razz Berry, Pomeg Berry, Tamato Berry, Spelon Berry, Occa Berry, Chople Berry, Haban Berry, Liechi Berry, Lansat Berry, Custap Berry

Spewpa: Pecha Berry, Persim Berry, Mago Berry, Nanab Berry, Magost Berry, Watmel Berry, Petaya Berry, Roseli Berry

Volbeat: Oran Berry, Kelpsy Berry, Passho Berry, Yache Berry, Coba Berry, Apicot Berry, Rowap Berry, Maranga Berry

Berry tree locations

You can't plant Berry trees if you don't have any Berries. The friendly old farmer gives you some Berries when you first visit the Berry fields, but there are many more types of Berry out there. To get started, use the following table to find Berry trees throughout the Kalos region. Each yields one Berry a week.

> **NOTE** *Many other types of Berry can be discovered during your adventure. Sometimes the wild Pokémon that you catch will be holding Berries, and they can also be received from friendly people around the Kalos region or as prizes in some battle facilities. This table provides a reliable source for finding Berries that grow naturally on wild trees each week.*

Aguav Berry tree	Route 6	Leppa Berry tree	Route 15	Roseli Berry tree	Route 14
Aspear Berry tree	Route 12	Lum Berry tree	Route 16	Sitrus Berry tree	Route 11
Figy Berry tree	Route 21	Mago Berry tree	Route 8	Tanga Berry tree	Route 22
Iapapa Berry tree	Route 10	Oran Berry tree	Route 5	Wacan Berry tree	Route 18
Kasib Berry tree	Route 20	Persim Berry tree	Route 7	Yache Berry tree	Route 19

Juice Shoppe

Berries can be blended into a variety of special juices that boast welcome benefits. Just pop by the Juice Shoppe on Autumnal Avenue in Lumiose City, and you can mix different Berries to make one of 10 special juices. Each juice can have various effects on a Pokémon's base stats, levels, or friendship.

The following chart reveals the effects of all 10 juices, along with the Berry combinations you need to make them.

Berry juice chart

Juice name	Pokémon effect	How to make
Colorful Shake	Makes it more friendly	Use different color Berries
Yellow Juice	Raises its base Defense stat	Use yellow Berries
Red Juice	Raises its base Attack stat	Use red Berries
Purple Juice	Raises its base HP stat	Use purple Berries
Pink Juice	Raises its base Speed stat	Use pink Berries
Blue Juice	Raises its base Sp. Atk stat	Use blue Berries
Green Juice	Raises its base Sp. Def stat	Use green Berries
Rare Soda	Raises its level slightly	Use Lansat Berry and Starf Berry
Perilous Soup	Resets all of its base stats to 0	Use Kee Berry and Maranga Berry

Berry color chart

Color	Berry name
Blue	Apicot Berry, Coba Berry, Kelpsy Berry, Maranga Berry, Oran Berry, Passho Berry, Rowap Berry, Yache Berry
Green	Aguav Berry, Babiri Berry, Durin Berry, Hondew Berry, Kebia Berry, Lum Berry, Micle Berry, Rabuta Berry, Rawst Berry, Rindo Berry, Salac Berry, Starf Berry, Tanga Berry, Wepear Berry
Pink	Mago Berry, Magost Berry, Nanab Berry, Pecha Berry, Persim Berry, Petaya Berry, Roseli Berry, Watmel Berry
Purple	Belue Berry, Bluk Berry, Chesto Berry, Colbur Berry, Cornn Berry, Ganlon Berry, Kasib Berry, Pamtre Berry, Payapa Berry, Wiki Berry
Red	Cheri Berry, Chople Berry, Custap Berry, Figy Berry, Haban Berry, Lansat Berry, Leppa Berry, Liechi Berry, Occa Berry, Pomeg Berry, Spelon Berry, Tamato Berry
Yellow	Aspear Berry, Charti Berry, Chilan Berry, Grepa Berry, Iapapa Berry, Jaboca Berry, Kee Berry, Nomel Berry, Pinap Berry, Qualot Berry, Shuca Berry, Sitrus Berry, Wacan Berry

Photo Spots

The beautiful Kalos region is filled with marvelous sights. Wouldn't it be great if you could take photos of your journey as you explore this wondrous land? Well, once you get your first Gym Badge and find a photo spot, you can do exactly that!

Phil the Photo Guy

Take a photo
View a photo
About the camera
Good-bye

Hey!
What do you want to do?

Look for this special sign, which indicates that you're standing near a photo spot. Inspect the sign, and you'll have the option to call Phil the Photo Guy. Tell Phil that you'd like to take a photo, and he'll set up his camera and get to work.

Camera controls

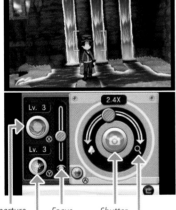

Aperture   Focus   Shutter
    Brightness   Zoom

In order to take the perfect shot, you need to master the camera controls. You can adjust all of these on the Touch Screen, of course, by tapping them directly. Or you can learn to manipulate them all using your Nintendo 3DS system's buttons. Here's how they work.

Button	Action
Ⓐ	Toggle between Auto and Manual mode
Ⓡ	Take a photo
Ⓛ	Toggle on-screen guide on or off
✚ / ✚	Adjust the focus (Manual mode)
✚ / ✚	Adjust the zoom
Ⓧ	Adjust aperture (Manual mode)
Ⓨ	Adjust brightness (Manual mode)
SELECT / START	Reset the angle
Ⓑ	Exit shooting mode

Camera functions

Below is a quick and easy guide to the adjustments you can make using manual mode.

Zoom	Allows you to zoom in or out.
Focus	Allows you to adjust the focus, so that different parts of the screen appear crisp and clear. You can move the focus from the foreground (things closer to the camera) to the background (things farther from the camera).
Aperture	Allows you to adjust the depth of field, which decides how much of the screen is in focus (the higher the aperture value, the clearer the picture will be).
Brightness	Allows you to adjust the brightness of objects in the background.

Reviewing photos

After you've taken at least one photo, you can ask Phil to view your photos. Phil will only show you one photo, however: the latest one he took of you. Don't worry, as all of your photos are saved to your Nintendo 3DS Camera. You can browse through all of your photos there.

Uploading photos to the Pokémon Global Link

By using the Game Sync function, you can send your photos to the Pokémon Global Link, known as the PGL (www.pokemon-gl.com). Use the PSS (Player Search System) to access Game Sync, then send the latest photo you took. Take a great photo and dazzle everyone!

Picture-perfect prizes

Taking photos of your adventures across the Kalos region can be more than fun. It can also be profitable. Visit the Shutterbug Café, located on Lumiose City's South Boulevard, and a man will give you items based on how many photos you've taken. If you like, you can take multiple photos at the same photo spot in order to earn these prizes quickly.

- Wide Lens (1–14 photos)
- Scope Lens (15–29 photos)
- Zoom Lens (30+ photos)

Photo spots

Wondering where you can find photo spots? Here's a guided tour!

- Aquacorde Town
- Parfum Palace
- Route 7 (Rivière Walk)
- Geosenge Town
- Shalour City
- Azure Bay
- Lumiose City
- Frost Cavern
- Anistar City
- Couriway Town
- Snowbelle City
- Pokémon League

Restaurants

Dining doesn't get any finer than in Lumiose City. Four restaurants can be visited in the Kalos region's crown city, but it isn't just their exquisite menus that makes these establishments so irresistible. It's the epic Pokémon battles that you experience as you wait for each course to be ready to consume! You won't be able to switch Pokémon between battles, so think about your team carefully before you agree to dine.

Restaurant Le Nah

This one-star restaurant is located along Lumiose City's South Boulevard. It offers a three-course meal, and the Chef will entertain you with Double Battles at each course.

Base cost: 3,000
Average Pokémon level: Lv. 10
Prizes: Tiny Mushrooms

Restaurant Le Yeah

A two-star establishment, Restaurant Le Yeah is located on Autumnal Avenue. You can enjoy a delightful four-course banquet. You also have your choice of entertainment at each course: Triple Battles or Rotation Battles.

Base cost: 15,000
Average Pokémon level: Lv. 31
Prizes: Big Mushrooms

NOTE *Each of these restaurant's prices is given as a base cost. The reason why is simple—how stylish you are will determine how much you pay! See page 119 for more on what it means to be stylish in Lumiose City, but for now, just remember that the more you do in Lumiose, the better the chance that you might get a nice discount at these restaurants!*

Restaurant Le Wow

This critically acclaimed three-star restaurant is located on Hibernal Avenue, but it only becomes available after you enter the Hall of Fame. Expect to pay a premium fee to enjoy the amazing dining experience here! You'll be able to take on the staff in Double Battles, Triple Battles, or Rotation Battles during the five courses of the fantastic meals served here.

Base cost: 100,000
Average Pokémon level: Lv. 63
Prizes: Balm Mushrooms

Sushi High Roller

This high-class restaurant is tucked away in an alley between North Boulevard and Rouge Plaza. It serves an incredible meal, but to dine in this exclusive restaurant, you not only have to be the Champion of the Kalos region, but you have to be very stylish as well (p. 119 and p. 395). Visit the restaurant after exploring Lumiose City and perhaps you'll be able to get in the door to experience their five-course feast of Double Battles, Triple Battles, or Rotation Battles.

Base cost: 500,000
Average Pokémon level: 65
Prizes: Big Nuggets

Restaurant Battles

No matter where you choose to chow, or which battles you prefer to partake of, all restaurants share a few things in common. For starters, you must pay for your meal up front. After you're shown to your seat, you're given a goal—a number of turns in which to finish each battle. If you can manage to complete each battle in exactly the requested number of turns, you'll earn greater rewards by the meal's end.

What will Pikachu do?

Whether or not you win the battle, and whether or not you succeed in hitting the goal, your Pokémon are always healed at the end of battle. You can also use items during battles, if you need to. Since these are real battles, any items you use will be consumed and disappear from your Bag—but at the same time, any Experience Points that your Pokémon earn and any prize money that you gain will also be yours to keep. Now, enjoy your delicious dish while you wait for the next course!

Thank you again for dining with us this evening. I will leave your receipt here with you.

When the entire meal is over, you'll be given the receipt. It itemizes how well you performed in each battle. The number of prize items you get will be based on how close you are to that designated number of turns and how many of your Pokémon faint. You can earn up to five items for each battle, so that means up to 25 items for a five-course meal!

So we're having a meal together as men. Nothing wrong with that.

After examining your receipt, you're free to get up and wander around the restaurant. Go ahead and talk to each patron to see how they feel about the place. You paid for the privilege, after all!

Restaurant battle prizes and their worth

Prize	Value
Tiny Mushroom(s)	Can be sold at shops for 250 each
Big Mushroom(s)	Can be sold at shops for 2,500 each
Balm Mushroom(s)	Can be sold at shops for 6,250 each
Big Nugget(s)	Can be sold at shops for 10,000 each

PR Video Studio

Trainer PR Videos are neat little videos that you can create and customize. These videos let you show off with your Pokémon. You can share them over the PSS (Player Search System) so that other players can marvel at your style and filmmaking talent!

Creating Trainer PR Videos

Creating Trainer PR Videos is fun and easy. Just enter the PR Video Studio on Lumiose City's South Boulevard and speak to the clerk on the left. For your first video, the studio staff will start shooting soon after you choose your favorite style. Later on, you will be able to choose between "Surprise me," to have the studio direct your video once again, or "Create by yourself," to shoot your own video. You're then whisked away to the recording studio to begin filming. Before you begin filming, though, you may want to fix up your look. There is a convenient fitting room right there in the studio where you can change your outfit and your contact lenses. There is also a green room, which is worth a visit. Girls can apply various kinds of makeup, including eye shadow, mascara, blush, and lipstick, and boys can spruce up their looks with facial hair, temporary tattoos, and more!

Customization options

When shooting your own Trainer PR Videos, you have plenty of options and lots of creative freedom. Although Trainer PR Videos are only 10 seconds long, you can edit them in each individual second if you like. See the next page for a breakdown of all your options.

Backgrounds: Change the background for your video.

Poses: Choose from a selection of poses.

Facial expressions: Alter your facial expression.

Music: Select the background music.

Sound effects: Sprinkle in some sound effects.

Pokémon: Cast your favorite Pokémon to appear in the video.

Effects: Make use of cool visual effects, like spotlights and speed lines.

Camera: Change the camera angle. Use lots of angles to really spice things up!

Captions: Make text captions appear during your video.

Reset: Undo all changes and reset the selected portion back to its default setting.

Remember, you can change all of these options for each second of your video. For example, you can take on multiple poses, facial expressions, and camera angles throughout the video, or make the background, sound effects, and music change as the video plays. Get creative and see how dynamic your Trainer PR Videos can be!

NOTE *After you've filmed a Trainer PR Video at the PR Video Studio in Lumiose City, you can edit the video by logging on to any PC around the Kalos region.*

Unlock more options

There are well over 200 options for you to adjust when making a Trainer PR Video. But wait, there's more! As your fame grows and you become more stylish, you'll be able to unlock new background music, visual effects, poses, and backgrounds. Special options will also appear when various conditions are met, such as entering the Hall of Fame, getting affectionate with your Pokémon, using the PSS a lot, and dozens of other accomplishments. You can also get new captions for your videos every day, if you're deemed stylish enough, by talking to a copywriter in North Boulevard's Café Action! He may not be the only one in that café to reward you for your style, either!

Being stylish in Kalos

You've probably noticed by now, but aesthetics are king in the Kalos region. The more stylish you are thought to be by others, the more options will open to you—and what better way to get stylish than by spending lots of time in the most fashionable city in the world? Everything you do in Lumiose City will make you seem more polished and worldly in the eyes of Lumiose residents. Some of the ways that you can make yourself seem more stylish include shopping at all of the stores, using the transportation options, visiting all of the facilities, dining at all of the restaurants, and talking to various people around the city. Don't miss out on a single thing to do in Lumiose City if you want to live the truly high life.

Being perceived as stylish can change the way that people talk to you and treat you. You can get discounts on services and in shops, meet new people, unlock new options at places like the PR Video Studio, Friseur Furfrou, and the hair salon, purchase special items at different shops, and more. The more that you do in Lumiose, the more you'll be able to do in Lumiose!

Hotel Richissime Minigames

No hotel in the Kalos region can compare to the lavish luxury of Lumiose City's Hotel Richissime. Located on North Boulevard, this swanky hotel features thick marble columns and the most exquisite accommodations that money can buy.

A place as big as Hotel Richissime can always use a little extra help. Speak to the hotel receptionist in the lobby, and she'll offer to hire you for some part-time work. You can perform three part-time jobs each day, and the better your performance, the more challenging the tasks you will be assigned. If you reach the highest level, you could be making a lot of money. Keep coming back each day to prove your worth!

NOTE *If you earn enough, why not consider a stay at Hotel Richissime as a guest? It is not cheap, but it will restore the health of your team Pokémon and even make them more affectionate! Go on and spoil yourself and your team sometime!*

Room Service

In the Room Service minigame, your goal is to answer the phone, memorize every detail of the guest's order, and then relay the order back to the kitchen staff. If you make any mistakes, the guest won't be thrilled, and your compensation will drop accordingly. As you become more experienced, you will have to remember one to four orders at a time.

Making Beds

In the Making Beds minigame, you must race around one of the hotel's floors and make every bed as fast as you can. Simply run up to each bed and press Ⓐ to make it. Depending on how experienced you are, you will have anywhere from a generous 75 seconds to a scant 35 seconds to make all of the beds. There, that room looks much more tidy!

Lost and Found

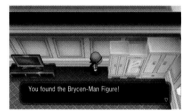

In the Lost and Found minigame, your task is to carefully search a room for a missing item. You can't see the lost item, so go slow and press Ⓐ to search after every step. There's no time limit to worry about, so take your time. If you run around the room without being careful, you're likely to step on the fragile item you're looking for! You'll have to find one to four items, depending on how experienced you are. When you're still learning, you'll be forgiven for treading slightly on an item, but once you become an expert worker, you won't get away with such rookie mistakes.

Other hotels

While Hotel Richissime is easily the grandest hotel in the Kalos region, it is hardly the only one. Tourists flock to Kalos by the hundreds, and there are hotels in many cities and towns. You can reap some special rewards if you visit them regularly.

Get to know your fellow travelers

You may notice some familiar faces if you frequent the hotels in the Kalos region. Seven travelers from various regions around the world are circling Kalos, just as you are. Keep talking to them each time that you meet them, and after you get to know each other a bit, they will each reward you in some way. These travelers can always be found in the western room on 2F of the hotel.

Trainer	Homeland	Reward
Hiker	Kanto region	Trades you a Magikarp
Garçon	Johto region	Gives you a Rage Candy Bar
Madame	Hoenn region	Gives you a Lava Cookie
Maid	Sinnoh region	Trades you an Eevee
Tourist	Unova region	Tells you more about the Gym Leaders
Backpacker	Unknown region	Gives you a Strange Souvenir

Get Ribbons on different days

Another Tourist can be found around the Kalos region's hotels on different days. She loves to share her Ribbons with you, to capture her mood on any given day. Visit each hotel on the day specified to get a Ribbon for your lead Pokémon. She can always be found in the middle room in the hotel's 2F.

Ribbon name	Day of the week	Location
Alert Ribbon	Monday	Hotel Ambrette
Shock Ribbon	Tuesday	Hotel Camphrier
Downcast Ribbon	Wednesday	Hotel Marine Snow
Careless Ribbon	Thursday	Coumarine Hotel
Relax Ribbon	Friday	Couriway Hotel
Snooze Ribbon	Saturday	Hotel Cyllage
Smile Ribbon	Sunday	Coumarine Hotel

Roller Skate Tricks

To help you navigate the vast reaches of the Kalos region, you'll receive a flashy pair of Roller Skates fairly early in your adventure. Roller Skates are great for quickly getting around Kalos, and they become even more fun to use after you've learned a few slick tricks.

TIP *Simply use the Circle Pad to slap on your Roller Skates and start zipping around. Roller Skates can be used practically anywhere outdoors, but they often aren't available when exploring indoor areas.*

Learning tricks

I'll teach you a technique that's perfect for a master trickster like you!

Roller skating is a pretty big deal in the Kalos region, and lots of talented skaters have devised a number of cool tricks that you can learn. These are just for fun, mind you, but they're also just that—fun! You may be able to figure out some of the tricks on your own, but if you're not sure, just speak to Roller Skaters in the Kalos region. They are very happy to help you learn awesome tricks.

Trick	Action	Controls	Teacher Location
Spin	Spin in a circle	Rotate the Circle Pad to the right or left	Can be used from the start
Dash	Kick off the ground to speed up	Slide the Circle Pad hard in one direction	Can be used from the start
Parallel swizzle	Swing your body left and right	Press lightly on the Circle Pad	Lumiose City (South Boulevard, Office Building 1F)
Drift-and-dash	Change directions and double your speed	Slide the Circle Pad in the opposite direction	Lumiose City (Vert Plaza)
Backflip*	Backflip over a ledge	Go off a ledge while dashing or doing a parallel swizzle	Lumiose City (North Boulevard)
The 360*	Turn a full circle over a ledge	Jump over a ledge while rotating the Circle Pad	Lumiose City (Estival Avenue, Café Rouleau)
Cosmic flip**	Spin and flip over a ledge	Go off a ledge while doing a drift-and-dash	Lost Hotel on Route 15

*You need to learn these tricks by speaking to the Roller Skaters.
**You must know the backflip and the 360 to learn this trick.

Rail grinding

Although it's not technically considered a trick, you can also use your Roller Skates to grind along special rails that appear in certain areas around Kalos. No one needs to teach you this skill. It's available from the moment you obtain your Roller Skates. Grinding on rails lets you cross obstacles and reach items that you otherwise couldn't get. Whenever you spot a rail, slap on your Roller Skates and see where it leads!

 Some rails feature small kinks, and you'll fall while grinding along them if you don't have enough speed.

Battle Chateau

The Battle Chateau is a large, fancy estate that's located along Route 7. Here you can test your battle skills against noble Trainers who seek to become the region's Champion. Sounds like a good place to sharpen your skills, eh?

Battle Chateau ranks

When you first enter the Battle Chateau, you're given the lowly rank of Baroness/Baron. In order to increase your rank, you must battle other Trainers in the Chateau. Battling Trainers in the Chateau is fun. More than that, it's a money-maker. You earn prize money after every battle. Spend some time in the Battle Chateau and try to increase your rank!

Rank increase notifications

you have been granted the title of Viscount.

You won't realize that your rank has increased until you attempt to leave the Battle Chateau. At that point, if you've done enough battling, one of the servants will inform you of your new title and standing. It's a very aristocratic way of doing things! From lowest to highest, below are the ranks you can attain in the Battle Chateau.

1. Baron / Baroness
2. Viscount / Viscountess
3. Earl / Countess
4. Marquis / Marchioness
5. Duke / Duchess
6. Grand Duke / Grand Duchess*

*Only a Trainer as strong as the Champion of Kalos can obtain these ranks.

Special visitors

Even as a Marchioness, I'm still always looking for the perfect shot.

As you gain ranks and begin to make a name for yourself at the Battle Chateau, you'll start seeing special visitors, like Leader Viola of the Santalune City Gym. Other major characters will appear at the Battle Chateau as well, so keep on battling!

Battle Chateau prizes

In addition to winning prize money and earning Experience Points for your Pokémon, your opponents may give you special prizes. This chart lists the prizes you may receive. The higher your opponent's rank, the more likely it becomes that you will receive a special prize.

Your opponent's rank	Prize
Baron / Baroness	Pearl
Viscount / Viscountess	Stardust
Earl / Countess	Big Pearl
Marquis / Marchioness	Star Piece / Nugget / Pearl String
Duke / Duchess	Nugget / Big Nugget*
Grand Duke / Grand Duchess	Comet Shard

*Duke Hennessy may give you this after battle.

Issuing Writs

How might I be of service today?

Send a Writ
About Writs 1
About Writs 2
Cancel

If you have the funds to spare, consider issuing a Writ at the Battle Chateau. Although they're costly, Writs will entice more Trainers to challenge you at the Battle Chateau. This means you'll increase your rank even faster. Note that any Writs you issue will expire at midnight, so don't issue one unless you're planning to devote some time to improving your standing at the Battle Chateau that day.

Writ costs and details

Writ	Price	Details
Writ of Invitation	50,000	Invite more Trainers than usual to come and accept your challenge at the Battle Chateau
Silver Writ of Invitation	100,000	Invite far more Trainers than usual to come and accept your challenge at the Battle Chateau
Gold Writ of Invitation	100,000	Increase the prize money received by 50%
Writ of Challenge	50,000	Raise the level of opposing Trainers' party Pokémon by 5
Blue Writ of Challenge	10,000	Lower the level of opposing Trainers' party Pokémon by 10
Red Writ of Challenge	100,000	Raise the level of opposing Trainers' party Pokémon by 10
Black Writ of Challenge	300,000	Raise the level of opposing Trainers' party Pokémon by 20

NOTE *Not all of these Writs will be available to you from the start. You have to prove your worth to unlock them all. Becoming a Viscount or Viscountess will unlock the Writ of Challenge. Becoming an Earl or Countess will unlock the Gold Writ of Invitation. Becoming a Marquis or Marchioness will unlock the Silver Writ of Invitation. Becoming a Duke or Duchess will unlock the Blue and Red Writs of Challenge. And becoming the Grand Duke or Grand Duchess will unlock the Black Writ of Challenge.*

Cafés

Cafés are laid-back hangouts where friends can gather to enjoy a fresh beverage or a tasty treat. More important, cafés are great places to visit when you want to catch up on the latest rumors and gossip types: the ones in Lumiose, which are free to enter, and the ones in other towns which you must pay to visit.

Lumiose City cafés

Lumiose City's cafés are straightforward places, but, wow, there sure are a lot of them! It won't cost you a thing to visit these cafés, and you can hear plenty of interesting stories by talking to everyone inside. These cafés have naturally developed into popular hangouts for different types of people over the years, and you'll find that they are filled by enthusiasts with a variety of hobbies and lifestyles.

Other Kalos region cafés

The few cafés that you find in other cities and towns are a bit different. For starters, you must pay in order to enter these establishments. Depending on how much you're willing to spend, you can choose to sit at the counter, get a table, or enjoy the atmosphere on the terrace.

Once you've taken a seat, you're served the café's signature drink. Afterward, you're free to get up and walk around the immediate area. Talk to any patrons you see, and they'll show off their favorite Pokémon, registering them in your Pokédex. If you pay to sit at the counter (500), you will be able to see one Pokémon. If you pay to get a table (1,000), you will be shown two Pokémon. If you pay to sit on the terrace (5,000), you will see just one Pokémon, but it will for sure be one that is not yet registered in your Pokédex.

Lumiose City cafés

Name	Location	Special features
Café Cyclone	Vert Plaza	A café where many show off their unique skills in the hope of receiving tips
Café Introversion	South Boulevard	A popular hangout for those who love communications features
Café Classe	Vernal Avenue	A popular hangout for fashion-lovers
Café Woof	Vernal Avenue	A popular hangout for Furfrou admirers
Café Soleil	South Boulevard	A perfectly normal café, popular with the movie star Diantha
Shutterbug Café	South Boulevard	A popular hangout for aspiring photographers
Café Rouleau	Estival Avenue	A popular hangout for Roller Skate enthusiasts
Café Gallant	Estival Avenue	A café popular with the ladies, thanks to the all-male staff
Café Triste	North Boulevard	A sad café without many customers. Perhaps you can make it more popular if you're stylish enough...
Lysandre Café	Magenta Plaza	The café run by the wealthy inventor Lysandre
Café Pokémon-Amie	Autumnal Avenue	A popular hangout for those who love Pokémon-Amie
Café Ultimo	North Boulevard	A popular hangout for those who love Super Training
Café Kizuna	Hibernal Avenue	A popular hangout for those who like to bond with their Pokémon partners
Café Action!	North Boulevard	A popular hangout for those who hope to be Trainer PR Video stars
Café Bataille	North Boulevard	A popular hangout for those who love Pokémon battle above all else

Other cafés

Cyllage City	The northwest building
Laverre City	The northeast building
Anistar City	The northern building

Pokémon Global Link

When you're looking to expand your online battle experiences, consider checking out the Pokémon Global Link (PGL). That's where you'll find competitive players who participate in Online Competitions. Think you've got what it takes to battle the best from around the world? Then the PGL is the place for you!

PGL features

Just visit www.pokemon-gl.com and you'll be able to create a PGL account, where you can register your Pokémon game(s) with the Game Sync ID issued within the game and start enjoying everything that the PGL has to offer. Here's a quick peek at some of the very cool things the PGL brings to you.

Screenshot image subject to change.

1 **Quick links:** Use this list of buttons to quickly access your profile and account settings, or to access the PokéMileage Club, Rating Battles, and Online Competitions.

2 **Announcements:** Any special announcements or particularly important PGL information is shown here, at the top of the PGL home page.

3 **This week's events:** All special events that are on the horizon are listed here. Stay connected to the PGL and you won't miss a thing!

4 **Support:** Need a little help navigating the PGL website? No problem! Just click "Support" to receive more information about the site's many features.

5 **Featured content:** Special content and features get the spotlight treatment here. Click on any feature to find out more!

6 **News:** All news and announcements are featured here, from newest to oldest. Check here for everything that's happening on the PGL.

7 **Top 10 Trainer rankings:** Check out the top 10 Trainers ranked in all formats of Rating Battles from around the world.

Get started on the PGL

The first thing to do at the PGL is set up an account. Do this through the PGL website by choosing a username and password. You may then choose to register up to one copy each of *Pokémon X* and *Pokémon Y*. Please note that you can't register multiple copies of the same game on a single account, so if you change Game Cards of the same version for any reason, you'll need to deactivate your old game before you register your new one. To register a game in the PGL, start by generating a Game Sync ID in your game using the PSS.

Open the PSS menu by tapping the icon at the top of the main PSS screen. On the second page of the menu, select Game Sync. You'll be asked if you want to connect to the Internet and then to save your game. If you're not currently in an environment where you can connect to the Internet, you won't be able to connect to Game Sync.

Choose "Create your Game Sync ID" from the menu that appears, and then select "Yes." Your game will be authenticated online and you will be issued a Game Sync ID. Your Game Sync ID will be a 16-digit series of letters and numbers, which you will need to enter at the PGL website to connect your game. For more information about how to use the Game Sync feature, choose "Info" from the Game Sync menu.

You can change your Game Sync settings by selecting "Settings" from the Game Sync menu. Choose whether or not you want your game to Game Sync automatically whenever it has an Internet connection. Indicate your choice by toggling the Auto Sync option on or off. You can also choose whether or not to send the Poké Miles that you've earned in the game to the PGL, where they can be used for minigames and other activities. You could keep them instead to exchange for items in Lumiose City's South Pokémon Center in your game.

What can be seen on your profile

Your profile displays a variety of data regarding your game. Here's an overview of what can be seen on your PGL profile:

- Game software information
- Friend list
- Global Battle Union (GBU) statistics
- Medals you've earned

- Poké Miles, including a usage history and remaining Poké Mile balance
- Current items due to be sent to your game at the next Game Sync
- Information about Pokémon trades

 If you don't want to reveal all of this info to others on the PGL, you can manage your privacy settings.

Connect to your social networks

You can now share information on your favorite social networking sites, such as Facebook and Twitter, via the new PGL site. Here are some examples of the type of content you can share:

- Updates about your progress in the game
- Online Tournament participation information

- GBU Rankings
- Photos you've taken
- Medals you've earned

NOTE *The PGL's social networking functions will be disabled for players who do not meet the age restriction for Facebook and Twitter.*

View GBU and GTS stats

The PGL tracks a variety of important stats for you regarding your performance in the Global Battle Union and your trades at the Global Trade Station.

Global Battle Union (GBU) stats
- Your personal battle stats are displayed in the PGL.
- GBU stats are updated regularly and displayed per Battle format (Single, Double, Triple, Rotation, and Special).
- You can view other players' stats sorted by region.
- Detailed stats are shown for Pokémon used in battles, Battle Box Pokémon, and popular moves.

Online Competition results and stats
- Online Competition data will be displayed in the PGL for *Pokémon X* and *Pokémon Y* players.
- You can sort the ranking stats page to view your personal standing in the rankings.

Global Trade Station (GTS) stats
- Trade history can be viewed (not including infrared trades).
- You can view trade data sorted by region.

Earn Medals for your accomplishments

You can earn Medals for your actions in the *Pokémon X* and *Pokémon Y* games. Earned Medals will appear in your list of updates from your game. The more Medals you have, the more you can do in the PGL. Your Medal count will affect how you play, such as by opening up new ways to play minigames and increasing the items available to be exchanged for your Poké Miles.

The PokéMileage Club

The PokéMileage Club is a part of the PGL where you can exchange your Poké Miles to obtain items. You earn Poké Miles in the game by traveling around the Kalos region. You can also obtain Poké Miles by passing by other players by StreetPass, or even by trading with them. For more about earning Poké Miles, please see page 409.

 NOTE *There is a limit to how many items you can store on the PGL, after which you must transfer your items back to your game via Game Sync before you can obtain more.*

Check out the PGL mobile website

No access to a PC? No problem! With the PGL mobile website, you can access your favorite PGL features anywhere, anytime. This version of the site is specifically designed to work on smaller screens and still allow you all the ease of access you would find on the standard site. Visit the PGL mobile site today using your smart phone or other mobile device!

Poké Miles

Just what are Poké Miles, anyway? This special stat slowly increases as you wander around the Kalos region. Press Ⓧ and check out the Trainer Info menu to see how many Poké Miles you've accumulated. You'll also accumulate Poké Miles much faster when you trade Pokémon with other players or pass by other players by StreetPass. In these instances, the number of Poké Miles you get will depend on the distance between the two regions registered on the Nintendo 3DS systems. The greater the distance, the more Poké Miles you'll receive. This is another great reason to trade with players from other countries. Not only will those Pokémon gain more Experience Points than other Pokémon, but they'll also earn you more Poké Miles!

What can you do with Poké Miles? In *Pokémon X* and *Pokémon Y*, you can speak to the PokéMileage representative in the Pokémon Center on Lumiose City's South Boulevard, and you'll be able to trade in your Poké Miles for valuable prizes. This includes the fantastic Discount Coupon that will get you up to 50% off in clothing boutiques around the Kalos region!

Poké Mile Prizes (Available in Lumiose City's South Pokémon Center)	
Berry Juice	10
Ether	120
Full Heal	30
Full Restore	300
Hyper Potion	60
Max Potion	125
Max Repel	35
Max Revive	400
Moomoo Milk	20
PP Up	1,000
Rare Candy	500
Ultra Ball	60

Data Lists

The last few pages of this guide provide quick-reference data lists.

Poké Mart items

These tables list all the items that can be purchased at every Poké Mart around the Kalos region. Smart Trainers stop and shop at the Poké Mart!

Items available from the clerk on the left

The following items are available at all Poké Marts. When two Poké Mart clerks are present, these items are always sold by the clerk on the left. Note that more and more items become available at all Poké Marts as you collect Gym Badges.

Left Clerk			
Items available from the start		**Items added after obtaining the second Gym Badge**	
Poké Ball	200	Hyper Potion	1,200
Potion	300	Revive	1,500
Items added after obtaining the first Gym Badge		Super Repel	500
		Items added after obtaining the third Gym Badge	
Antidote	100	Full Heal	600
Awakening	250	Max Repel	700
Burn Heal	250	Ultra Ball	1,200
Escape Rope	550	**Items added after obtaining the fourth Gym Badge**	
Great Ball	600	Max Potion	2,500
Ice Heal	250	**Items added after obtaining the fifth Gym Badge**	
Paralyze Heal	200		
Repel	350	Full Restore	3,000
Super Potion	700		

Unique items available from the clerk on the right

The following items are available at Poké Marts in certain cities. When two Poké Mart clerks are present, these items are always sold by the clerk on the right.

Santalune City	
Dire Hit	650
Guard Spec.	700
X Accuracy	950
X Attack	500
X Defense	550
X Sp. Atk	350
X Sp. Def	350
X Speed	350

Lumiose City (South Pokémon Center)	
TM11 Sunny Day	50,000
TM18 Rain Dance	50,000
TM75 Swords Dance	10,000
TM76 Struggle Bug	10,000
TM78 Bulldoze	10,000

Cyllage City

Dusk Ball	1,000
Nest Ball	1,000
Net Ball	1,000

Coumarine City

Quick Ball	1,000
Timer Ball	1,000
Repeat Ball	1,000

Anistar City

TM14 Blizzard	70,000
TM15 Hyper Beam	70,000
TM25 Thunder	70,000
TM38 Fire Blast	70,000
TM52 Focus Blast	70,000

Shalour City

TM07 Hail	50,000
TM20 Safeguard	30,000
TM28 Dig	10,000
TM37 Sandstorm	50,000
TM84 Poison Jab	10,000

Laverre City

Calcium	9,800
Carbos	9,800
HP Up	9,800
Iron	9,800
Protein	9,800
Zinc	9,800

Snowbelle City

Dusk Ball	1,000
Heal Ball	300
Nest Ball	1,000
Net Ball	1,000
Quick Ball	1,000
Repeat Ball	1,000
Timer Ball	1,000

Lumiose City (North Pokémon Center)

Heal Ball	300
Nest Ball	1,000
Net Ball	1,000

TM locations

This table lists the location of every TM and HM to be found in the Kalos region. Some cannot be received before beating the game, but if you are diligent, you will eventually have all 100 TMs in your possession!

Move	How to obtain	Move	How to obtain
TM01 Hone Claws	Route 5	TM11 Sunny Day	Lumiose City (South Boulevard Poké Mart)
TM02 Dragon Claw	Victory Road	TM12 Taunt	Lysandre Labs
TM03 Psyshock	Victory Road	TM13 Ice Beam	Snowbelle City Gym
TM04 Calm Mind	Anistar City Gym	TM14 Blizzard	Anistar City Poké Mart
TM05 —	Available after beating the game	TM15 Hyper Beam	Anistar City Poké Mart
TM06 Toxic	Route 14	TM16 —	Available after beating the game
TM07 Hail	Shalour City Poké Mart	TM17 Protect	Parfum Palace
TM08 Bulk Up	Snowbelle City	TM18 Rain Dance	Lumiose City (South Boulevard Poké Mart)
TM09 Venoshock	Route 6	TM19 Roost	Route 8
TM10 Hidden Power	Anistar City	TM20 Safeguard	Shalour City Poké Mart

Move	How to obtain	Move	How to obtain
TM21 Frustration	Connecting Cave	TM42 Facade	Dendemille Town
TM22 Solar Beam	Route 21	TM43 Flame Charge	Kalos Power Plant
TM23 —	Available after beating the game	TM44 Rest	Cyllage City
TM24 Thunderbolt	Lumiose City Gym	TM45 Attract	Route 12
TM25 Thunder	Anistar City Poké Mart	TM46 Thief	Camphrier Town
TM26 Earthquake	Route 22	TM47 Low Sweep	Shalour City (Tower of Mastery)
TM27 Return	Lumiose City (Route 4 Gate)	TM48 —	Available after beating the game
TM28 Dig	Shalour City Poké Mart	TM49 Echoed Voice	Lumiose City (Hotel Richissime)
TM29 Psychic	Pokémon Village	TM50 —	Available after beating the game
TM30 Shadow Ball	Terminus Cave	TM51 —	Available after beating the game
TM31 Brick Break	Terminus Cave	TM52 Focus Blast	Anistar City Poké Mart
TM32 Double Team	Anistar City	TM53 Energy Ball	Route 20
TM33 —	Available after beating the game	TM54 False Swipe	Lumiose City (Sycamore Pokémon Lab)
TM34 —	Available after beating the game	TM55 Scald	Couriway Town
TM35 Flamethrower	Anistar City	TM56 Fling	Lost Hotel
TM36 Sludge Bomb	Route 19	TM57 Charge Beam	Route 13
TM37 Sandstorm	Shalour City Poké Mart	TM58 —	Available after beating the game
TM38 Fire Blast	Anistar City Poké Mart	TM59 —	Available after beating the game
TM39 Rock Tomb	Cyllage City Gym	TM60 —	Available after beating the game
TM40 Aerial Ace	Connecting Cave	TM61 Will-O-Wisp	Route 14
TM41 Torment	Laverre City	TM62 Acrobatics	Coumarine City

Move	How to obtain	Move	How to obtain
TM63 Embargo	Coumarine City	TM85 —	Available after beating the game
TM64 —	Available after beating the game	TM86 Grass Knot	Coumarine City Gym
TM65 Shadow Claw	Glittering Cave	TM87 —	Available after beating the game
TM66 Payback	Geosenge Town	TM88 Sleep Talk	Cyllage City
TM67 —	Available after beating the game	TM89 U-turn	Couriway Town
TM68 —	Available after beating the game	TM90 Substitute	Anistar City
TM69 Rock Polish	Route 11	TM91 —	Available after beating the game
TM70 Flash	Reflection Cave	TM92 Trick Room	Coumarine City
TM71 Stone Edge	Frost Cavern	TM93 —	Available after beating the game
TM72 —	Available after beating the game	TM94 Rock Smash	Ambrette Town
TM73 Thunder Wave	Route 10	TM95 Snarl	Lost Hotel
TM74 Gyro Ball	Reflection Cave	TM96 Nature Power	Ambrette Town
TM75 Swords Dance	Lumiose City (South Boulevard Poké Mart)	TM97 Dark Pulse	Route 15
TM76 Struggle Bug	Lumiose City (South Boulevard Poké Mart)	TM98 Power-Up Punch	Shalour City Gym
TM77 Psych Up	Anistar City	TM99 Dazzling Gleam	Laverre City Gym
TM78 Bulldoze	Lumiose City (South Boulevard Poké Mart)	TM100 Confide	Coumarine City
TM79 Frost Breath	Frost Cavern	HM01 Cut	Parfum Palace
TM80 Rock Slide	Couriway Town	HM02 Fly	Coumarine City
TM81 X-Scissor	Azure Bay	HM03 Surf	Shalour City
TM82 Dragon Tail	Lumiose City (Museum)	HM04 Strength	Cyllage City
TM83 Infestation	Santalune City Gym	HM05 Waterfall	Route 19
TM84 Poison Jab	Shalour City Poké Mart		

Type Matchup Chart

Types are assigned both to moves and to the Pokémon themselves. These types can greatly affect the amount of damage dealt or received in battle, so if you learn how they line up against one another, you'll give yourself an edge in battle.

Defending Pokémon's Type →
Attacking Pokémon's Move Type ↓

Move \ Def	Normal	Fire	Water	Grass	Electric	Ice	Fighting	Poison	Ground	Flying	Psychic	Bug	Rock	Ghost	Dragon	Dark	Steel	Fairy
Normal													▲	✕			▲	
Fire		▲	▲	◉		◉						◉	▲		▲		◉	
Water		◉	▲	▲					◉				◉		▲			
Grass		▲	◉	▲				▲	◉	▲		▲	◉		▲		▲	
Electric			◉	▲	▲				✕	◉					▲			
Ice		▲	▲	◉		▲			◉	◉					◉		▲	
Fighting	◉					◉		▲		▲	▲	▲	◉	✕		◉	◉	▲
Poison				◉				▲	▲				▲	▲			✕	◉
Ground		◉		▲	◉			◉		✕		▲	◉				◉	
Flying				◉	▲		◉					◉	▲				▲	
Psychic							◉	◉			▲					✕	▲	
Bug		▲		◉			▲	▲		▲	◉			▲		◉	▲	▲
Rock		◉				◉	▲		▲	◉		◉					▲	
Ghost	✕										◉			◉		▲		
Dragon															◉		▲	✕
Dark							▲				◉			◉		▲		▲
Steel		▲	▲		▲	◉							◉				▲	◉
Fairy		▲					◉	▲							◉	◉	▲	

Key

◉	Very effective — "It's super effective!"	× 2
No icon	Normal damage	× 1
▲	Not too effective — "It's not very effective…"	× ½
✕	No effect — "It doesn't affect…"	× 0

- Fire-type Pokémon cannot be afflicted with the Burned condition.
- Grass-type Pokémon are immune to Leech Seed and powder and spore moves.
- Electric-type Pokémon cannot be afflicted with the Paralyzed condition.
- Ice-type Pokémon are immune to the Frozen condition and take no damage from hail.
- Poison-type Pokémon are immune to the Poison and Badly Poisoned conditions, even when switching in with Toxic Spikes in play. Poison-type Pokémon nullify Toxic Spikes (unless these Pokémon are also Flying type or have the Levitate Ability).
- Ground-type Pokémon are immune to Thunder Wave and take no damage from a sandstorm.
- Flying-type Pokémon cannot be damaged by Spikes when switching in, nor become afflicted with the Poison or Badly Poisoned conditions due to switching in with Toxic Spikes in play.
- Rock-type Pokémon take no damage from a sandstorm. Their Sp. Def also goes up in a sandstorm.
- Ghost-type Pokémon are not affected by moves that prevent Pokémon from fleeing from battle.
- Steel-type Pokémon take no damage from a sandstorm. They are also immune to the Poison and Badly Poisoned conditions. Even if switched in with Toxic Spikes in play, they will not be afflicted with the Poison or Badly Poisoned conditions.

Credits

WRITER
Steve Stratton (Prima Games)

EDITORS
Wolfgang Baur
Kellyn Ballard
Blaise Selby
Eric Haddock
Rachel Payne (Bridge Consulting)

RESEARCHERS
Hisato Yamamori
Mikiko Ryu
Jillian Nonaka
Sayuri Munday

SCREENSHOTS
Antoin Johnson
Aaron Campion (Aerotek)
Jeff Hines (Bridge Consulting)

COVER DESIGNERS
Eric Medalle
Bridget O'Neill

PROJECT MANAGER
Emily Luty

DESIGN & PRODUCTION
Prima Games
Donato Tica
Jamie Knight Bryson
Mark Hughes
Melissa Jeneé Smith
Shaida Boroumand

ACKNOWLEDGEMENTS
Chris Franc
Doug Wohlfeil (Bridge Consulting)
Heather Dalgleish
Hiromi Kimura
J.C. Smith
John Moore
Kenji Okubo
Misty Thomas
Phaedra Long
Traci Thomson
Yasuhiro Usui

Writer **Steve Stratton** fell in love with gaming at age six, and he fondly recalls repeatedly saving the universe from the brink of destruction. More recently, Steve has written more than 60 official strategy guides. Like a well-raised Pokémon, his skills have steadily evolved through years of hard work and plenty of help from family and friends. Steve grew up in central Vermont and attended the Rochester Institute of Technology in 1998.